The Doulton Figure Collectors Handbook

Fourth Edition

London
1 870703-41-3

Acknowledgements

I am indebted to several people without whose help and encouragement I would never have been involved in collecting Doulton let alone had the courage to go into print. First and foremost my wife, Alison, whose family's interest in Doulton figures brought them to my attention in the first place, and whose support and encouragement allowed me a dramatic career change. She also deserves mention for her heroic deciphering of my original manuscript and correcting my spelling. Jocelyn Lukins for her friendship and sharing of her knowledge. Louise Irvine who determinedly persuaded me to start writing about Doulton. Nick Tzimas for being, well, Nick Tzimas! Frank Salmon for having the courage to take me on as editor of *Collecting Doulton* and asking me to write for Francis Joseph Publications. Finally thanks to all the specialist dealers and collectors too numerous to mention who have sustained my interest in Doulton over the years.

A special note of appreciation must go to Kevin Pearson for his great efforts with the first three editions of this book. Without his prevous work, this book would not be possible.

Published in the UK by
Francis Joseph Publications
15 St Swithuns Road, London SE13 6RW
Telephone: 0181 318 9580

Production: Francis Salmon
Photography: Trevor Leak

Typeset by E J Folkard Computer Services
199 Station Road, Crayford, Kent DA1 3QF

Printed in Great Britain by
The Greenwich Press, London SE7

ISBN 1-870703-41-3

Contents

Introduction 4
Why Collect Doulton Figures? 6
From Ink Bottles to Figures 8
Creating a Collection 13
Designers 17
Designer Gallery
Charles Vyse 25
Leslie Harradine 26
Charles Noke 44
Richard Garbe 46
Peggy Davies 47
Mary Nicholl 52
William K Harper/Douglas V Tootle 54
Eric Griffiths/Robert Jefferson/Pauline Parsons 55
Peter Gee/Robert Tabbenor 58
Nada Pedley 59
Alan Maslankowski/John Bromley 60
Valerie Annand/Miscellaneous 61
How a Doulton Figure is Made 65
Buying Royal Doulton Figures 68
Care of Your Collection 73
Displaying Your Collection 74
Dating and Backstamps 75
Listing and Price Guide 78

Introduction

This book should start with a confession – I have not always approved of price guides and have been heard to say so in rather strong tones! So what am I doing writing one? The answer is quite simply that while I still do not approve of the slavish following of what usually amounts to one person's idea of the value of an object, I do think a guide, (and guide is the most important word here) to the relative values of pieces is a useful tool in the collecting world. This is particularly true when it comes to collecting Royal Doulton figures. When faced with the three thousand plus HN numbers, even the most ardent collector can be a little non-plussed. A price guide can help sort the not-so-common from the commonplace, and nobody really likes to pay 'over the odds' for anything!' But it should be borne in mind that any object is only worth what somebody is prepared to pay for it at a given time. An item can be extremely rare but if there is no market for it, its commercial value will not reflect its rarity no matter how wonderful the piece may be. This is true even of Royal Doulton figures.

This book, it must be emphasised, is intended as a guide. The prices contained within it are not the final word. All manner of factors can affect the equation which determines a price but in the end, it is the basic law of supply and demand which rules.

The market for out of production Royal Doulton figures is surprisingly strong given the world wide economic problems of recent years. During the last year, prices at auction for some Royal Doulton figures, notably and perhaps predictably the art deco models, have risen once more to the heady heights of the mid to late 1980s. The comparatively rare crinoline ladies from the 1930s have also enjoyed a resurgence of interest with an associated rise in their value, as have some of the rarer early character figures. With a few exceptions later models have more or less kept pace with their equivalent in-production models. What has become noticeable is a slowing down in the numbers of good quality figures coming on the market. Coupled with a strong demand for pieces this has resulted in some very high prices being paid. On the auction front, the situation has been exacerbated by the growth of the computer based finder services which, for a subscription, provide countrywide details of auctions containing specified items, thus resulting in potential buyers being able to bid by telephone anywhere in the country. The resutling extra competition can obviously inflate prices.

In some respects over high prices can be a little worrying. There is always a danger of the market 'over-heating' which can have a detrimental effect on the whole market, not just the highly priced items. Collectors can be frightened away when they consider they can no longer afford to collect. There will always be pieces which command high values. This is fine as it gives collectors an incentive to continue to collect, but when prices are almost artificially hyped to unrealistic levels, it can be bad for the market. At present the market for out of production Royal Doulton figures has not fallen foul of this trap, it has happened with other collectables but collectors, dealers and auction houses should be aware of the danger of artificially high prices.

I hope that collectors will find this book useful. It has been my intention to provide not only a guide to prices but also a basic guide to the whys and wherefores to collecting Royal Doulton figures, their history, creators and methods of production. Collecting is always a very personal matter, every collector will have different tastes and preferences and by extension every collection will be unique. What is common to all is the pleasure, excitement and sense of belonging to an almost worldwide enthusiasm that collecting Royal Doulton figures can bring.

Enjoy collecting, enjoy your collection.

Scotland (HN 3629). One of the Ladies of the British Isles. Modelled by Valerie Annand. Picture Royal Doulton

Why Collect Doulton Figures?

As you have probably already bought this book, you have made up your mind to collect Doulton figures. But why?

Royal Doulton is one of the most collectable names of today and its figurines are the most popular items to have emerged from the Doulton factory. Why should it be that these figures have surpassed in the popularity stakes the multitude of other Doulton collectables? Furthermore, why should Royal Doulton figures and not those of other manufacturers exert such a powerful hold over collectors from all over the world? I do not pretend to have come up with the definitive answer – it would be unrealistic to suppose that there are just one or two reasons. What follows are a few ideas. I am sure that every collector will be able to add their own personal reasons to the list. Indeed, perhaps this is in itself a major factor in their appeal.

Quality is fundamental to Doulton figures. A particular figurine may not be to one's taste but almost without exception there is something to be admired. The lustrous glazes and assured painting are very easy to take for granted. However it is only when one remembers that these objects are mass produced, albeit of the highest craftsmanship, and not the limited product of a studio potter that the true quality of Doulton figures is realised. The fine modelling and attention to the smallest detail are inherent features of all Doulton figures. This has been the case from their inception to the present day. Compare a Doulton figure with a similar piece from virtually any other factory; the Doulton model will stand out as being special in an indefinable way. This can only partly be explained by the proven quality of the figures. They have a certain magic all their own.

A huge variety of subjects make up the collection, robust character studies, coy children, art deco fantasies and perhaps the most famous of all, the pretty ladies; in fact something for all tastes. If the collector has limited space or a liking for the miniature, there are small scale figures (the M series – usually a smaller version of a full size figure). There were also several models, such as *Erminie* (M 40) and *Robin* (M 28) which were only ever issued as miniatures.

At the other end of the scale for collectors with more space and larger cheque books there are impressive prestige pieces which seem to stretch the skills of the ceramic craftsman to the limit.

There are very few Doulton figures in contemporary dress. Even in the 1920s and 1930s there were only a handful of figurines, such as *Miss 1926* and *Irish Colleen*, which could be thought of as being representations of the fashions of the day. The Peggy Davies set of 1950s style figures really evoke the feel of the period rather than the style of dress. This lack of contemporary fashion perhaps gives a clue to the attraction of Doulton figures for some collectors. By appearing to come from an age of elegance and grace, (attributes some might think have been lost by the twentieth century), the Doulton lady dressed in a pastiche of eighteenth or nineteenth century fashion, strikes a note of yearning for a more gentle, refined age. The eighteenth and nineteenth centuries were not idyllic for most of the population, but Doulton figures were never meant to be part of a history lesson, so does it really matter that they present an idealised view of days gone by?

It may sound like a statement of the obvious but it is much easier to form a collection if the would-be collector knows exactly what constitutes the collection. Information is the key to successful collecting. In recent years the Doulton collector certainly cannot complain of a lack of publications on their passion. These books have helped the established collector and fired the enthusiasm of many a new collector. This abundance of information can be something of a double-edged sword. Pioneer figure collectors in the United States still talk of the halcyon days in the early 1970s when out of production models all tended to fall in the same price bracket. There was then no conception of rarities, as there was very little published information on the subject. Many collectors, thirsty for knowledge, began corresponding with one another , passing on information gleaned from all manner of sources. Some rather dubious theories were expounded and it was not until 1978, when 'Royal Doulton Figures' by Desmond Eyles was available, that competition then became fierce for some of the rarest figures. The figure book was by no means complete and since its publication many previously unseen models have come to light and have been included in subsequent editions with six figures still unaccounted for*. Every day brings surprises in the Doulton world and this is another appealing aspect of the subject.

Availability is an important consideration when embarking on any collecting project. There is very little point in setting out on an impossible quest for collectables which are known to exist in minute numbers. It is much more satisfactory to collect something which is known to exist in appreciable numbers, knowing that one stands a fair chance of amassing a reasonable selection of the chosen articles. This is the case with Doulton figures. While it is undeniable that certain figures are very rare and when and, (if they ever surface), command a king's ransom, the majority do seem to turn up eventually – as many a collectors bank balance will testify.

Psychologists would doubtlessly be able to suggest a whole range of different theories to explain the fascination of these 'poem's in pottery' (as Doulton figures were described in the 1930s catalogues). But whatever the true reason for their appeal, I cannot help but think that the best reason for the success of Doulton figures was that given to me by an enthusiastic collector from England. When I asked her why she had filled her home with an army of china ladies, she simply said, "Because I like them".

**The six ellusive figures are: Carpet Vendor (2nd version) HN 38 (with long carpet); Dancing Figure HN 311; Cavalier (1st version) HN 369; Lady and Blackamoor HN 375, 377, 470; Despair HN 596 and Toys HN 1316.*

From Ink Bottles to Figures – A Brief History of Royal Doulton

The story of Doulton's rise from humble beginnings as just another Thames-side pottery to a world famous ceramics giant is well documented in many other publications but perhaps the quantum leap from producing blacking bottles to making fine bone china tableware and figurines via drainpipes and art pottery needs some explanation.

It can almost be explained by the mention of one man, Sir Henry Doulton. It was he who took the quite ordinary pottery and made it something quite extraordinary. It was said that Henry Doulton made a fortune from drains and spent it on art. In a way this is true. The fortune was accumulated by Sir Henry having the foresight to see that saltglazed stoneware, the material used by Doultons for making ink bottles and the like, was an ideal substance in which to make the drain and sewer pipes which were desperately needed to alleviate the appalling insanitary conditions in the worlds post-industrial revolution cities and towns. The conurbations had rapidly expanded but the means to deal with the increasing amounts of effluence had not. Furthermore he also had the drive to invest in and install the latest machinery for the manufacture of the much needed pipes. Consequently the company prospered.

When approached by John Sparks, the principal of the Lambeth School of Art, requesting that students from the nearby school should be allowed to attempt the making of art pottery at the factory, Henry Doulton was in a position to let the experiment take place. He did not agree immediately, it was the prospect of prestige which might ensue if the project succeeded which swayed him. Even so his initial investment was modest. The students could only use materials already at the factory and the facilities provided could best be described as basic. But as the world knows the experiment succeeded and a full-blown art pottery studio was established at Doulton's Lambeth factory. The studio survived with varying degrees of success, until the mid 1950s. The building, the sole survivor of the once huge Doulton complex is still there today but used for more mundane purposes.

Henry Doulton, in common with many other Victorian entrepreneurs thrived on challenge. It could be argued that his biggest challenge was to take on the potters of Staffordshire. Despite its world wide fame, the area around Stoke on Trent known as the Potteries was remarkably insular, indeed to some extent it still is, and the prospect of that 'stoneware fellow from London' setting up a business in their midst was not greeted with widespread enthusiasm. Henry Doulton was well aware of the resentment felt towards outsiders. His often quoted remark "in their view we Londoners know little about God and nothing about pottery" sums up the feeling of the time in Stoke. Rather than establishing a completely new Doulton operation in Staffordshire Henry Doulton took a more cautious approach. In 1877 he bought an interest in an already established concern. The firm chosen was Pinder, Bourne and Co. of

Nile Street, Burslem – manufacturers of earthenwares, tablewares and artwares in a style typical of the period. The Pinder Bourne-Doulton partnership was not an easy one. Henry Doulton's drive was somewhat stifled by the conservative attitudes of his new associates. In 1882 Shadford Pinder finally retired and the company was renamed Doulton and Co. It is roughly from this point that the Staffordshire arm of the Doulton organisation began to take on an identity of its own. With hindsight, we can say that the greatest asset Henry Doulton acquired with his new company was its decorating manager, John Slater. As he had done with his Lambeth employees Henry Doulton encouraged John Slater to develop new ideas and techniques. A young man called John Bailey was appointed as General Manager of the new factory and he proved to be an equally valuable appointment. The new team, with the full support of Henry Doulton, set about rationalising the product range and introducing new innovations. Gradually a new Doulton style and quality emerged from the Victorian clutter of the Pinder, Bourne heritage. It was not an overnight transformation as the company continued to produce wares which were still based in the traditions of the area.

Beefeater toasting The Queen – vellum figure c1899.

By about 1900 the Doulton Burslem style was easily recognisable. Henry Doulton obviously had a talent for choosing the right personnel for his company. The most important recruit as far as the story of Royal Doulton figures is concerned was Charles Noke who joined the company in 1889. Noke began his career at the Royal Worcester factory where he worked for fifteen years before John Slater persuaded him to join the company as Chief Modeller at Nile Street. He was to remain at Doulton for the rest of his career.

The world at large first saw evidence of Noke's modelling talent in the pieces exhibited at the Chicago Exhibition of 1893. Although a few free standing figures were shown, it was the large spectacular vases which commanded the most interest, many of which included modelled figures in their design. It is known, however, that about six figures were shown at Chicago but very little attention was drawn to them. In the next few years other figures were added to the range available from Burslem, including some models which were later

The Mermaid HN 97. An early figure designed by Harry Tittensor.

destined to become part of the now familiar HN range. These early figures were in a 'vellum' finish decorated in a very restricted palette very similar to those produced by Royal Worcester. They were generally on a much larger scale to the later HN range. The figures were also rather expensive. These factors probably accounted for their rather limited success at the time. They were certainly not made in large quantities. It is only very recently that they have been reappraised by collectors although their modest renaissance as collectable Doulton figures is tiny compared with the interest shown in the HN range models.

From about 1897 until 1909, Noke's energies were taken up developing new projects, and figure production took a back seat. Staffordshire had a tradition of figure making but by the early years of the twentieth century it was rather neglected and the quality of much of the production of traditional Staffordshire figures was questionable. By about 1909 Charles Noke decided the time had come to revive the tradition with something relevant to the new century. He was also aware that it was a considerable undertaking. Other English factories had not had a great deal of financial success producing figurines, (most specialist factories seemed to go bankrupt alarmingly quickly). Noke was shrewd enough to realise that if Doulton was to succeed where others had failed, a great deal of preparation and experimentation would be necessary before any figures could be launched on an unsuspecting market. Having obtained the approval and backing of Henry Doulton's son and successor, Noke set about producing a 'trial run' of figures. Rather than having the new figures designed 'in house' he approached a number of well known sculptors of the day and commissioned designs for the projected range. He met with a mixed response but eventually five sculptors submitted designs. Noke also designed some models himself. By 1912 twenty models were ready. Although different in concept to the earlier vellum range these figures were still not in the style so easily recognisable today and are, on the whole, much more solid looking and not so brightly coloured.

A visit to the Nile Street factory by King George V and Queen Mary was planned for April 1913. The launch of the new figurines was held back for this auspicious occasion. Had the Royal visit not taken place a figure still on sale today, albeit in a smaller scale, would be named 'Bedtime' rather than 'Darling'. When shown the new figures, Queen Mary picked up Bedtime, a model of a small boy in a nightshirt, and exclaimed 'isn't he a darling!' so Bedtime became *Darling* by Royal patronage. The Queen ordered copies of the figure for herself and her friends. *Darling* was the work of Charles Vyse and it is rather ironic that this figure, which is so completely different from his usual style, should have proved to be his most commercially successful.

Queen Mary's enthusiasm for *Darling* was to be mirrored by the public as he proved to be by far the most popular of the first figures, easily outselling all the others. This is not to say that the new Royal Doulton figures were instantly successful. In four years from their public launch in 1913 only just under 700 figures were made. Of these *Darling* accounted for almost a quarter. It is not really fair to judge the new figure range on these stark statistics alone as their appearance in the market coincided with the First World War. This rather restricted their marketing both at home and across the world. Royal Doulton kept faith with the project though and new models were introduced during the war years, but it was not until 1920 that figures made any real impact on the market. Even so production was still on a limited scale. At this time a new designer was employed who was to have a profound effect on Royal Doulton figures. His name was Leslie Harradine. Throughout the 1920s and 1930s and even on to the post 2nd World War years Harradine was responsible for designing the lion's share of the collection. Some of his models are still available today. It is with the advent of Harradine that Royal Doulton figures take on the style, both in modelling and colouring, which has appealed to collectors ever since.

The figure department at Burslem had been expanded over the years. Even so by 1939 there were still only twenty seven painters. Given that the range of figures had also grown it becomes obvious that even for the most popular models production was still quite limited. Exact production figures are not available but it has been said that an averagely popular pre-war figure would have been made in much smaller quantities than a modern limited edition. Some models were withdrawn from production in the mid 1930s, others in 1938 but it was the outbreak of the Second World War and the restrictions which it brought which caused the deletions from the range of the majority of the existing figures. Some production continued for export and it is possible to find figures date-coded for the early 1940s. When production was resumed after the war only a handful of pre-war designs were kept in the collection. At first the majority of the new introductions were the work of Harradine but a new talent was on the Doulton horizon who was to have an equally important influence in Royal Doulton figures. The new talent was Margaret May Davies, perhaps better known to collectors as Peggy Davies. She had joined Royal Doulton in 1939 as an assistant to C.J.Noke. After the interruptions of the war Peggy returned to the company but as an independent artist under contract to Royal Doulton. She created many, many figures for the HN range. Her most famous creations are the 'Pretty Ladies' but she also designed prestige series such as **The Dancers of the World** and **Les Femmes Fatales**. Together with the character studies modelled by Mary Nicholl, Peggy Davies' figures formed the backbone of the range for many years. This almost brings the story of Royal Doulton figures up to the present day.

Eric Griffiths was appointed Head of Ceramic Sculpture at Royal Doulton in 1972. It became obvious to him that if figure production was to continue to flourish at Burslem, new talent needed to be nurtured. Freelance artists such as William K. (Bill) Harper and Robert Jefferson submitted designs and apprentice modellers such as Peter Gee and Robert Tabbenor, began work but this time 'in house'. The pool of designers was swelled by Pauline Parsons, Adrian Hughes and Nada Pedley, each with their own particular interpretation of the Doulton figure. Eric Griffiths retired at the end of 1990. He was succeeded by his deputy, Amanda Dickson who is the current Director of Art and Design for all Royal Doulton studios. Under her auspices Alan Maslankowski joined Royal Doulton as a resident artist, while Valerie Annand works on a freelance basis.

Fisherwoman HN 80 designed by Charles Noke (photo Sothebys)

Since 1913 there have been many changes of style and direction within the Royal Doulton figure collection reflecting the different tastes and fashions of the century. Other manufacturers have imitated the Doulton style but none have achieved the success with the genre which remains peculiar to Royal Doulton. Even so it should be remembered that despite their fame and collectability Royal Doulton figures represent only one small part of the company's output.

Creating a Collection

Collections of Royal Doulton figures are put together for innumerable reasons, some almost by accident, others with great purpose and determination. Only on very rare occasions do collectors set out to assemble the entire HN collection. Given the rarity of some early pieces, this would seem an almost impossible task and in practice, an unrealistic goal. Conveniently the HN collection breaks down into manageable sub-collections. Some are quite obvious divisions while others are more subtle and personal to the collector in question.

There are , of course, collectors who are happy just to collect Royal Doulton figures. Their collections will contain a cross section of the figure range with no discernable theme or link between the pieces other than that they were all made by Royal Doulton. These collectors simply like Doulton figures and are not too bothered if the assembled figurines do not seem to 'gel' as an overall collection. This type of collection illustrates what I consider is the first rule of collecting – only buy what you like. Of course your tastes may change over the years but fortunately there is at present a healthy secondary market in Royal Doulton figures, and therefore it is usually possible to sell on figures should they become superfluous to requirements. A word of warning – there are a very few figures which, shall we say, are not as popular as others and could possibly be more difficult to sell, therefore before buying it is wise to ask yourself the questions 'Do I like this figure?' and 'am I prepared to have it in my home forever?' If the answer is in the affirmative, fine, buy it. If the answer is 'no', do not buy it no matter how much of a bargain it may seem to be because you might just be stuck with a piece you don't like and what is worse, you have paid good money for it.

As in everything there are exceptions. For example, if you are collecting a set of figures and there is one model in the set you do not like, it may still be worth buying it to complete the set. Forget your opinion of that one item because a complete collection can be worth more than the sum of the constituent parts. Ironically the least appealing figure may ultimately become the most valuable as its general lack of appeal may have resulted in poor sales rendering it the rarest and most difficult to find.

Collections often start with a gift, usually a current figure. It should be remembered that Royal Doulton market their figures as 'gift-ware'. The initial gift might set the theme of a collection or equally it might just spark their interest, allowing the embryonic collector to pursue the style of collection which most appeals to them. It must be said there are as many collection themes as there are collections. No two are ever exactly the same which proves the scope there is to be found in the HN collection. Here are a few suggestions.

By artist

Given the long history of Royal Doulton figures, there have been surprisingly few designers. There are more artists currently working on the collection than has been usual in the past. Never the less despite designing within an overall

'Doulton style' each artist has brought their own particular quality to the range, thus making it possible to easily differentiate between, say, a Leslie Harradine piece and a Mary Nicholl design. A collection by artist might still be too broad a division, but with most artists work it is possible to be more specific still. For example a collector may decide only to collect Mary Nicholl's sea-faring characters and not her land based models.

By colour

This category can be split into two variations. Firstly some collectors only buy figures dressed in certain colours — pretty ladies in blue dresses, for example. Secondly, some try to amass every colour variation of one figure such as all fifteen versions of *A Victorian Lady*.

There is also a more subtle variation of collecting by colour. In the 1930s Royal Doulton used very similar colour schemes on different figures. There is a colourway which features two shades of green, a dark bottle green and a lighter pale leaf green with trimmings picked out in a bright bluey-pink. This colour scheme is to be found on *A Victorian Lady* (HN 1452), *Sweet Anne* (HN 1453) *Patricia* (HN 1462) *Paisley Shawl* (HN 1460), *Barbara* (HN 1461), *Miss Demure* (1463), *Pearly Boy* (HN 1347) and *Pearly Girl* (HN 1348). There are other repeated colourways within the HN collection. Once again, the scope for an interesting collection is obvious.

Historical Characters

Within the HN collection there are numerous historical personages, such as *Sir Walter Raleigh* and *King Charles I*. Some are fictional but based on a period from history like *Janice*, a tudor lady in all but name or the miniature *Man in a Tudor Costume*. A sizeable collection could be assembled linked by the common factor of historical dress.

Royalty

This is really a subdivision of the above. In the 1980s Royal Doulton issued a series of limited edition portrait figures of the more attractive members of the

The British Royal Family as seen by Royal Doulton.

present British Royal family. The 1990s have not been so royal. Either the pool of suitable subjects has run dry or the current problems besetting the Royal family, have in Royal Doulton's view, rendered them commercially unviable to be immortalised in bone china.

However there are other Kings and Queens to be discovered in the HN collection which pre-date today's royals. Some are straight forward 'portrait' figures and are named accordingly but others need a certain amount of detective work to identify them. These figures are usually based on well known historical portraits but for some reason have been given different names. The collector once again has scope to form an impressive collection with a linking theme.

Characters From Literature (etc)

Charles Noke had a passion for the works of Charles Dickens. Almost certainly due to this interest there are many characters from this authors work in the HN and M collections. However Dickens does not have the monopoly. Shakespeares' Falstaff has been portrayed three times and the recent **Shakespeares' Ladies Collection** included many of the Bards more attractive creations. In the 1980s the **Characters from Childrens Literature** series featured six familiar literary characters. We must not forget the twelve **Tolkien** figures from the same period nor the eighteen models inspired by the works of **Kate Greenaway**.

The world of theatre and cinema could also be included in a literary collection. Apart from his enthusiasm for Dickens, Charles Noke was also a theatre buff, which probably accounts for the inclusion of such figures as *Doris Keene as Cavalini* and *W. S. Penley as Charley's Aunt* in the early part of the collection. The theatrical connection has continued with *Lord Olivier as Richard III* (HN 2881). There are few figurines directly taken from the cinema, although the recently launched **Disney Princess** collection is an exception. *Pirouette* (HN 2216) is widely believed to be based on Marilyn Monroe in the The Seven Year Itch and *Gypsy Dance* (HN 2230) is thought to be a tribute to Ava Gardner in The Barefoot Contessa.

The Ballerina (HN 2116) with her brightly coloured footwear is contemporary with the film The Red Shoes which starred ballerina Moira Shearer and leads the collector into the world of dance and ballet. There are a number of ballet inspired figures in the collection which are the work of Peggy Davies. Peggy was a fan of the ballet and fully admitted that some of her figures were based on Margot Fonteyn. Therefore these figures could also be included in a theatrical collection.

This also illustrates how one 'themed' collection can lead seamlessly to another. On the face of it there is very little connection between *Sairey Gamp* and *Les Sylphides* but with a little imagination, in the world of collecting Doulton, there can be!

By Accessory

Some enterprising collectors have set out to collect figures which include a particular accessory as part of their design. Lady figures with bonnets or modelled flowers are favourites but handkerchiefs, parasols, animals, cups and saucers, handbags, fans and even whips have their devotees.

By Size

At face value this would seem to be a very limited collecting category as basically there are only two sizes of figures, full size at about seven inches high and miniature between three and four inches. However there are the usual exceptions. The early figures in the HN collection are considerably bigger than most later models, and in the 1930s there was a range of larger earthenware figures such as *Margery* (HN 1413). The **Haute Ensemble Collectio**n of the 1970s were about 12 inches tall and many of the limited edition series are also on a larger scale. So if the collector has an interest in the large scale there is again scope for a collection.

Not everyone has the space to collect the larger models and the diminutive M series and the later HN miniatures fit the bill here. As do the many child figures that are usually on a smaller scale. Some collectors restrict themselves to the tall, thin, elegant figures such as *Karen* (HN 1994), *Harmony* (HN 2824) and *Lorna* (HN 2311).

I hope that I have demonstrated that by putting some restrictions on your collection to make it more manageable, you need not end up with a boring collection. Indeed the opposite is true. Not only does the collection take on some unifying form but with a little imagination it is possible to create a unique selection of models. It can also add to the pleasure of collecting by supplying an extra element of fun as you decide first what your 'theme' is to be and then search them out.

As I said earlier there are probably as many reasons for collecting as there are collectors. The list of ideas for collection is endless. However I make no apologies for repeating myself when I say my strongest piece of advice is collect only what you like!

Reflections HN 1820; Blighty HN 323 and Out for a Walk HN 86. Three figures which demonstrate the range of styles to be found in the HN collection.

Designers

Until recent times there have been surprisingly few designers responsible for Royal Doulton's HN figure range. The first collection of figures launched in 1913 was the work of five designers plus Charles Noke. This select band had been carefully selected by Noke and were all well established artists in their own right, but with the exception of Noke, their contribution to the collection was relatively short-lived. Only *Darling*, designed by Charles Vyse, has stood the commercial test of time. However from the late 1920s until the 1950s, virtually all the new introductions to the range were the work of one man, Leslie Harradine. In the post war years, the pretty ladies and prestige models of Peggy Davies reigned supreme together with the strong character studies created by Mary Nicholl. Both these ladies indulged in a little role reversal. Peggy produced the occasional character figure and Mary, the occasional pretty lady. During Eric Griffith's time as Director of Ceramic Sculpture, it was decided that in order to secure the future success of the collection, the design team should be considerably expanded. This policy continues today under the leadership of Amanda Dickson with a team of designers who have each developed their own styles and specialities.

The current collection is therefore made up of a number of artists' work rather than being the showcase for one or two designers.

To do further justice to the lives and work of the talented people who, over the years have contributed models to the HN collection, would take more space than is available here. However I am sure that a little background knowledge of the designers is helpful to the figure enthusiast in their appreciation of their collections. What follows are brief lives of the major contributors.

Charles Noke

The photographs of Charles Noke which have appeared in various publications over the years show a rather stern old gentleman usually surrounded with examples of his models. This rather dour image probably says more about the then current style of photographic portraiture than the man. Noke was born in Worcester. From a remarkably early age he wanted to be a ceramic modeller and during school holidays he often visited the local Worcester China factory to watch the artists at work. In 1874, at the age of 16, Noke joined the company. He was to stay at Worcester until 1889 when he moved to Doulton's Burslem studio. His work had reached the attention of John Slater, the art Director at Burslem, who invited him to move to the potteries. At first Noke was employed on modelling prestige pieces for the various international exhibitions of the time. His gift for modelling figures soon became apparent, although initially the figures were incorporated into the large and imposing vases which were produced as centre pieces for the exhibitions. At the Chicago Exhibition of 1893, a few free standing figures modelled by Noke were shown but very little attention was drawn to them. In the next few years more of his figures were added to the range. These were in general larger than the later HN series models and decorated in a much more muted and restricted palette. Around 1909 Charles Noke turned his attention to reviving the tradition of figure making in Staffordshire. This culminated with the launch of the HN Collection in 1913. Of the models designed by Noke, many reflect the interests of the man. From his photographs it is hard to imagine that Noke had a passion for the theatre but this interest manifested itself in the HN collection with such models as *Doris Keane as Cavallini* (HN 90 and HN 96), *Ellen Terry as Queen Catherine* (HN 379) and *Henry Irving as Cardinal Wolsey* (HN 344). (The last two being adaptations of the earlier 'vellum' figures). Noke was also fascinated by jesters and these too appeared in the HN collection. His *Jester* (HN 2016) is still available today.

Perhaps Charles Noke's delight in the works of Charles Dickens was to have the greatest influence on his choice of subjects for Doulton's various ranges. *Tony Weller* (HN 346), the earliest Dickensian character in the HN collection was designed by him, as were the majority of the many 'eastern' subjects which were a feature of the early years of the collection and reflect Noke's interest in what can be loosely termed 'the orient'.

The threads of Charles Nokes' many and varied interests can be traced through the pre-war HN collection but it is not just figure production which was to be so influenced. Noke's fertile mind was responsible for the introduction of Series wares, character jugs, Kingsware and the myriad of special glazes developed at Burslem. Throughout all these ranges similar subjects are to be found reflecting the interests and tastes of Charles Noke.

Charles Noke spent the rest of his life working at Doulton being succeeded as Art Director by his son, Cecil Jack. He died in 1941, aged 83.

Leslie Harradine

If Charles Noke was responsible for the revival of figure making at Burslem, it was Leslie Harradine who caught the public's taste in figurines and ensured the success of the collection. Arthur Leslie Harradine was born in 1887. In 1902 he joined Doulton's Lambeth studio where he worked at various times under the guidance of such Lambeth luminaries as George Tinworth, John Broad and Mark Marshall. Never the less, Harradine spent more time than he liked designing pots for reproduction rather than on ceramic sculptures. Despite this feeling he did produce a series of salt-glazed spirit flasks and a number of figures including a set of characters taken from the works of Charles Dickens. These figures attracted the attention of Charles Noke.

At the end of 1912, Harradine abruptly left the urban confines of Lambeth for the wide open spaces of Canada. With his brother, Percy, Harradine acquired 4000 acres of farming land in Saskatchewan. The self sufficient life style suited the brothers. Leslie continued to make models but was unable to fire them successfully. The outbreak of the First World War signalled the end of the Harradine brothers' rural idyll, at least it did for Leslie. By 1916 both had enlisted in Lord Strachcona's Horse Regiment and had seen action in France. Leslie had two horses shot from under him. On the second occasion the horse fell on him, badly damaging one of his legs, resulting in long spells in hospital.

By the time the peace was signed, Harradine was married and had a child. The privations of his life in Canada were thought to be unsuitable for his young family and Leslie made over his share in the Canadian farm to his brother. His intention was now to stay in Britain and establish his own studio and work as an independent artist.

Scotties HN 1281 by Leslie Harradine.

Charles Noke, hearing of Harradine's return, contacted him with a view to his joining the Burslem studio. Despite Noke's entreaties, Harradine refused to be tied to the restrictions of Burslem. His alternative suggestion was that he would model some figures at his studio and send them to Burslem to see if they could be produced in bone china. The models were indeed suitable for reproduction and an association between Leslie Harradine and Royal Doulton Burslem began which was to last for almost forty years. The fruitful partnership produced some of the most commercially successful figurines ever made. *The Old Balloon Seller, Top O'The Hill* or *Autumn Breezes* were all created by Harradine at his studio and sent to Burslem. He was equally at home designing child studies, robust character models, alluring art deco ladies, (there is an often repeated story that the models for these figures were ladies of his acquaintance and indeed several of the figures have similar faces) and archetypal crinoline ladies which were to become synonymous with Royal Doulton. The quality of his modelling remained constant despite the sheer volume of his output.

Leslie Harradine died in Gibraltar in 1965. The basic facts of his life are well known but there are many questions about his life which remain unanswered and in some ways he remains a rather shadowy figure despite his fame in the Doulton figure collecting world. Perhaps, one day a full biography will be written.

Peggy Davies

Margaret May Davies, aka Peggy, was born in Burslem in the heart of the Potteries. Her childhood was dominated by illness. To be exact, bovine

Character studies by Mary Nicholl and Peggy Davies. Top Row: A Good Catch HN 2258; Sailors Holiday HN 2442; Sea Harvest HN 2257; Lobster Man HN 2317; Shore Leave HN 2254; Second Row: Long Silver HN 2204; Tall Story HN 2248; Jolly Sailor HN 2172; Horn Pipes HN 2161. Third Row: Friar Tuck HN 2143; Coachman HN 2282; Cellist HN 2226, Town Crier HN 2119; Fiddler HN 2171.

tuberculosis caused by unpasteurised milk. Peggy spent more of her time in a series of hospitals and convalescent homes than at school. It was during one of her hospital stays that her artistic skills were discovered. Her detailed drawing of a mermaid caused quite a stir amongst the staff who were more used to childish doodles.

When she eventually returned to school she was way behind her classmates. However an enlightened teacher encouraged Peggy's artistic leanings rather than pushing her to catch up academically with her contemporaries. Still a delicate child Peggy was sent to live with her grandparents who, it was felt, could better look after her. Her grandfather was an engineer at a pot bank and the young Peggy was soon well acquainted with the world of the potteries. At twelve years old she won a scholarship to the Burslem College of Art but the circumstances of her family meant that Peggy had to earn some money while still attending the College on a part-time basis. She became assistant to Clarice Cliff. Later in her life Peggy made it clear to me that she did not exactly hold this lady in high regard. On her first day working for Clarice she was told to model some wall masks. By lunchtime she had achieved what she considered to be some rough designs. Clarice swept in from a good lunch, inspected what Peggy had modelled and despite Peggy's protestations that they were not finished ordered the masks to be put into production. Naturally the finished products carried the Clarice Cliff backstamp. When Peggy told me this story some forty years later, it was obvious that she was still rather displeased!

Peggy Davies first worked at Royal Doulton's Burslem studios in 1939. She was engaged as an assistant to Charles Noke. This association was not to last long. Her studio was destroyed by a bomb and Peggy decided she could be more use to the war effort by becoming a nurse. Given her diminutive stature and past medical history the authorities took more than a little persuading that Peggy was up to the job. They reckoned without her determination. Peggy became a nurse.

After the war Peggy did not return to Nile Street. She became an independent artist but secured a contract with Royal Doulton to provide figures for the HN collection. The rest, as they say, is history. Her particular style of pretty lady figures became a firm favourite with collectors all over the world. It should be remembered that she also produced a limited number of character studies – she was fond of telling how her husband endured posing with his mouth wide open for the *Town Crier*, and also the meticulously researched and detailed limited edition and prestige pieces.

As far as her many fans were concerned Peggy 'retired' far too soon. Judging from her comments, her working relationship with Eric Griffiths, the new Head of Ceramic Sculpture, was not an easy one and this may have contributed to her decision to leave Royal Doulton and concentrate on her own Pottery. Sadly Peggy died in 1989 but the legacy of her work and the delight her figures bring to collectors lives on as indeed does the Peggy Davies Studio which still thrives under the direction of her son, Rodrhi.

Mary Nicholl

If Peggy Davies was the doyen of Royal Doulton pretty lady designs then Mary Nicholl certainly held the same position when it came to character figures.

Like Peggy Davies, Mary Nicholl's artistic talents came to light at an early age, her first commission coming when she was only twelve years old. Her father, Gordon Nicholl, was a well known painter. He encouraged Mary's talent and supervised her artistic education. It was also thanks to him that Mary's modelling skills were brought to the attention of Royal Doulton. Gordon Nicholl had provided illustrations for two books written by Desmond Eyles. The two men became friends and one day Gordon Nicholls showed Desmond some terracotta figures to see if he thought they might be of interest to Royal Doulton. The figures were the work of his daughter, Mary. Desmond Eyles, while having reservations as to their suitability, was sufficiently impressed to arrange for Mary to travel from her West country home to Burslem to meet Jack Noke, the then Art Director at Burslem. Desmond's reservations were proved correct. Jack Noke considered the style of her figures unsuitable for reproduction in bone china or earthenware but he was impressed with Mary's undoubted modelling talents. It was arranged for her to spend some time at Burslem to study the techniques and style which were required for Royal Doulton figures. Mary was able to adapt her style and another successful and fruitful collaboration began.

Mary Nicholl died in 1974 at the early age of 52 but in common with Peggy Davies, her creations live on in collections all over the world. She is perhaps best known for her seafaring characters which still bring a salty tang of her Devonshire home wherever in the world they might be.

Douglas V Tootle

Doug Tootle is another artist who was trained at the Burslem School of Art. He joined Royal Doulton in the late 1960s as a modeller. His first figures to be added to the HN collection were launched in 1973. Among these was the dramatic and different *Masque* (HN 2554). Doug left Royal Doulton in 1974 to pursue a freelance career. However a collection of figures modelled by Doug but inspired by Leslie Harradine's figures of the 1930s was issued in the 1980s. He has also contributed figures for the **Images** and **Reflection** ranges, but his most spectacular models must be the large scale *Columbine* and *Harlequin* figures which were introduced in 1982 with an alternative colourway being issued in 1993.

Eric Griffiths

Eric Griffiths spent his childhood in North Wales. An accident, which nearly killed him, ultimately led him into his future career. In common with Peggy Davies, it was during a long period of convalescence that his artistic skills surfaced. More formal training was courtesy of the Shrewsbury Art School and Wolverhampton Art College. After a rather abortive attempt to earn his living as a portrait painter, Griffiths put his modelling talents to good use and began a career as a sculptor in industry. Before being appointed Director of Sculpture at Royal Doulton, he worked in a varied selection of industries ranging from toy soldiers to tractors.

Apart from his brief to expand Royal Doulton's pool of modelling talent, Eric Griffiths also contributed a number of models to the HN collection, notably the Royal Family portrait figures as well as designs for the **Haute Ensemble**, **Images** and **Reflections** series which illustrate his innovative stylised approach to Doulton figures. Eric Griffiths retired at the end of 1990.

William K Harper

Bill Harper joined Royal Doulton as a freelance modeller in 1973. He had previously worked as a designer with a number of other ceramics companies including Wade. At Royal Doulton character studies became his forte. A number of his figures followed on smoothly from the styles and themes set by Mary Nicholls but are indisputedly in Bill's own style. He is also responsible for the London series and portrait figures of *Charlie Chaplin* and *Groucho Marx*.

A friendly, charming man, Bill often attends Doulton Fairs and collectors meetings where he delights in talking to collectors about his figures and the stories behind them.

Robert Jefferson

Another freelance modeller who began working with Royal Doulton in the early 1970s, Robert Jefferson had previously enjoyed a career as a tableware designer. His first figure for the HN collection was the very distinctive *Harmony*. Subsequently his considerable talents have been put to good use in creating many of the prestige limited edition series such as **Les Saisons** and **The Great Lovers**, as well as stylish models for the **Images** and **Reflection** series.

Pauline Parsons

A sculpture graduate from the Manchester School of Art, Pauline Parsons first approached Royal Doulton in 1977 with a view to modelling character models for the HN collection. Her first figure to be issued was *The Lawyer*. However she eventually turned her attention to pretty lady figures contributing several to the Vanity Fair range. Perhaps her most famous figure is *Sleepy Darling*, the first figure to be commissioned solely for members of the Royal Doulton International Collectors Club. More recently her historical style limited edition figures such as **The Queens of the Realm** and **The Tudor Princesses** have found favour with collectors.

Peter Gee

Peter applied for a job as caster at the Royal Crown Derby factory. At his interview some clay models he brought with him caused a considerable amount of interest. The interest was transformed into an apprenticeship and Peter's first figure, *Rachel* was introduced in 1981. Since then Peter has demonstrated his versatility by modelling a wide range of figures ranging from *The Balloon Boy* to the **Reynolds Ladies** and **Gainsborough Ladies** by way of *Isadora* and probably the most popular of the **Figures of the Year**, *Amy*.

Robert Tabbenor

Robert Tabbenor always wanted an artistic career but although he is a native of Stoke-on-Trent, before joining Royal Doulton he had no experience of the pottery industry. The idea of sculpture fascinated him and under the guidance of Eric Griffiths, his talent flourished. His first figure was introduced in 1982. He had modelled several character figures as Royal Doulton International Collectors Club exclusives as well as child studies and several Images figures. Robert also worked on experimental projects at the factory and is now Studio Head.

Adrian Hughes

Adrian Hughes taught at the Derby College of Art and in several schools before opening his own design studio. He joined Royal Doulton as a freelance modeller in 1982. His versatility has been demonstrated with a wide range of figures which includes virtually every type of figure to be found in the HN collection.

Nada Pedley

Nada Pedley is another freelance modeller whose style has made its mark on the HN collection. She studied art in evening classes in Germany and England. Modelling started as a hobby but soon became her primary interest. Her first

Royal Doulton figure was *Bunny's Bedtime* which was once again an exclusive offer to members of the Royal Doulton International Collectors Club. She has now contributed many child studies and pretty lady figures for the collection in her own distinctive style.

Alan Maslankowski

It was Alan Maslankowski's mother who encouraged his interest in modelling. At 15, recognising his future potential, Royal Doulton sent him to art school for five years. Even during this period he produced several animal models which were accepted for production. After leaving art school he worked for a time at the John Beswick studio. He then left to pursue a freelance career but did not entirely sever his connections with Royal Doulton. In 1990 Alan returned to Royal Doulton as a resident artist. His figures include *The Wizard*, *Napoleon* and a number of child studies.

Patricia HN 3365. The 1993 figure of the year designed by Valerie Annand. Photo Royal Doulton

Valerie Annand

Valerie has developed a very particular style of Royal Doulton figures. Her ladies are a fantasy of frills and movement, attributes well loved by many collectors. Unlike her formally trained colleagues, Glasgow born Valerie is a self taught artist who came to figure modelling by way of designing greeting cards. Her flowing designs are to be found in both the standard collection and in various limited edition series such as **The British Sporting Heritage** and the 1996 **Figure of the Year**, *Belle*.

Charles Vyse

A group of Child Studies. Bedtime HN 1978; Sleepy Darling HN 2953; Darling (2nd version) HN 1985; Darling (1st version) HN 1319. Charles Vyse's design for Darling launched the HN collection in 1913.

Leslie Harradine

The Balloon Man HN 1954, an early example – note the blue balloon which was later replaced by a green one. The Old Balloon Seller HN 1315.

Odds and Ends HN 1844; Biddy Penny Farthing HN 1843. These figures were made as a pair but only the latter has remained in production. Early examples do not have balloons.

Bonnie Lassie HN 1626.

Curly Knob HN 1627.

Romany Sue HN 1757, HN 1758.

Daffy Down Dilly HN 1712, HN 1713.

London Cry – Strawberries HN 749; London Cry – Parsnips and Carrots HN 752.

Granny's Heritage HN 1874, HN 1873.

Spring Flowers HN 1807.

Covent Garden (1st version) HN 1339.

The Orange Lady HN 1759.

The Flower Sellers' Children HN 1342.

Old Lavender Seller HN 1492.

Primrose HN 1617.

All-A- Blooming HN 1466.

Sweet Lavender HN 1373.

The Flower Seller HN 789.

The Balloon Seller HN 583.

A group of Art Deco figures. Marietta HN 1446; Columbine (1st version) HN 1296; Angela (1st version) HN1204; Harlequinade HN 635; Clothilde HN 1599; The Bather (1st version) HN 687.

More Art Deco figures: Butterfuly HN 720; Pierrette HN 643; Sunshine Girl HN 1348, Carmen (1st version) HN 1267; Marietta HN 1341.

A Victorian Lady HN 1277.

Sweet Anne HN 1330.

Priscilla HN 1340.

Camille (1st version) HN 1586.

Two examples of Janet HN 1537. The figure on the left was made in 1995, the one on the right is dated 1935. The differences clearly illustrate the modifications which can occur during a long production run.

Top O' the Hill HN 1834. One of the all time classic Doulton Ladies.

Top O' the Hill HN 2127 in Australian national colours to celebrate the country's bicentennial in 1988.

Marguerite HN 1928.

Blithe Morning HN 2021.

Kate Hardcastle HN 1719.

Fleurette HN 1587.

Veronica HN 1517.

Gwendolen HN 1503

Pamela (1st version) HN 1468.

Irene HN 1621.

Daydreams HN 1731.

Rosebud (2nd version) HN 1983.

Penelope HN 1901.

Derrick HN 1398.

Rose HN 1368; Marie HN 1370. Both these figures are date coded for 1932.

Dinky Do HN 1678; Tinkle Bell HN 1677.

Bo Beep (2nd version) HN 1811.

Lily (1st version) HN 1798.

Cissie HN 1809.

Cissie HN 1808.

Lucy Ann HN 1502.

She Loves Me Not HN 2045; He Loves Me HN 2046.

Monica HN 1467.

Pearly Girl (1st version) HN 1483.

Peggy HN 2038.

Lavinia HN 1955.

Wendy HN 2109.

Ivy HN 1768.

Pied Piper HN 2102.

The Emir HN 1604.

Milkmaid HN 2057.

Charles Noke

The Jester HN 2016. The Jester originally appeared as a Vellum figure and was adapted for the HN collection in 1913.

King Charles HN 2084. This figure from the Prestige range was designed by Noke and Harry Tittensor.

Richard Garbe

Spring (3rd version) HN 1774. This figure was produced in a limited edition of 100. A coloured version was also available in an unlimited edition.

Peggy Davies

Janice (1st version) HN 2165.

Alison HN 2336.

Hilary HN 2335.

Nina HN 2347. This figure was produced with a matt glaze.

Gypsy Dance HN 2230.

Sunday Morning HN 2184.

Victoria HN 3416. Usually available in pink, this striking colourway was produced for sale at Royal Doulton Roadshow events.

Kelly Hn 2478. A Peggy Davies design given the Vanity Fair treatment.

Noelle HN 2179.

Monte Carlo HN 2332; Deauville HN 2344. These figures make up the 'Sweet and Twenties' collection.

The Young Master HN 2872.

Affection HN 2236.

Belle (2nd version) HN 2340.

Valerie HN 2107.

Vanity HN 2475.

Choir Boy HN 2141.

Eleanor of Provence HN 2009. One of a set of eight figures of important ladies in English history.

Mary Nicholl

Jovial Monk HN 2144. Usually associated with pretty lady figures, Peggy Davies also contributed some character studies to the collection. This is one.

The Carpenter HN 2678.

Sea Harvest HN 2257.

Lobster Man HN 2317.

Huntsman (3rd version) HN 2492.

Past Glory HN 2484.

Good Morning HN 2671. One of a group of character figures issued in a matt glaze. Not popular with collectors, these figures were withdrawn after only a few years.

The Judge HN 2443. Another matt glazed figure. When the other matt figures were withdrawn this model was reissued with a gloss finish.

Make Believe HN 2225. Unusually this child study was designed by Mary Nicholl.

William K. Harper

Pearly Boy (3rd version) HN 2767.

Douglas V. Tootle

Laurianne HN 2719.

Masque HN 2554. The figure illustrated is the early version with the right hand modelled away from the body.

Eric Griffiths

Old Ben HN 3190.

H.M. Queen Elizabeth the Queen Mother (3rd version) HN 3189.

Robert Jefferson

Harmony HN 2824.

Pauline Parsons

Sharon (1st version) HN 3047.

Snow White HN 3678.

Cinderella HN 3677.

Cherry Blossom HN 3092.

Geisha (3rd version) HN 3229.

Queens of the Realm: Queen Victoria HN 3125; Queen Anne HN 3141; Mary, Queen of Scots (2nd version) HN 3142; Queen Elizabeth I HN 3099.

Peter Gee

Celeste (2nd version) HN 3322. This is a renamed colourway of Isadora.

Hon. Frances Duncombe HN 3009; Sophia Charlotte, Lady Sheffield HN 3008. Two figures from the Gainsborough Ladies Collection.

Robert Tabbenor

Prized Possessions HN 2942.

Pride and Joy HN 2945.

The Auctioneer HN 2988.

Tom Brown HN 2941. A figure from the Characters from Children's Literature Series.

For Adrian Hughes' designs see Miscellaneous Section

Nada Pedley

Charlotte (2nd version) HN 3658. This figure was produced for Great Universal Stores and unusually is not a colourway of an existing figure.

Best Wishes HN 3426.

Alan Maslankowski

The Wizard HN 2877.

Little Ballerina HN 3395. This figure is shown in a colourway made the US market.

John Bromley

Janine HN 2461.

Francine HN 2422.

Valerie Annand

L'Ambittieuse HN 3359. This figure, made for members of the Royal Doulton International Collectors Club, introduced Valerie's flambuoyant style to collectors.

Miscellaneous

Gandulf HN 2911 – a figure from the Tolkein Series modelled by David Lyttleton.

The Four Seasons Collection made for the RDICC: Springtime HN 3033 (designed by Adrian Hughes); Summertime HN 3137 (designed by Pauline Parsons); Autumntime HN 3231 (designed by Pauline Parsons); Wintertime HN 3060 (designed by Adrian Hughes).

Grossmith's Tsang Ihang – Perfume of Tibet HN 582. This advertising figure dates from the 1920s. Unusually the example illustrated does not bear the name of the product. The designer is unknown.

Yardley's Old English Lavender. Although not strictly part of the HN collection – it was never allocated an HN number – this advertising figure is popular with collectors. The designer is unknown.

Clothilde HN 1598 table lamp. This art deco lampbase is rare and only appears to have been used for Clothilde.

Victorian Lady HN 727 table lamp. In the 1920s and 1930s figures from the HN collection could be purchased from Royal Doulton mounted as table lamps.

A group of 1930s miniature figures: Sweet Anne M6; Sweet Anne M27; Bridesmaid M12; Victorian Lady M2; Victorian Lady M25. All designed by Leslie Harradine.

The three colourways of Paisley Shawl, M3, M4, M26. All designed by Leslie Harradine.

Three of the rarer miniature figures, Monica M22; Janet M68;Windflower M78. All designed by Leslie Harradine.

A group of 1930s miniature figures: Patricia M7; Pantalettes M16; Chloe M9; Pantalettes M31; Polly Peachum HN 699. All designed by Leslie Harradine.

Two 'classic' Doulton Ladies in miniature. Leslie Harradine's Top O' the Hill re-introduced miniature figures to the HN Collection in 1988. Christmas Morn HN 3212 was originally created by Peggy Davies.

The Michael Doulton Signature Collection of Miniature Figures: Sara HN 3249; Southern Belle HN 3244; Ninette HN 3248; Elaine HN 3247; Kirsty HN 3246; Fragrance HN 3250. All designed by Peggy Davies.

Miniature character figures, Jester HN 3335 (designed by Charles Noke); Town Crier HN 3261 (designed by Peggy Davies); The Balloon Seller HN 2130 (designed by Leslie Harradine); Guy Fawkes HN 3271 (designed by Charles Noke); Good King Wenceslas HN 3262 (designed by Peggy Davies); Falstaff HN 3236 (designed by Charles Noke).

How a Royal Doulton Figure is Made

To the uninitiated, today's Royal Doulton figures seem expensive. They were never cheap. In the 1930s a Doulton lady could cost 37/6d (£1.17.6d) or in modern terms £1.87,which to us seems a ludicrously small amount. In 1930 this could represent more than a weeks wage. In the early 1970s I worked a day's overtime (for which I was paid £11.00 which I though was reasonable), in order to buy my wife her first Doulton lady. The figure was *Masque* (HN 2554) and the figure cost me almost that amount.

Taken at face value, the materials used to produce a china figurine cost very little. Even allowing for the various profit margins and taxes, the price still seems high until one considers how the figures are made and how much of a very expensive commodity was invested in even the simplest model. This pricey commodity is time, manhours (should that be 'person' hours to be politically correct?) call it what you will but a Royal Doulton figure is not a product which can be churned out of a machine. Indeed on my first visit to the Burslem factory I was struck by the fact that the most mechanical object I saw was a tap. So how is a Doulton figure made?

Any figure starts as an idea in the modellers mind. This idea is then made solid in the form of a clay, or sometimes wax model. Assuming that this model passes Doulton's selection process, it is given to the mould-maker in order for him to make the master mould or block. During the selection process the designers original concept can be drastically altered for reasons of practicality, aesthetics, marketing or cost. Sometimes this is not always an improvement! As it is only possible to cast the most basic figure from a single mould, the original model must be cut into as many pieces as is necessary to retain the shape and detail in reproducable form. As the original model is destroyed at this stage, the block makers job is extremely skilled. The resulting parts must fit exactly when assembled to recreate copies of the original model. From the master mould, plaster of paris moulds are made which are used for the casting of the figure. The liquid clay or slip is carefully poured into these moulds. (This is when the tap comes into the picture.) The plaster of paris absorbs water from the clay forming a layer of 'set clay' on the inner surface of the mould. After a carefully monitored period of time the excess slip is poured off. This timing is critical to ensure the cast pieces are of the exact required thickness. Today this does not appear to be too much of a problem but figures from earlier periods of production are sometimes found which have become victims of stress cracks. A figure suffering badly from stress cracks often weighs more than a comparable figure of the correct thickness. For example: I have two copies of *Daffy Down Dilly* , one perfect, one badly cracked. The perfect example, dating from about 1970 weighs 481 grams, the cracked one, dated 1937, weighs 659 grams.

Once the excess slip is removed the moulds are opened and the pieces of the figure are removed and trimmed. The cast figures are then assembled, the pieces being glued together with more slip. This process is highly skilled. At this stage the figures are extremely brittle and if too much pressure is exerted, the figure will be crushed. The assembled figure is then allowed to dry before receiving its first firing in the kilns. The first firing, known as the biscuit firing, is at a temperature of 1240° Centigrade. The kilns are slowly brought up to temperature and once at the correct heat they are kept at this temperature for six hours. The kilns and the china are then allowed to cool before the kilns are emptied. It is at this firing that the figures shrink by about one eighth of their volume. This is due to the evaporation of water contained in the clay. Until this stage the figures are treated the same, whether they are destined to become 'pretty ladies' or 'character studies' although the composition of the slip will be different. Most character figures are made of 'English Porcelain', which was formally known as English Translucent China, a Royal Doulton development dating from about 1960. Prior to that, character figures were usually made of earthenware. Where there is a choice, many collectors prefer to have an earthenware version of a figure as they consider the figures 'crisper' with the features more defined. The 'pretty lady' figures are still made from fine bone china.

The Royal Doulton prestige figure Columbine being assembled. This figue is made in 20 separate pieces and then each part is individually assembled and is then ready for the first 'biscuit firing. Photo Royal Doulton.

After the biscuit firing character studies, which are painted under glaze, are ready for painting. Once painted the figures are allowed to dry for about twelve hours before they are fired again to harden the paint and dry off the oils. The next stage is to immerse the figures in a vat of glaze before they receive their final firing at 1100° Centigrade for eleven hours.

The difference between under glazed and on glaze decoration has been likened to the difference between oil painting and watercolour. Pretty lady figures require, on the whole, a much more subtle look, like a water colour painting, and are therefore painted on glaze.

After the initial biscuit firing the bone china 'lady' figures are dipped by hand into a vat of glaze. They are then fired again emerging with a smooth sheen. If the subject includes hand made flowers they are added at this point. The figures are now ready for decoration to commence. Working from a completed figure as a guide, the body painter begins by painting the dresses and accessories. The colours are built up carefully to achieve the desired subtlety of tone. As different colours require different firing temperatures, some figures will be fired many times in the enamel kilns before the process is complete.

The body painting completed, the figures are then passed to the skilled face painters for the final part of their decoration. Yet another firing takes place and the figures are finished.

Although the production of Royal Doulton figures involves a large number of people, each figure is actually only handled by three craftsmen, the caster, the body painter and the face painter. Of course they could not carry out their tasks without the back-up provided in the factory by the skilled members of the team.

The above is only a brief description of the methods used in the production of Royal Doulton figures. If at all possible collectors should visit the factory or if this is not practical obtain one of the excellent videos which have been made that includes footage of the factory at work. Only by seeing the figures being made does one truly appreciate their magic.

Royal Doulton Fair Lady figures are decorated by the traditional and delicate skills of the figure painter, who chooses from a wide range of ceramic colours to achieve the delicate blend of shades and realistic skin tones of Royal Doulton figures. As different colours withstand different temperatures, some figures need to be fired several times in the enamel kilns during the handpainting process, to obtain the correct colourways. Photo Royal Doulton.

Buying Royal Doulton Figures

For collectors of current Royal Doulton figures there is no real problem in finding the models you require. Even if the desired figure is not on the china store shelves it can be ordered from the factory. It might take some weeks to arrive but in due course it will come. For collectors of out of production models it is not quite so easy. I know of no warehouse that is full to bursting point with desirable discontinued figures. But all is not lost, there is a thriving secondary market in out of production Royal Doulton figures. At first it can be a little daunting for the new collector to tap into it.

So where does the collector start? The Royal Doulton company is as good a place as any. They issue lists of specialist dealers and auction houses who hold regular sales which include Royal Doulton figures. It is very worthwhile making contact with a specialist dealer as they will usually have a good stock of Doulton. Even if they do not have the figure you want it is a good idea to give the dealer your list of wants. The dealer will then keep an eye out for the pieces in question and contact you when an example is available. In particular, if the item is quite rare or unusual it is unlikely that you will find it sitting on a shelf, as often there is a waiting list of collectors for the choicest pieces. Consequently the only way to be sure of obtaining the figure is to get onto a dealers' list. Most specialist dealers jealously guard their reputations and by buying from them, you have the added advantage that they will guarantee their stock. Needless to say that you should always be aware of what you are buying. Ask for a written receipt stating the figure's HN number, condition and price. If the dealer refuses to do this, then it is probably time to find a different dealer! Most dealers will also be happy to part-exchange figures or other items but remember the dealer is in business to make a profit, so don't expect the dealer to buy back a figure (or anything else come to that) at its current selling price. He has to sell it again and to stay in business a profit has to be made! Get to know your dealer(s), some will have shops, others will only exhibit at Antique Fairs, others stick to the specialist Doulton Fairs – some will be at all these places, whilst others deal by mail order. Search them out, talk to them and let them know what you are looking for. They are usually only too pleased to help. These then are the advantages of specialist dealers. The reverse side of the coin is that because a specialist dealer is very much in tune with the market, it is unlikely you will find the bargain of the century on his shelves. It has happened but only very rarely. There again it is equally unlikely that you will pay 'over the odds' for a piece. There is just too much competition in the market place and collectors soon would be aware of being 'overcharged'.

What are the other alternatives? General Antiques dealers at Antiques fairs, flea markets and of course, in their shops will often have Doulton in stock. They probably will not have a deep specialist knowledge of Doulton figures, which can work both to the advantage and disadvantage of the collector. The main advantage is that the general dealer may not appreciate the fine shading of the Doulton market. This could mean that a very good figure is only priced as an average piece. However Doulton figures are very well marked and it does not take too much detective work to discover the current market value of a particular figure. The disadvantage of buying from a general dealer is that a figure can be just as easily be overpriced — pricing based on the premise that 'if its Doulton it must be valuable' is all too common. Also the lack of detailed knowledge can mean obvious faults and flaws can be genuinely overlooked (and sometimes, it must be said, not so genuinely). But there are still bargains to be found if you look for them.

Another good source of Doulton figures is at auction. For the careful this is a very good method of adding pieces to the collection. But I must emphasise that it can also be a minefield for the unwary. I have seen many disappointed collectors who have been tempted to buy at auction and have ended up paying too much for damaged or restored items. Some auction houses, usually the larger ones, state in their catalogues when an item has been restored but in general lots are sold 'as seen' on the 'buyer beware' principle. This means that the prospective purchaser must thoroughly inspect the piece at the auction viewing. Auction rooms are rarely the most well lit of places and it is very easy to miss damage and restoration. Remember, once the hammer comes down, the piece is yours, which possibly means faults and all! The other danger is 'auction fever'. It is very easy to get carried away with the bidding and go over what you intended to pay. This overspend is then compounded by the auction house's commission (buyer's premium) and any taxes which might be due on the sale. Even a 'good buy' at hammer price can be transferred into not such a good deal by these often forgotten extras.

The third main source of Royal Doulton figures is other collectors. As collections grow and change, the collector can find that he (or she) has figures which no longer fit into the collection. Both Collecting Doulton magazine and Gallery, the magazine of the Royal Doulton International Collectors Club have free 'For sale and wanted' columns where private collectors can 'deal' amongst themselves.

Doulton Fairs

There is one place where you are guaranteed to find a good selection of out of production Royal Doulton figures and that is a specialised Doulton Fair. These originated in the United States in the 1970s and soon spread to the United Kingdom. The first UK Doulton Collectors Fair was organised by Nick Tzimas at the Park Lane Hotel in London. The success of this annual event resulted in other Doulton Fairs springing up. First of all came 20th Century Fairs International Doulton Fair held every year in Stafford and then the Doulton and Beswick Dealers Association Fair held twice a year at the National Motorcycle Museum in Birmingham. The Park Lane event has now been moved to the Queensway Hall in Dunstable making at present, a total of four Doulton Fairs in the UK every year. In the United States Doulton Fairs are currently organised in Ohio, Chicago and California.

At all these events the collector is assailed by a huge variety of Doulton wares which naturally includes hundreds of figures. Probably the biggest problem facing the collector is making the final choice of what to buy! Some collectors seem worried that at this type of event prices will be high. This is not usually the case. Of course there will be expensive items on sale but the fact that the dealers are all in competition with each other for sales means that it is not practical for them to charge anything other than the usual going rate. Indeed, in my experience, there are often bargains to be found.

Damage and Restoration

This is a very difficult subject and is an area in which collectors must decide for themselves if damage and/or restoration is acceptable in their collection. What follows are some guide lines and my own observations on the topic.

It goes without saying that if a figure is sold as perfect it should be just that —- no restorations or damage. It should be borne in mind, however, that Royal Doulton figures are handmade and were never intended for very close scrutiny under a strong magnifying glass. Almost inevitably some imperfections will be visible if one inspects them closely. Unless these blemishes are so bad as to disfigure the piece, in which case the figure is probably a second, they have to be accepted as part and parcel of the figure. If any imperfection, no matter how small, renders the piece unacceptable to you , then I can only suggest you collect something else!

I know there are many collectors who will not accept restoration on a figure in any shape or form. I think this is a rather short sighted view. There are some ceramic items I would not recommend buying in anything other than perfect condition. This is not necessarily the case with Doulton figures. Providing the figure is bought as 'restored' and at a suitably reduced price and is professionally restored, I can see no problem. One reason often given for not buying a restored figure is that it would be difficult to sell again. In my experience there are plenty of people, myself included, who cannot afford a perfect example of, say, an art deco figure. A well repaired example would be perfectly acceptable. There is a market in restored figures, therefore should it be necessary to sell it, you can be confident there would be someone else prepared to buy it from you.

There are a number of pre-war figures which because of their shape, rarely if ever, survived in perfect condition. It would seem that the technology of the 1930s was not up to some of Leslie Harradines designs, consequently stress cracks can appear and open. For example, Teresa (HN 1682/3) is particularly prone to this type of damage. The corners of the square base can crack, the cracks sometimes spreading into the body of the figure. It is a rare figure in any condition, a truly perfect copy is extremely rare. Thus by rejecting restored figures out of hand, the collector could be restricting his choice of figures. Ultimately it is the collector who must decide their position on restoration but remember 1) there are some figures which hardly ever come on the market in perfect condition 2) a restored figure can fill a gap in a collection until a perfect example is available 3) buying a good figure which has been restored can cut the cost of collecting 4) no matter how good a restoration may be, the figure will never again be 'perfect'.

Many of the same criteria also apply to damaged but unrestored figures and again it is for the collector to decide what is acceptable to them.

Detecting Restoration

Everybody seems to have their own special way of checking for restoration. With modern restoration techniques it is not always easy to spot restoration, even professionals can make mistakes. Here are a few tips you might find useful.

In every figure there are areas which are more prone to damage. When examining a figure start by checking these areas.

1) The neck.
2) Outstretched limbs including hands and feet.
3) Modelled flowers (these are so vulnerable that the odd tiny chip might be classed as fair wear and tear.
4) Bases – particularly the corners of square bases, look for cracks.
5) Thin waists.
6) Any part of the figure which projects from the main body of the figure.

Methods of Detection

By touch

The glaze which covers Royal Doulton figures is a type of glass. Restoration glazes are synthetic. An unrestored figure will therefore have the cold touch of glass, an area of restoration will have the warmer feel of plastic.

There is another 'touch' method of detection. Run the fleshy part of your hand at the base of the thumb across the suspect area. If there is no restoration your hand will run smoothly over the glaze. If restoration is present, you will feel a slight resistance on your skin, the skin will feel as if it is being slightly pulled back. This may sound bizarre but in my experience it works, but only with that part of the hand. Strange but true!

By sight

Old restorations can discolour with age and are therefore easy to find. Newer repairs can sometimes be noticed by a slight change of tone and the presence of little bubbles in the new glaze. With bone china figures which are translucent, cracks and glue marks from breaks can be spotted by holding the figure against a strong light and looking through the hole in the base of the figure. The damage will be visible in the form of brown lines.

By teeth

Not a method I use or recommend but it explains why on occasions you see people apparently chewing china! The principle of this method is that if you lightly tap your teeth on a suspect area of china, you will hear a slight dull thud, whereas if the piece is perfect you will get more of a ringing sound. I am told this is particularly good for finding cracks. I think the same result can be achieved by lightly tapping the piece with your fingernails which is probably more hygienic!

By metal object

Definitely not a recommended method under any circumstances. Based on the premise that the original glaze is hard and glass-like and restoration glaze is softer, a metal object, a pin, car keys etc. will either sink into the restoration or scratch it but not harm a perfect piece. This method of detection also destroys, to a greater or lesser extent, the restoration.

By light

Most restorations show up as dark patches when viewed under Ultra Violet light. There are various gadgets on the market to provide the ultra light. The idea sounds foolproof but it is not entirely so. Some modern restoration glazes do not show up and it is not always convenient to exclude sufficient light for the ultra violet to do its job

Ultimately nothing beats experience so the more you become familiar with and handle Royal Doulton figures the more you will be able to develop your own sixth sense for the detection of restoration.

A Final Word on Restoration

A restored figure should be cheaper than a perfect example. The difference in price depends on the rarity of the figure and the extent of the restoration. As a rule of thumb the rarer the figure, the closer to the perfect price you can expect to pay. A reasonably restored example of a common figure – for instance a pink *Autumn Breezes* (HN 1911) should be 40-50% of its perfect price, an extremely rare figure with only slight restoration could be 80-90% of the perfect price. Each purchase should be individually judged by the prospective purchaser.

Care of your Collection

Generally Royal Doulton figures are a lot tougher than most people think but having said that I am sure collectors need no reminding that any ceramic item can be broken or damaged, so treat your valuable figures with respect.

In my experience, most accidental damage to figures seems to occur when they are being dusted. It is very easy to catch the duster on a finger or flower and break it off or, even worse, figures have been dropped or smashed when picked up for dusting. Ban the duster! If you must dust your figures between washings, either just blow on them or use a soft brush to carefully flick the dust off. What I prefer to do is to let the figures get good and dusty and then wash them in warm soapy water using a small, soft paint brush. Do not immerse them. I then rinse off the soap with clean water and leave the figure to dry naturally – drying up cloths are just as bad as dusters for catching on protruding parts of figures. Do not wash your figures too often. The more often you handle them, the more the risk of accidental damage. If you are worried about dust and dirt, keep the figures in a cabinet.

Glass shelves are not considered by some to be suitable for displaying china as small chips can occur when the china is placed on the harder surface of glass.

Do not place your figures near a source of heat, this includes near windows which can magnify the heat of the sun. A sudden change of temperature can, in extreme circumstances, cause a figure to crack.

Do keep a list of your collection, noting any information you can about the piece (limited edition numbers, damage or restoration), which can help identify it should you have the misfortune to have it stolen.

Do not display your collection where it can be seen from outside your home, and remember, at night a lit room without drawn curtains or blinds will become even more visible from outside.

Displaying your Collection

There are no hard and fast rules for displaying your collection. Every collection is different and every collectors' home will be individual. No matter how extensive or how modest your collection may be, with a little imagination it can be viewed to its best advantage.

Some collections are housed in cabinets, others scattered around the home. Some really serious collectors have even built special rooms to house their collections. It is just a matter of personal taste but sometimes collections can take over your home and you begin to wonder if you are living in a warehouse!

A few basic ideas can transform your collection. Grouping your figures can be a good idea, groups of similar colour or type look well together. Try and keep the scale of the figures the same. Not all Royal Doulton figures are made to the same scale. Estelle (HN 1566) is a child model but at 8inches, she is considerably larger than most other child studies and will tower over them if placed with them. Equally as an over large child she will look out of place with average sized lady figures. 'Conversational' groups will also add interest.

Using plastic 'bridges' or covered wooden blocks to raise some of the figures to another level are a useful way of making a double row of figures into an attractive display. Without the extra height afforded by these blocks, all you would see of the back row would be a row of heads. They also allow more figures to be displayed in the same space.

Be adventurous, why not put some figures in places you would not normally expect to find them, in the bathroom or the kitchen for instance. Link your Royal Doulton figures with other compatible objects in your home – a group of figures with books would look appropriate near your bookshelves or some 'rustic' characters might look good in the conservatory.

Good lighting is important. One of the most appealing aspects of Royal Doulton figures is their vibrant glazes. To see the figures at their best advantage, they should be well lit. A strategically placed spotlight can work wonders. If spotlights are inappropriate, tablelamps can help. If you do not want to lose the Doulton theme to your collection, there are even Doulton figure lamps which were sold in the 1930s. These sometimes appear on the market but usually need a certain amount of work done to them to ensure they are safe to use. If you are lucky you might find a fully restored lamp on sale.

A word of warning —NEVER display your figures or any other valuables) where they can clearly be seen from outside. It is an invitation to burglars.

Your collecting is to be enjoyed, do not just have it scattered around your home or arranged in serried ranks on shelves. Round it up, let your imagination run a little wild and display your collection with style.

Dating and Backstamps

Most collectors like to know when their Royal Doulton figures were made. Sometimes it is possible to identify the exact year of manufacture but in most cases it is only feasible to be accurate within a band of likely dates.

A date coding system was introduced in the late 1920s. It seems to have petered out by the 1950s. The coding was very simple and is the only way of being sure of a figure's date of manufacture. A numeral was printed beside the Royal Doulton backstamp (Roman numerals were used until 1930, arabic figures thereafter) by adding this figure to the base year, 1927, the date of manufacture can be obtained. For instance, a figure with a '5' beside the backstamp will have been made in 1932 (5+27=32).

Sometimes it is possible to detect other numbers impressed in the base of some figures. One set of numbers will be the model number (not the same as the HN number), another set of numbers will look like a date (eg. 2.32). It is a date but not necessarily the date the figure was made. It is the date on which the mould from which the figure was cast was made. As moulds quickly wear out it is more than likely to be the same as the date of manufacture but it is not always so.

Royal Doulton have changed the style of marking their figures on a number of occasions over the years. The Royal Doulton 'lion and crown' backstamp has remained more or less constant but the form in which other information is presented has changed. By knowing the production dates of a particular figure and also the dates the markings changed, it is possible to be a little more specific as to the date of manufacture. It is worth remembering that although it is often stated that certain pre-war figures ceased production 'by 1949' production often ended long before this date. 1949 was taken as a convenient cut off point but in fact figure production was phased out rather than coming to shuddering halt as the war time restriction of decorative china production took hold. Therefore some figures introduced in the mid to late 1930s had a very short production run. For '1949' it is probably more realistic to think of 1940 as the deletion date. A very few figures continued in production throughout the war years for sale in overseas markets to help the war effort by earning dollars.

Backstamps

All dates must be considered approximate. A version of the standard Lion and Crown Royal Doulton mark is used throughout. The words 'Bone China' are omitted when the figure is made in earthenware or fine china.

Typical backstamp used on M Series figures.

1. 1913-c1920

Handwritten title, HN number, Potted by Doulton and Co. 'Gothic' style script. Name of designer included

2. c1920-1930

Handwritten title, HN number, Potted by Doulton and Co. Designers name omitted.

3. 1930-c1945

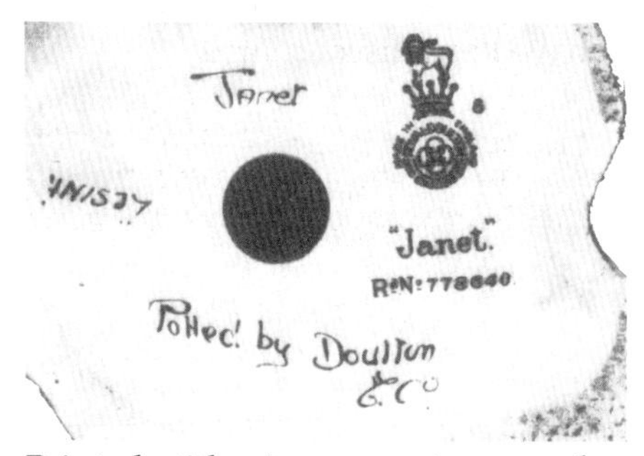

Printed title in quotation marks, design registration numbers. Handwritten HN number, Potted by Doulton. Often found with date code.

Picture shows figure date coded for 1935 (27+8)

4. 1945-1959

Printed title in quotation marks and design registration numbers. Copyright date added, also Doulton and Co. Limited. Handwritten HN number.

5. 1959-1976

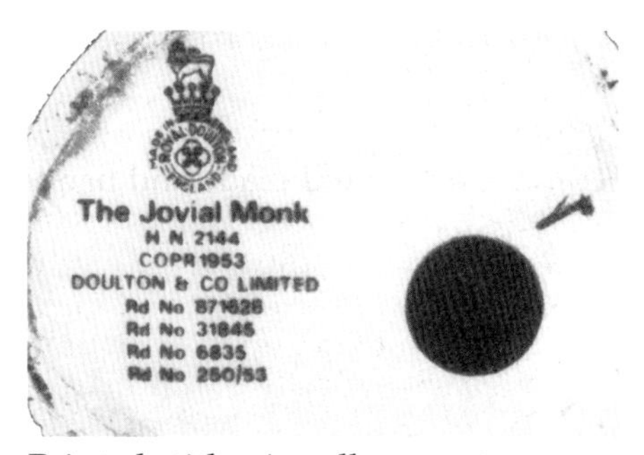

Printed title (smaller, neater type face), registration numbers and HN number. DOULTON AND CO. LIMITED.

6. 1977-1978

As Number 5 but registration numbers removed.

7. 1979-1981

Printed title in upper case type, printed HN number. © ROYAL DOULTON TABLEWARE LTD.

8. 1982

Printed Royal Doulton added below mark, title in smaller upper case type. Printed HN number 'Hand made and Hand decorated' added. © ROYAL DOULTON LTD.

9. 1983

Printed mark. Hand made and hand decorated in semi-circular form around Royal Doulton mark. HN number above title. Title in larger print than in No 8. Facsimile signature of modeller added. © ROYAL DOULTON TABLEWARE LIMITED.

10. 1984

As Number 9 except (UK) replaces TABLEWARE LIMITED.

11. 1985

As Number 10 except registered trade symbol added to Royal Doulton.

12. 1986-CURRENT

As Number 11 except (UK) removed. Note that the first year of issue was recorded around 1993 but now seems to have been discontinued.

There are various variations to be found on specially commissioned figures These are self explanatory.

Listings and Price Guide

As I reviewed the current values of the HN and M collection figures it became evident that in today's market conditions it is impossible to determine a definite price for many of the figures. This is particularly true of the desirable early figures and the stylish art deco models. It should also be borne in mind that there are still six figures which have yet to be re-discovered. Obviously having never appeared on the secondary market their commercial value has never really been determined. If and when any of these elusive figures should be offered for sale, one can only speculate what price they might command. Therefore the collector should remember that the prices listed in this guide are just that – *a guide*. At any particular time any number of factors can affect the value of a figure. For instance at a recent specialist Doulton auction at least three high spending collectors were more than a little interested in the art deco figures. This high octane competition backed up with suitably high performance cheque books resulted in some startlingly high prices. But once these wealthy collectors' demands have been satisfied, there are no guarantees that the prices achieved on that day will be repeated. So what is the real value of these figures? In truth, only time will tell.

In the following pages a number of titles have been marked *. This indicates that these models are both rare and in demand by collectors. This heady combination of factors is likely to lead to volatile prices. The market value of these pieces will ultimately be determined by market forces in operation at the time. Notes in smaller type refer to the figure immediately above it unless otherwise indicated. Currency values given are in Pounds Sterling and US Dollars.

If you are selling to a dealer, remember that he has to have some profit for his labours. 30%-40% is reasonable, but if the dealer has a lot of that item in stock, or finds it difficult to sell, he may want to pay less. Shop around. Dealers are human beings and are tied by market conditions, the same as collectors are.

RRP means Recommended Retail Price, as this piece is still being sold by retailers (at the time of going to press). Every effort is made to give a price which reflects the market generally. Some price guides are written by dealers who have a vested interest in recording prices higher than the market trend. This creates lack of confidence in the market if prices realised at auction or at trade fairs are much lower than the ones quoted in their books. All Francis Joseph books, including this one, give *general market* prices, which collectors should use as a basis for their collecting.

We are not talking about the market for tinned garden peas! Prices vary and collector interest varies and the market changes over time. Use this guide as a *general* guide, paying more for some items, less for others – and enjoy buying and selling.

HN No *Ver* *Prod Dates* *Market Values*

A LA MODE
Haute Ensemble Series
Designer: Eric J Griffiths
HN 2544 1 1974-79 £200-£250 $430-$535

"A LITTLE BOY CALLED LOVE . . ."
Designer: Unknown
HN 1545 1 1933-49 £180-£250 $385-$535

A POSY FOR YOU
Designer: Nada Pedley
HN 3606 1 1994 RRP RRP

ABDULLAH
Designer: Leslie Harradine
HN 1410 1 1930-38 £430-£560 $920-$1200
HN 2104 1 1953-62 £250-£280 $535-$600

A'COURTING
Designer: Leslie Harradine
HN 2004 1 1947-53 £200-£250 $430-$535

ACE, The
Designer: Robert Tabbenor
HN 3398 1 1991-95 £100-£120 $215-$255

ADELE
Designer: Peggy Davies
HN 2480 1 1987-92 £100-£120 $165-$200
Colourway of Margaret (2nd version).

ADORNMENT
Gentle Arts Series
Designer: Pauline Parsons. Ltd Ed: 750
HN 3015 1 1989 £450-£500 $965-$1075

ADRIENNE
Designer: Peggy Davies
HN 2152 1 1964-76 £120-£160 $255-$345
HN 2304 1 1964-91 £100-£140 $215-$300
Later variations known as Joan and Fiona.

AFFECTION
Designer: Peggy Davies
HN 2236 1 1962-94 £70-£90 $150-$195

AFTERNOON CALL, The
Designer: Ernest W Light
HN 82* 1 1918-38 £870-£1130 $1865-$2425
Also known as Lady with Ermine Muff

AFTERNOON TEA
Designer: P Railston
HN 1747* 1 1935-82 £250-£300 $535-$645
HN 1748* 1 1935-49 £300-£350 $645-$750

AILEEN
Designer: Leslie Harradine
HN 1645* 1 1934-38 £500-£550 $1075-$1180
HN 1664* 1 1934-38 £500-£550 $1075-$1180
HN 1803* 1 1937-49 £500-£550 $1075-$1180

ALCHEMIST, The
Designer: Leslie Harradine
HN 1259* 1 1927-38 £600-£650 $1285-$1395
HN 1282* 1 1928-38 £600-£650 $1285-$1395

ALEXANDRA
Designer: Peggy Davies
HN 2398 1 1970-76 £120-£140 $255-$300
Designer: Douglas V Tootle
HN 3286 2 1990 RRP RRP

ALFRED JINGLE
Dickens Series
Designer: Leslie Harradine
HN 541 1 1922-32 £55-£60 $120-$130
M 52 1 1932-81 £40-£60 $85-$130

ALFRED THE GREAT
Designer: Douglas V Tootle
HN 3821 1 1996 RRP RRP

ALICE
Designer: Peggy Davies
HN 2158 1 1960-81 £110-£130 $235-$280
Designer: Nada Pedley
HN 3368 2 1991 RRP RRP

ALISON
Designer: Peggy Davies
HN 2336 1 1966-92 £100-£130 $215-$280
HN 3264 1 1989-93 £100-£120 $215-$255

ALL ABOARD
Designer: Robert Tabbenor
HN 2940 1 1982-86 £130-£150 $280-$320

ALL-A-BLOOMING
Designer: Leslie Harradine
HN 1457 1 1931-38 £600-£650 $1285-$1395
HN 1466 1 1931-38 £600-£650 $1285-$1395

ALLURE
Reflections Series
Designer: Eric J Griffiths
HN 3080 1 1985-89 £80-£100 $170-$215

ALMOST GROWN
Designer: Nada Pedley
HN 3425 1 1993 RRP RRP

AMANDA
Designer: Robert Tabbenor
HN 3406 1 1993 RRP RRP
HN 3632 1 1994 RRP RRP
HN 3634 1 1996 RRP RRP
Colourway for Young of Canada
HN 3635 1 1995-96 £25 $55
Colourway for RDICC
Vanity Fair Children Series
HN 2996 1 1986 RRP RRP
There have been 17 versions of this figure under various different names!

HN No *Ver* *Prod Dates* *Market Values*

AMY
Kate Greenaway Series
Designer: Peggy Davies
HN 2958 1 1982-87 £130-£150 $280-$320
Figure of the Year Series
Designer: Peter Gee
HN 3316 2 1991 £300-£350 $645-$750
Designer: Tim Potts
HN 3854 3 1996 RRP RRP

AMY'S SISTER
Designer: Peter Gee
HN 445 1 1993 RRP RRP

AN ARAB
See also *The Moor*
Designer: Charles J Noke
HN 33* 1 1913-38 £750-£850 $1610-$1825
HN 343* 1 1919-38 £850-£900 $1825-$1930
HN 378* 1 1920-38 £750-£850 $1610-$1825

AND ONE FOR YOU
Childhood Days Series
Designer: Adrian Hughes
HN 2970 1 1982-85 £100-£120 $215-$255

AND SO TO BED
Childhood Days Series
Designer: Pauline Parsons
HN 2966 1 1982-85 £130-£150 $280-$320

ANDREA
Vanity Fair Children Series
Designer: Robert Tabbenor
HN 3058 1 1985-95 £40-£50 $85-$105

ANGELA
Designer: Leslie Harradine
HN 1204 1 1926-38 £500-£750 $1075-$1610
HN 1303 1 1928-38 £500-£750 $1075-$1610
Vanity Fair Series
Designer: Peggy Davies
HN 2389 2 1983-86 £100-£120 $215-$255
Michael Doulton Exclusive Series
Designer: Nada Pedley
HN 3419 3 1992 £150-£180 $320-$385
HN 3690 4 1996 RRP RRP
Colourway of Sweet Sixteen for Great Universal Stores

ANGELINA
Designer: Leslie Harradine
HN 2013 1 1948-51 £250-£300 $535-$645

ANITA
Designer: Nada Pedley
HN 3766 1 1996 RRP RRP
Colourway for Great Universal Stores

ANN
Vanity Fair Series
Designer: Douglas V Tootle
HN 2739 1 1983-85 £120-£140 $255-$300
HN 3259 2 1990 RRP RRP

ANNA
Kate Greenaway Series
Designer: Peggy Davies
HN 2802 1 1976-82 £120-£150 $255-$320

ANNABEL
Designer: Robert Tabbenor
HN 3273 1 1989-92 £130-£150 $280-$320

ANNABELLA
Designer: Leslie Harradine
HN 1871 1 1938-49 £500-£550 $1075-$1180
HN 1872 1 1938-49 £500-£550 $1075-$1180
HN 1875 1 1938-49 £500-£550 $1075-$1180

ANNE BOLEYN
King Henry VIII's Wives Series
Designer: Pauline Parsons. Ltd Ed: 9500
HN 3232 1 1990 RRP RRP

ANNE OF CLEVES
King Henry VIII's Wives Series
Designer: Pauline Parsons. Ltd Ed: 9500
HN 3356 1 1991 RRP RRP

ANNETTE
Designer: Leslie Harradine
HN 1471 1 1931-38 £180-£200 $385-$430
HN 1472 1 1931-49 £180-£200 $385-$430
HN 1550 1 1933-49 £180-£200 $385-$430
Designer: Peggy Davis
HN 3495 2 1993 £100-£130 $215-$280
Colourway of Sandra for Great Universal Stores

ANNIVERSARY
Designer: Valerie Annand
HN 3625 1 1994 RRP RRP

ANTHEA
Designer: Leslie Harradine
HN 1526* 1 1932-38 £500-£550 $1075-$1180
HN 1527* 1 1932-49 £500-£550 $1075-$1180
HN 1669* 1 1934-38 £500-£550 $1075-$1180

ANTOINETTE
Designer: Leslie Harradine.
HN 1850* 1 1938-49 £650-£700 $1395-$1500
HN 1851* 1 1938-49 £650-£700 $1395-$1500
Designer: Peggy Davies
HN 2326 2 1967-79 £130-£150 $280-$320

ANTONY AND CLEOPATRA
Great Lovers Collection Series
Designer: Robert Jefferson. Ltd Ed: 150
HN 3114 1 1996 RRP RRP

APERITIF
Reflections Series
Designer: Robert Tabbenor
HN 2998 1 1988 RRP RRP
Commissioned by Home Shopping Network

APPLE MAID, The
Designer: Leslie Harradine
HN 2160 1 1957-62 £220-£250 $470-$535

HN No *Ver* *Prod Dates* *Market Values*

APRIL
Figure of the Month Series
Designer: Peggy Davies. Ltd Ed: 950
HN 2708 1 1987 £140-£160 $300-$345
For Home Shopping Network, USA
Designer: Robert Tabbenor
HN 3333 2 1990 £100-£130 $215-$280
Colourway of Amanda. USA only
Wild Flower of the Month Series
Designer: Peggy Davis
HN 3344 3 1991 £130-£150 $280-$320
Colourway of Beatrice for Sears of Canada
Designer: Nada Pedley
HN 3693 4 1995 RRP RRP

APRIL SHOWER
Enchantment Series
Designer: Robert Jefferson
HN 3024 1 1983-86 £140-£165 $300-$355

ARAGORN
Tolkien Series
Designer: David Lyttleton
HN 2916 1 1981-84 £60-£80 $130-$170

ARIEL
Disney Princesses Series
Designer: Pauline Parsons. Ltd Ed: 2000
HN 3831 1 1996 RRP RRP
For Disney stores, selected markets only

ARTFUL DODGER, The
Dickens Series
Designer: Leslie Harradine
HN 546 1 1922-32 £55-£60 $120-$130
M 55 1 1932-83 £40-£60 $85-$130

AS GOOD AS NEW
Childhood Days Series
Designer: Adrian Hughes
HN 2971 1 1982-85 £100-£130 $215-$280

ASCOT
Designer: Mary Nicoll
HN 2356 1 1968-95 £100-£120 $215-$255
British Sporting Heritage Series
Designer: Valerie Annand. Ltd Ed: 5000
HN 3471 2 1993 RRP RRP

ASHLEY
Vanity Fair Series
Designer: Nada Pedley
HN 3420 1 1992 RRP RRP

AT EASE
Designer: Peggy Davies
HN 2473 1 1973-79 £160-£180 $345-$385

AU REVOIR
Elegance Series
Designer: Alan Maslankowski
HN 3723 1 1995 RRP RRP
Sentiments Series
HN 3729 2 1996 RRP RRP

AUCTIONEER, The
RDICC Exclusive Series
Designer: Robert Tabbenor
HN 2988 1 1986 £160-£180 $345-$385

AUGUST
Figure of the Month Series
Designer: Peggy Davies
HN 3165 1 1987 £140-£160 $300-$345
For Home Shopping Network, USA
Designer: Robert Tabbenor
HN 3325 2 1990 £100-£130 $215-$280
Colourway of Amanda. USA only
Wild Flower of the Month Series
Designer: Peggy Davis
HN 3408 3 1991 £130-£150 $280-$320
Colourway of Beatrice for Sears of Canada

AUTOMNE
Les Saisons Series
Designer: Robert Jefferson. Ltd Ed: 500
HN 3068 1 1986 £450-£500 $965-$1075

AUTUMN
Designer: Unknown
HN 314 1 1918-38 £600-£650 $1285-$1395
HN 474 1 1921-38 £620-£680 $1330-$1460
Designer: Peggy Davies
HN 2087 2 1952-59 £250-£280 $535-$600

AUTUMN ATTRACTION
Designer: Peggy Davis
HN 3612 1 1993 RRP RRP
Colourway of Michele for Guild of Specialist Retailers

AUTUMN BREEZES
Designer: Leslie Harradine
HN 1911 1 1939-76 £130-£150 $280-$320
HN 1913 1 1939-71 £140-£160 $300-$345
HN 1934 1 1940 RRP RRP
HN 2131 1 1990-94 £120-£140 $255-$300
HN 2147 1 1955-71 £250-£280 $535-$600
Miniature Series
HN 2176 1 1991-95 RRP RRP
Michael Doulton Miniature Series
HN 2180 1 1991 RRP RRP

AUTUMN GLORY
Reflections Series
Designer: Robert Tabbenor
HN 2766 1 1988 RRP RRP
Commissioned by Home Shopping Network

AUTUMNTIME
RDICC Exclusive Series
Designer: Pauline Parsons
HN 3231 1 1989 £100-£120 $215-$255
Four Seasons Series
Designer: Valerie Annand
HN 3621 2 1994 RRP RRP

AWAKENING, The
Designer: Leslie Harradine
HN 1927 1 1940-49 £950-£1200 $2040-$2575

HN No	Ver	Prod Dates	Market Values	

AWAKENING
Images Series Series
Designer: Peggy Davies

HN 2837	2	1981	RRP	RRP
HN 2875	2	1981	RRP	RRP

BABA
Designer: Leslie Harradine

HN 1230	1	1927-38	£260-£310	$555-$665
HN 1243	1	1927-38	£260-£310	$555-$665
HN 1244	1	1927-38	£260-£310	$555-$665
HN 1245	1	1927-38	£260-£310	$555-$665
HN 1246	1	1927-38	£260-£310	$555-$665
HN 1247	1	1927-38	£260-£310	$555-$665
HN 1248	1	1927-38	£260-£310	$555-$665

BABETTE
Designer: Leslie Harradine

HN 1423	1	1930-38	£370-£440	$795-$945
HN 1424	1	1930-38	£370-£440	$795-$945

BABIE
Designer: Leslie Harradine

HN 1679	1	1935-92	£70-£85	$150-$180
HN 1842*	1	1938-49	£120-£150	$255-$320
HN 2121	1	1983-92	£70-£85	$150-$180

BABY
Designer: Charles J Noke

HN 12	1	1913-38	£750-£1000	$1610-$2145

BABY BUNTING
Designer: Peggy Davies

HN 2108	1	1953-59	£160-£170	$345-$365

BACHELOR, The
Designer: Mary Nicoll

HN 2319	1	1964-75	£200-£250	$430-$535

BALINESE DANCER
Dancers of the World Series
Designer: Peggy Davies. Ltd Ed: 750

HN 2808	1	1982	£300-£350	$645-$750

BALLAD SELLER
Designer: Peggy Davies

HN 2266	1	1968-73	£150-£180	$320-$385

BALLERINA
Designer: Peggy Davies

HN 2116	1	1953-73	£160-£190	$345-$405

Reflections Series
Designer: Adrian Hughes. Ltd Ed: 500

HN 3197	2	1988	RRP	RRP

Commissioned by Home Shopping Network

BALLET CLASS
Reflections Series
Designer: Pauline Parsons

HN 3134	1	1987-92	£100-£130	$215-$280

BALLET SHOES
Designer: Alan Maslankowski

HN 3434	1	1993	RRP	RRP

BALLOON BOY
Designer: Peter Gee

HN 2934	1	1984	RRP	RRP

BALLOON CLOWN
Designer: William K Harper

HN 2894	1	1986-92	£130-£150	$280-$320

BALLOON GIRL
Designer: William K Harper

HN 2818	1	1982	RRP	RRP

BALLOON LADY
Designer: Peter Gee

HN 2935	1	1984	RRP	RRP

BALLOON MAN, The
Designer: Leslie Harradine

HN 1954	1	1940	RRP	RRP

BALLOON SELLER, The
Designer: Leslie Harradine

HN 479*	1	1921-38	£1060-£1190	$2275-$2555
HN 486*	1	1921-38	£680-£750	$1460-$1610
HN 548	1	1922-38	£380-£440	$815-$945
HN 583	1	1923-49	£220-£280	$470-$600
HN 697	1	1925-38	£160-£160	$345-$345

Miniature Series

HN 2130	1	1989-91	£130-£150	$280-$320

BALLOONS
Reflections Series
Designer: Eric J Griffiths

HN 3187	1	1988	RRP	RRP

Commissioned by Home Shopping Network

BARBARA
Designer: Leslie Harradine

HN 1421	1	1930-38	£450-£500	$965-$1075
HN 1432	1	1930-38	£450-£500	$965-$1075
HN 1461	1	1931-38	£450-£500	$965-$1075

Designer: Pauline Parsons

HN 2962	2	1982-84	£130-£150	$280-$320

Designer: Peter Gee. Ltd Ed: 9500

HN 3441	3	1994	RRP	RRP

RDICC

BARLIMAN BUTTERBUR
Tolkien Series
Designer: David Lyttleton

HN 2923	1	1982-84	£200-£250	$430-$535

BASKET WEAVER, The
Designer: Mary Nicoll

HN 2245	1	1959-62	£250-£300	$535-$645

BATHER, The
Designer: Leslie Harradine

HN 597	1	1924-38	£600-£650	$1285-$1395
HN 687	1	1924-49	£450-£500	$965-$1075
HN 781	1	1926-38	£600-£650	$1285-$1395
HN 782	1	1926-38	£600-£650	$1285-$1395
HN 1238	1	1927-38	£600-£650	$1285-$1395
HN 1708	1	1935-38	£750-£1000	$1610-$2145

Has bathing suit painted on

HN No Ver Prod Dates Market Values

HN 773 2 1925-38 £600-£650 $1285-$1395
HN 774 2 1925-38 £600-£650 $1285-$1395
HN 1227 2 1927-38 £600-£650 $1285-$1395

BATHING BEAUTY
Reflections Series
Designer: Adrian Hughes
HN 3156 1 1987-89 £150-£180 $320-$385
USA only

BEACHCOMBER
Designer: Mary Nicoll
HN 2487 1 1973-76 £130-£150 $280-$320

BEAT YOU TO IT
Designer: Peggy Davies
HN 2871 1 1980-87 £180-£200 $385-$430

BEATRICE
Designer: Peggy Davies
HN 3263 1 1989 RRP RRP
There have been 18 versions of this figure under various names
HN 3631 1 1994 RRP RRP

BECKY
Designer: Douglas V Tootle
HN 2740 1 1987-92 £130-£150 $280-$320

BEDTIME
Designer: Leslie Harradine.
HN 1978 1 1945 RRP RRP
HN 2219 1 1992 RRP RRP
Colourway commissioned by Peter Jones
Designer: Nada Pedley. Ltd Ed: 9500
HN 3418 2 1991 RRP RRP
Lawleys by Post

BEDTIME STORY, The
Designer: Leslie Harradine
HN 2059 1 1950-96 £150-£180 $320-$385

BEETHOVEN
Designer: Richard Garbe. Ltd Ed: 25
HN 1778 1 1933 £1750-£2250 $3755-$4830

BEGGAR, The
Beggar's Opera Series
Designer: Leslie Harradine
HN 526 1 1921-49 £220-£300 $470-$645
HN 591 1 1924-49 £220-£3000 $470-$6440
HN 2175 2 1956-62 £200-£275 $430-$590

BELLE, The
Designer: Leslie Harradine
HN 754* 1 1925-38 £500-£550 $1075-$1180
HN 776* 1 1925-38 £500-£550 $1075-$1180

BELLE
Designer: Peggy Davies
HN 2340 2 1968-88 £60-£80 $130-$170
Figure of the Year Series
Designer: Valerie Annand
HN 3703 3 1996 RRP RRP
Disney Princesses Series
Designer: Pauline Parsons. Ltd Ed: 2000
HN 3830 4 1996 RRP RRP
For Disney stores, selected markets only

BELLE O' THE BALL
Designer: Leslie Harradine
HN 1997 1 1947-79 £200-£220 $430-$470

BENMORE
Ships Figureheads Series
Designer: Sharon Keenan. Ltd Ed: 950
HN 2909 1 1980 £200-£250 $430-$535

BERNICE
Designer: Peggy Davies
HN 2071 1 1951-53 £500-£550 $1075-$1180

BESS
Designer: Leslie Harradine
HN 2002 1 1947-69 £180-£200 $385-$430
HN 2003* 1 1947-50 £250-£300 $535-$645

BEST WISHES
Designer: Nada Pedley
HN 3426 1 1993-95 £70-£90 $150-$195

BETH
Kate Greenaway Series
Designer: Peggy Davies
HN 2870 1 1979-83 £130-£150 $280-$320

BETSY
Designer: Leslie Harradine
HN 2111 1 1953-59 £200-£225 $430-$480

BETTY
Designer: Leslie Harradine
HN 402* 1 1920-38 £1300-£1370 $2790-$2940
HN 403* 1 1920-38 £1300-£1370 $2790-$2940
HN 435* 1 1921-38 £1300-£1370 $2790-$2940
HN 438* 1 1921-38 £1300-£1370 $2790-$2940
HN 477* 1 1921-38 £1300-£1600 $2790-$3435
HN 478* 1 1921-38 £1300-£1600 $2790-$3435
HN 1404 2 1930-38 £500-£550 $1075-$1180
HN 1405 2 1930-38 £500-£550 $1075-$1180
HN 1435 2 1930-38 £500-£550 $1075-$1180
HN 1436 2 1930-38 £500-£550 $1075-$1180

BIDDY
Designer: Leslie Harradine
HN 1445 1 1931-38 £160-£180 $345-$385
HN 1500 1 1932-38 £160-£180 $345-$385
HN 1513 1 1932-51 £120-£150 $255-$320

BIDDY PENNY FARTHING
Designer: Leslie Harradine
HN 1843 1 1938 RRP RRP

HN No *Ver* *Prod Dates* *Market Values*

BILBO
Tolkien Series
Designer: David Lyttleton
HN 2914 1 1980-84 £90-£110 $195-$235

BILL SIKES
Designer: Arthur Dobson
HN 3785 2 1996 RRP RRP
Resin

BILL SYKES
Dickens Series
Designer: Leslie Harradine
HN 537 1 1922-32 £55-£60 $120-$130
M 54 1 1932-81 £40-£60 $85-$130

BIRTHDAY GIRL
Designer: Nada Pedley
HN 3423 1 1993 RRP RRP

BLACKSMITH OF WILLIAMSBURG
Designer: Peggy Davies
HN 2240 1 1960-83 £100-£140 $215-$300

BLACKSMITH, The
Designer: William K Harper
HN 2782 1 1987-91 £130-£150 $280-$320

BLIGHTY
Designer: Ernest W Light
HN 323 1 1918-38 £700-£750 $1500-$1610

BLITHE MORNING
Designer: Leslie Harradine
HN 2021 1 1949-71 £150-£180 $320-$385
HN 2065 1 1950-73 £150-£180 $320-$385

BLOSSOM
Designer: Leslie Harradine
HN 1667* 1 1934-49 £600-£650 $1285-$1395

BLUE BIRD
Designer: Leslie Harradine
HN 1280* 1 1928-38 £310-£350 $665-$750

BLUEBEARD
Designer: Ernest W Light.
HN 75* 1 1917-38 £750-£1130 $1610-$2425
HN 410* 1 1920-38 £750-£1130 $1610-$2425
Designer: Leslie Harradine
HN 1528 2 1932-49 £250-£310 $535-$665
HN 2105 2 1953-92 £200-£250 $430-$535

BO-PEEP
Designer: Leslie Harradine
HN 777 1 1926-38 £430-£500 $920-$1075
HN 1202 1 1926-38 £370-£440 $795-$945
HN 1327 1 1929-38 £370-£440 $795-$945
HN 1328 1 1929-38 £370-£440 $795-$945
HN 1810 2 1937-49 £120-£150 $255-$320
HN 1811 2 1937-95 £60-£80 $130-$170
Miniature Series
M 82 2 1939-49 £250-£310 $535-$665
M 83 2 1939-49 £250-£310 $535-$665

BOATMAN, The
Designer: Mary Nicoll
HN 2417 1 1971-87 £130-£150 $280-$320

BOBBY
Designer: William W Harper
HN 2778 1 1992-95 £100-£120 $215-$255

BOLERO
Reflections Series
Designer: Adrian Hughes
HN 3076 1 1985-89 £70-£90 $150-$195

BON APPÉTIT
Designer: Mary Nicoll
HN 2444 1 1972-76 £120-£150 $255-$320

BON JOUR
Designer: Leslie Harradine
HN 1879* 1 1938-49 £310-£380 $665-$815
HN 1888* 1 1938-49 £310-£380 $665-$815

BONNIE LASSIE
Designer: Leslie Harradine
HN 1626 1 1934-53 £275-£325 $590-$695

BOROMIR
Tolkien Series
Designer: David Lyttleton
HN 2918 1 1981-84 £120-£160 $255-$345

BOUDOIR
Haute Ensemble Series
Designer: Eric J Griffiths
HN 2542 1 1974-79 £200-£250 $430-$535

BOUQUET, The
Designer: George Lambert
HN 406* 1 1920-38 £700-£750 $1500-$1610
HN 414* 1 1920-38 £700-£750 $1500-$1610
HN 422* 1 1920-38 £700-£750 $1500-$1610
HN 428* 1 1921-38 £700-£750 $1500-$1610
HN 429* 1 1921-38 £700-£750 $1500-$1610
HN 567* 1 1923-38 £700-£750 $1500-$1610
HN 794* 1 1926-38 £700-£750 $1500-$1610

BOWLS PLAYER
Designer: Joseph Joues
HN 3780 1 1996 RRP RRP
Resin

BOY EVACUEE, The
Children of the Blitz Series
Designer: Adrian Hughes. Ltd Ed: 9500
HN 3202 1 1989 £225-£275 $480-$590

BOY FROM WILLIAMSBURG
Designer: Peggy Davies
HN 2183 1 1969-83 £100-£120 $215-$255

BOY ON CROCODILE
Designer: Charles J Noke
HN 373* 1 1920-38 £1120-£1500 $2405-$3220

HN No *Ver* *Prod Dates* *Market Values*

BOY ON PIG
Designer: Charles J Noke
HN 1369 1 1930-38 £700-£800 $1500-$1715

BOY SCOUT
Designer: Adrian Hughes. Ltd Ed: 9500
HN 3462 1 1994-95 RRP RRP
Lawleys by Post

BOY WITH TURBAN
Designer: Leslie Harradine
HN 586* 1 1923-38 £340-£410 $730-$880
HN 587* 1 1923-38 £340-£410 $730-$880
HN 661* 1 1924-38 £340-£410 $730-$880
HN 662* 1 1924-38 £470-£530 $1010-$1135
HN 1210* 1 1926-38 £310-£380 $665-$815
HN 1212* 1 1926-38 £310-£380 $665-$815
HN 1213* 1 1926-38 £310-£380 $665-$815
HN 1214* 1 1926-38 £310-£380 $665-$815
HN 1225* 1 1927-38 £310-£380 $665-$815

BREEZY DAYS
Reflections Series
Designer: Adrian Hughes
HN 3162 1 1988-90 £100-£130 $215-$280
USA only

BRETON DANCER
Designer: Peggy Davies. Ltd Ed: 750
HN 2383 1 1981 £310-£380 $665-$815

BRIDE
Designer: Leslie Harradine.
HN 1588 1 1933-38 £300-£350 $645-$750
HN 1600 1 1933-49 £300-£350 $645-$750
HN 1762 1 1936-49 £350-£400 $750-$860
HN 1841 1 1938-49 £380-£400 $815-$860
Designer: Peggy Davies
HN 2166 2 1956-76 £120-£150 $255-$320
HN 2873 3 1980-89 £110-£130 $235-$280
Designer: Douglas V. Tootle
HN 3284 4 1990 RRP RRP
Designer: Douglas V Tootle
HN 3285 4 1990 RRP RRP

BRIDE AND GROOM
Images Series
Designer: Robert Tabbenor
HN 3281 1 1991 RRP RRP

BRIDE OF THE YEAR
Designer: Tim Potts
HN 3758 1 1996 RRP RRP
Colourway of Wedding Morn (2nd version) for Great Universal Stores

BRIDESMAID
Designer: Valerie Annand
HN 3476 6 1994 RRP RRP
See also Flower Girl

BRIDESMAID, The
Designer: Leslie Harradine
HN 1433 1 1930-51 £120-£150 $255-$320
HN 1434 1 1930-49 £150-£195 $320-$420
HN 1530 1 1932-38 £190-£220 $405-$470
M 11 1 1932-38 £180-£220 $385-$470
M 12 1 1932-45 £150-£200 $320-$430
M 30 1 1932-45 £150-£200 $320-$430
Designer: Peggy Davies
HN 2148 2 1955-59 £120-£150 $255-$320
HN 2196 3 1960-76 £80-£110 $170-$235
HN 2874 4 1980-89 £80-£100 $170-$215
Images Series
Designer: Robert Tabbenor
HN 3280 5 1991 RRP RRP

BRIDGET
Designer: Leslie Harradine
HN 2070 1 1951-73 £150-£190 $320-$405

BROKEN LANCE, The
Designer: Peggy Davies
HN 2041 1 1949-75 £300-£350 $645-$750

BROTHER AND SISTER
Images Series
Designer: Adrian Hughes
HN 3460 1 1993 RRP RRP

BROTHERS
Images Series
Designer: Eric J Griffiths
HN 3191 1 1991 RRP RRP

BUDDIES
Designer: Eric J Griffiths
HN 2546 1 1973-76 £80-£110 $170-$235
Vanity Fair Series
Designer: Alan Maslankowski
HN 3396 1 1992 RRP RRP

BUMBLE
Dickens Series
Designer: Leslie Harradine
M 76 1 1939-49 £40-£60 $85-$130

BUNNY
Designer: Peggy Davies
HN 2214 1 1960-75 £120-£140 $255-$300

BUNNY'S BEDTIME
RDICC Exclusive Series
Designer: Nada Pedley. Ltd Ed: 9500
HN 3370 1 1991 £130-£150 $280-$320

BUTTERCUP
Designer: Peggy Davies
HN 2309 1 1964 RRP RRP
HN 2399 1 1983 RRP RRP
Miniature Series
HN 3268 1 1990 RRP RRP

HN No — Ver — Prod Dates — Market Values

BUTTERFLY

Designer: Leslie Harradine

HN No	Ver	Prod Dates	Market Values	
HN 719*	1	1925-38	£750-£800	$1610-$1715
HN 720*	1	1925-38	£700-£750	$1500-$1610
HN 730*	1	1925-38	£700-£750	$1500-$1610
HN 1203*	1	1926-38	£1000-£1200	$2145-$2575
HN 1456*	1	1931-38	£1000-£1200	$2145-$2575

BUZ FUZ

Dickens Series

Designer: Leslie Harradine

HN No	Ver	Prod Dates	Market Values	
HN 538	1	1922-32	£55-£60	$120-$130
M 53	1	1932-83	£40-£60	$85-$130

CALUMET

Designer: Charles J Noke

HN No	Ver	Prod Dates	Market Values	
HN 1428	1	1930-49	£400-£500	$860-$1075
HN 1689	1	1935-49	£340-£410	$730-$880
HN 2068	1	1950-53	£340-£410	$730-$880

CAMELLIA

Designer: Peggy Davies

HN No	Ver	Prod Dates	Market Values	
HN 2222	1	1960-71	£160-£200	$345-$430

CAMELLIAS

Flowers of Love Series

Designer: Valerie Annand

HN No	Ver	Prod Dates	Market Values	
HN 3701	1	1995	RRP	RRP

CAMILLA

Designer: Leslie Harradine

HN No	Ver	Prod Dates	Market Values	
HN 1710	1	1935-49	£400-£470	$860-$1010
HN 1711	1	1935-49	£400-£470	$860-$1010

CAMILLE

Designer: Leslie Harradine

HN No	Ver	Prod Dates	Market Values	
HN 1586	1	1933-49	£350-£400	$750-$860
HN 1648	1	1934-49	£350-£400	$750-$860
HN 1736	1	1935-49	£350-£400	$750-$860

Designer: Peggy Davies

HN No	Ver	Prod Dates	Market Values	
HN 3171	2	1987	£100-£130	$215-$280

Commissioned by Marks and Spencers. Colourway of Margaret (2nd version)

CAPTAIN

Designer: Leslie Harradine

HN No	Ver	Prod Dates	Market Values	
HN 778*	1	1926-38	£620-£750	$1330-$1610

Designer: Mary Nicoll

HN No	Ver	Prod Dates	Market Values	
HN 2260	2	1965-82	£150-£180	$320-$385

CAPTAIN COOK

Designer: William K Harper

HN No	Ver	Prod Dates	Market Values	
HN 2889	1	1980-84	£200-£220	$430-$470

CAPTAIN CUTTLE

Dickens Series

Designer: Leslie Harradine

HN No	Ver	Prod Dates	Market Values	
M 77	1	1939-82	£40-£60	$85-$130

CAPTAIN HOOK

Designer: Robert Tabbenor

HN No	Ver	Prod Dates	Market Values	
HN 3636	1	1993	RRP	RRP

Resin

CAPTAIN MACHEATH

Beggar's Opera Series

Designer: Leslie Harradine

HN No	Ver	Prod Dates	Market Values	
HN 464*	1	1921-49	£250-£350	$535-$750
HN 590*	1	1924-49	£400-£450	$860-$965
HN 1256*	1	1927-49	£400-£450	$860-$965

CAPTAIN, 2nd NEW YORK REGIMENT 1775

Designer: Eric J Griffiths. Ltd Ed: 350

HN No	Ver	Prod Dates	Market Values	
HN 2755	1	1976-77	£400-£600	$860-$1285

CAREFREE

Images Series

Designer: Robert Jefferson

HN No	Ver	Prod Dates	Market Values	
HN 3026	1	1986	RRP	RRP
HN 3029	1	1986	RRP	RRP

CARMEN

Designer: Leslie Harradine

HN No	Ver	Prod Dates	Market Values	
HN 1267	1	1928-38	£370-£440	$795-$945
HN 1300	1	1928-38	£430-£560	$920-$1200

Haute Ensemble Series

Designer: Eric J Griffiths

HN No	Ver	Prod Dates	Market Values	
HN 2545	2	1974-79	£200-£240	$430-$515

CARNIVAL

Designer: Leslie Harradine

HN No	Ver	Prod Dates	Market Values	
HN 1260	1	1927-38	£1000-£1500	$2145-$3220
HN 1278	1	1928-38	£1000-£1500	$2145-$3220

CAROL

Vanity Fair Series

Designer: Pauline Parsons

HN No	Ver	Prod Dates	Market Values	
HN 2961	1	1982-95	£100-£120	$215-$255

CAROLINE

Designer: Peggy Davies

HN No	Ver	Prod Dates	Market Values	
HN 3170	1	1989-92	£100-£120	$215-$255

See also Winter Welcome

Designer: Nada Pedley

HN No	Ver	Prod Dates	Market Values	
HN 3694	2	1995	RRP	RRP

CAROLYN

Designer: Leslie Harradine

HN No	Ver	Prod Dates	Market Values	
HN 2112	1	1953-65	£180-£200	$385-$430

Designer: Adrian Hughes

HN No	Ver	Prod Dates	Market Values	
HN 2974	2	1984-86	£120-£160	$255-$345

CARPENTER, The

Designer: Mary Nicoll

HN No	Ver	Prod Dates	Market Values	
HN 2678	1	1986-92	£150-£180	$320-$385

CARPET SELLER, The

Designer: Leslie Harradine

HN No	Ver	Prod Dates	Market Values	
HN 1464	1	1929-69	£140-£175	$300-$375

Early versions have right hand outstretched

Flambé Series

Designer: William K Harper

HN No	Ver	Prod Dates	Market Values	
HN 2776	2	1990-95	£120-£160	$255-$345

Designer: Robert Tabbenor

HN No	Ver	Prod Dates	Market Values	
HN 3277	3	1990-95	£120-£160	$255-$345

HN No Ver Prod Dates Market Values

CARPET VENDOR, The
Designer: Charles J Noke

HN No	Ver	Prod Dates	Market Values	
HN 38	1	1914-38	£1500-£1880	$3220-$4035
HN 76	1	1917-38	£1500-£1880	$3220-$4035
HN 350	1	1919-38	£1125-£1500	$2415-$3220
HN 38A	2	1914-38	£1500-£1880	$3220-$4035
HN 348	2	1919-38	£500-£750	$1075-$1610

CARRIE
Kate Greenaway Series
Designer: Peggy Davies
HN 2800 1 1976-81 £140-£180 $300-$385

CASSIM
Designer: Leslie Harradine

HN No	Ver	Prod Dates	Market Values	
HN 1231	1	1927-38	£290-£350	$620-$750
HN 1232	1	1927-38	£290-£350	$620-$750
HN 1311	2	1929-38	£290-£350	$620-$750
HN 1312	2	1929-38	£290-£350	$620-$750

CATHERINE (In Spring)
Four Seasons Series
Designer: Peter Gee
HN 3006 2 1985 £100-£130 $215-$280
Commissioned by Danbury Mint

CATHERINE
Ladies of Covent Garden Series
Designer: Peggy Davies
HN 2395 1 1983-84 £120-£150 $255-$320
Produced for American Express
Vanity Fair Children Series
Designer: Pauline Parsons
HN 3044 3 1985-96 RRP RRP

CATHERINE HOWARD
King Henry VIII's Wives Series
Designer: Pauline Parsons. Ltd Ed: 9500
HN 3449 1 1992 RRP RRP

CATHERINE OF ARAGON
King Henry VIII's Wives Series
Designer: Pauline Parsons. Ltd Ed: 9500
HN 3233 1 1990 RRP RRP

CATHERINE PARR
King Henry VIII's Wives Series
Designer: Pauline Parsons. Ltd Ed: 9500
HN 3450 1 1992 RRP RRP

CAVALIER
Designer: Unknown
HN 369* 1 1920-38 £750-£1000 $1610-$2145
Designer: Eric J Griffiths
HN 2716 2 1976-82 £150-£180 $320-$385

CELESTE
Designer: Peggy Davies
HN 2237 1 1959-71 £120-£160 $255-$345
Designer: Peter Gee
HN 3322 2 1992 £120-£150 $255-$320
(Commissioned by Great Universal Stores). Colourway of Isadora

CELIA
Designer: Leslie Harradine

HN No	Ver	Prod Dates	Market Values	
HN 1726	1	1935-49	£600-£650	$1285-$1395
HN 1727	1	1935-49	£600-£650	$1285-$1395

CELLIST, The
Designer: Mary Nicoll
HN 2226 1 1960-67 £250-£300 $535-$645

CELLO
Lady Musicians Series
Designer: Peggy Davies. Ltd Ed: 750
HN 2331 1 1970 £370-£630 $795-$1350
Edwardian String Quartet Series
Designer: Valerie Annand. Ltd Ed: 1500
HN 3707 2 1995 RRP RRP
Lawleys by Post

CENTURION, The
Designer: William K Harper
HN 2726 1 1982-84 £120-£160 $255-$345

CERISE
Designer: Leslie Harradine
HN 1607 1 1933-49 £150-£190 $320-$405

CHARISMA
Reflections Series
Designer: Pauline Parsons
HN 3090 1 1986-90 £100-£130 $215-$280

CHARITY
Designer: Eric J Griffiths. Ltd Ed: 9500
HN 3087 1 1987 £100-£130 $215-$280

CHARLES DICKENS
Designer: Peter Gee. Ltd Ed: 1500
HN 3448 1 1994 RRP RRP
For Pascoe and Co

CHARLES II
Stuart Kings Series
Designer: Douglas V Tootle. Ltd Ed: 1500
HN 3825 1 1996 RRP RRP
Lawleys by Post

CHARLEY'S AUNT
Designer: A Toft
HN 35 1 1913-38 £200-£250 $430-$535
HN 640 1 1924-38 £200-£250 $430-$535
Designer: Harry Fenton
HN 1411* 2 1930-38 £750-£1000 $1610-$2145
HN 1554* 2 1933-38 £750-£1000 $1610-$2145
Designer: A Toft
HN 1703 3 1935-38 £750-£1000 $1610-$2145

CHARLIE CHAPLIN
Famous Movie Comedians Series
Designer: William K Harper. Ltd Ed: 9500
HN 2771 1 1989 £195-£250 $420-$535

HN No Ver Prod Dates Market Values

CHARLOTTE
Designer: John Bromley
HN 2421 1 1972-86 £120-£160 $255-$345
HN 2423 1 1986-92 £120-£160 $255-$345
Designer: Nada Pedley
HN 3658 2 1995 £120-£160 $255-$345
For Littlewoods
Charleston Series
Designer: Alan Maslankowski
HN 3810 3 1996 RRP RRP
Green version
HN 3811 3 1996 RRP RRP
Blue version
HN 3812 3 1996 RRP RRP
Pink version
HN 3813 3 1996 RRP RRP
Ivory version

CHARMIAN
Designer: Leslie Harradine
HN 1568 1 1933-38 £350-£400 $750-$860
HN 1569 1 1933-38 £350-£400 $750-$860
HN 1651 1 1934-38 £350-£400 $750-$860

CHELSEA PAIR (Female)
Designer: Leslie Harradine
HN 577 1 1923-38 £275-£325 $590-$695
HN 578 1 1923-38 £275-£325 $590-$695

CHELSEA PAIR (Male)
Designer: Leslie Harradine
HN 579 1 1923-38 £275-£325 $590-$695
HN 580 1 1923-38 £275-£325 $590-$695

CHELSEA PENSIONER
Designer: Leslie Harradine
HN 689 1 1924-38 £560-£630 $1200-$1350

CHERIE
Designer: Peggy Davies
HN 2341 1 1966-92 £80-£90 $170-$195

CHERRY BLOSSOM
Reflections Series
Designer: Pauline Parsons
HN 3092 1 1986-89 £80-£100 $170-$215

CHERYL
Designer: Douglas V Tootle
HN 3253 1 1989-94 £120-£140 $255-$300

CHIC
Reflections Series
Designer: Robert Tabbenor
HN 2997 1 1988-90 £100-£130 $215-$280

CHIEF, The
Designer: William K Harper
HN 2892 1 1979-88 £150-£175 $320-$375

CHIEFTAIN
Ships Figureheads Series
Designer: Sharon Keenan. Ltd Ed: 950
HN 2929 1 1982 £200-£250 $430-$535

CHILD FROM WILLIAMSBURG, A
Designer: Peggy Davies
HN 2154 1 1964-83 £90-£100 $195-$215

CHILD ON CRAB
Designer: Charles J Noke
HN 32* 1 1913-38 £1000-£1250 $2145-$2680

CHILD STUDY
Designer: Leslie Harradine
HN 603A 1 1924-38 £220-£250 $470-$535
HN 603B 1 1924-38 £220-£250 $470-$535
HN 605A 1 1924-38 £220-£250 $470-$535
HN 605B 1 1924-38 £220-£250 $470-$535
HN 606A 1 1924-38 £220-£250 $470-$535
HN 606B 1 1924-38 £220-£250 $470-$535
HN 1441 1 1931-38 £240-£260 $515-$555
HN 1442 1 1931-38 £240-£260 $515-$555
HN 1443* 1 1931-38 £240-£260 $515-$555

CHILD'S GRACE, A
Designer: Lawrence Perugini
HN 62* 1 1916-38 £500-£630 $1075-$1350
HN 62A* 1 1916-38 £560-£690 $1200-$1480
HN 510* 1 1921-38 £680-£810 $1460-$1740

CHINA REPAIRER, The
Designer: Robert Tabbenor
HN 2943 1 1983-88 £140-£180 $300-$385

CHINESE DANCER
Dancers of the World Series
Designer: Peggy Davies. Ltd Ed: 750
HN 2840 1 1980 £350-£400 $750-$860

CHITARRONE
Lady Musicians Series
Designer: Peggy Davies. Ltd Ed: 750
HN 2700 1 1974 £450-£500 $965-$1075

CHLOE
Designer: Leslie Harradine
HN 1470 1 1931-49 £200-£250 $430-$535
HN 1476 1 1931-38 £200-£250 $430-$535
HN 1479 1 1931-49 £200-£250 $430-$535
HN 1498 1 1932-38 £250-£280 $535-$600
HN 1765 1 1936-50 £250-£280 $535-$600
HN 1956 1 1940-49 £250-£280 $535-$600
M 9 1 1932-45 £200-£220 $430-$470
M 10 1 1932-45 £200-£220 $430-$470
M 29 1 1932-45 £200-£220 $430-$470

CHOICE, The
Designer: Leslie Harradine
HN 1959* 1 1941-49 £620-£750 $1330-$1610
HN 1960* 1 1941-49 £620-£750 $1330-$1610

CHOIR BOY
Designer: Peggy Davies
HN 2141 1 1954-75 £80-£100 $170-$215

CHORUS GIRL
Designer: Unknown
HN 1401* 1 1930-38 £680-£810 $1460-$1740
Also known as Harlequinnade

HN No Ver Prod Dates Market Values

CHRISTENING DAY
Designer: P Northcroft
HN 3210 1 1988-90 £100-£120 $215-$255
HN 3211 1 1988-90 £100-£120 $215-$255

CHRISTINE
Designer: Leslie Harradine
HN 1839 1 1938-49 £430-£500 $920-$1075
HN 1840 1 1938-49 £430-£500 $920-$1075
Designer: Peggy Davies
HN 2792 2 1978-94 £140-£160 $300-$345
. Ltd Ed: 1000
HN 3172 2 1988 RRP RRP
For Guild of China and Glass Retailers, UK
HN 3269 3 1990-94 RRP RRP
Miniature
Michael Doulton Miniature Series
HN 3337 3 1991 RRP RRP
Designer: Nada Pedley
HN 3767 4 1996 RRP RRP

CHRISTMAS ANGEL
Sentiments Collection Series
Designer: Alan Maslankowski
HN 3733 1 1996 RRP RRP

CHRISTMAS CAROLS
Sentiments Series
Designer: Alan Maslankowski
HN 3727 1 1995 RRP RRP

CHRISTMAS DAY
Sentiments Series
Designer: Alan Maslankowski
HN 3488 1 1993 RRP RRP

CHRISTMAS MORN
Designer: Peggy Davies
HN 1992 1 1947-96 £120-£140 $255-$300
A pilot figure wearing a blue dress sold for £800 at Louis Taylor's auction on 14 October 1985
HN 3212 1 1988 RRP RRP
Miniature
Michael Doulton Miniature Series
HN 3245 1 1991 RRP RRP

CHRISTMAS PARCELS
Designer: William K Harper
HN 2851 1 1978-82 £160-£190 $345-$405
Designer: Alan Maslankowski
HN 3493 2 1994 RRP RRP

CHRISTMAS TIME
Designer: Peggy Davies
HN 2110 1 1953-67 £240-£270 $515-$580

CHRISTOPHER COLUMBUS
Designer: Alan Maslankowski. Ltd Ed: 1492
HN 3392 1 1992 RRP RRP

CHU CHIN CHOW
Designer: Charles J Noke
HN 450 1 1921-38 £1500-£2000 $3220-$4290
HN 460 1 1921-38 £1500-£2000 $3220-$4290
HN 601 1 1921-38 £1500-£2000 $3220-$4290

CICELY
Designer: Leslie Harradine
HN 1516* 1 1932-49 £470-£560 $1010-$1200

CINDERELLA
Disney Princesses Series
Designer: Pauline Parsons. Ltd Ed: 2000
HN 3677 1 1995 RRP RRP
For Disney stores. Selected markets only

CIRCE
Designer: Leslie Harradine
HN 1249* 1 1927-38 £750-£800 $1610-$1715
HN 1250* 1 1927-38 £750-£800 $1610-$1715
HN 1254* 1 1927-38 £750-£800 $1610-$1715
HN 1255* 1 1927-38 £750-£800 $1610-$1715

CISSIE
Designer: Leslie Harradine
HN 1808 1 1937-51 £170-£230 $365-$495
HN 1809 1 1937-93 £60-£80 $130-$170

CLAIRE
Designer: Adrian Hughes
HN 3209 1 1990-92 £120-£140 $255-$300
Designer: Nada Pedley
HN 3646 2 1994 RRP RRP

CLARE
Designer: Peggy Davies
HN 2793 1 1980-84 £130-£150 $280-$320

CLARIBEL
Designer: Leslie Harradine
HN 1950 1 1940-49 £220-£260 $470-$555
HN 1951 1 1940-49 £220-£260 $470-$555

CLARINDA
Designer: William K Harper
HN 2724 1 1975-81 £130-£150 $280-$320

CLARISSA
Designer: Leslie Harradine
HN 1525 1 1932-38 £470-£530 $1010-$1135
HN 1687 1 1935-49 £470-£530 $1010-$1135
Designer: Peggy Davies
HN 2345 2 1968-81 £130-£150 $280-$320

CLAUDINE
Elegance Series
Designer: Adrian Hughes
HN 3055 1 1984 £200-£250 $430-$535
This figure was test marketed but not put into full production

CLEMENCY
Designer: Leslie Harradine
HN 1633 1 1934-38 £370-£440 $795-$945
HN 1634 1 1934-49 £370-£440 $795-$945
HN 1643 1 1934-38 £370-£440 $795-$945

CLEOPATRA
Les Femme Fatales Series
Designer: Peggy Davies. Ltd Ed: 750
HN 2868 1 1979 £600-£650 $1285-$1395

HN No	Ver	Prod Dates	Market Values	

CLOCKMAKER, The
Designer: Mary Nicoll

HN 2279	1	1961-75	£175-£225	$375-$480

CLOTHILDE
Designer: Leslie Harradine

HN 1598	1	1933-49	£400-£450	$860-$965
HN 1599	1	1933-49	£450-£500	$965-$1075

CLOUD, The
Designer: Richard Garbe

HN 1831*	1	1937-49	£1880-£2130	$4035-$4570

CLOWN, The
Designer: William K Harper

HN 2890	1	1979-88	£130-£150	$280-$320

CLOWNETTE
Previously known as *Lady Clown*
Designer: Leslie Harradine

HN 717*	1	1925-38	£800-£1000	$1715-$2145
HN 718*	1	1925-38	£800-£1000	$1715-$2145
HN 738*	1	1925-38	£800-£1000	$1715-$2145
HN 770*	1	1925-38	£800-£1000	$1715-$2145
HN 1263*	1	1927-38	£800-£1000	$1715-$2145

COACHMAN, The
Designer: Mary Nicoll

HN 2282	1	1963-71	£240-£295	$515-$635

COBBLER
Designer: Charles J Noke

HN 542	1	1922-39	£400-£450	$860-$965
HN 543	1	1922-38	£400-£450	$860-$965
HN 682	1	1924-38	£400-£450	$860-$965
HN 681	2	1924-38	£300-£380	$645-$815
HN 1251	2	1927-38	£300-£380	$645-$815
HN 1283	2	1928-49	£300-£380	$645-$815
HN 1705	3	1935-49	£250-£380	$535-$815
HN 1706	3	1935-69	£140-£160	$300-$345

COCKTAILS
Reflections Series
Designer: Adrian Hughes

HN 3070	1	1985-95	£100-£130	$215-$280

COLLINETTE
Designer: Leslie Harradine

HN 1998	1	1947-49	£250-£300	$535-$645
HN 1999	1	1947-49	£250-£300	$535-$645

COLONEL FAIRFAX
Gilbert & Sullivan Series
Designer: William K Harper

HN 2903	1	1982-85	£310-£340	$665-$730

COLUMBINE
Designer: Leslie Harradine

HN 1296	1	1928-38	£430-£500	$920-$1075
HN 1297	1	1928-38	£430-£500	$920-$1075
HN 1439	1	1930-38	£430-£500	$920-$1075

Designer: Peggy Davies

HN 2185	2	1957-69	£120-£160	$255-$345

Prestige Series
Designer: Douglas V Tootle

HN 2738	3	1982	RRP	RRP
HN 3288	3	1993	RRP	RRP

COMING OF SPRING, The
Designer: Leslie Harradine

HN 1722*	1	1935-49	£1000-£1250	$2145-$2680
HN 1723*	1	1935-49	£1000-£1250	$2145-$2680

CONFUCIUS
Flambé Series
Designer: Peter Gee

HN 3314	1	1990-95	£120-£160	$255-$345

CONGRATULATIONS
Images Series
Designer: Peter Gee

HN 3351	1	1991	RRP	RRP

CONSTANCE
Designer: Leslie Harradine

HN 1510*	1	1932-38	£620-£750	$1330-$1610
HN 1511*	1	1932-38	£620-£750	$1330-$1610

CONTEMPLATION
Images Series
Designer: Peggy Davies

HN 2213	1	1982-86	£80-£100	$170-$215
HN 2241	1	1982-86	£80-£100	$170-$215

CONTENTMENT
Designer: Leslie Harradine

HN 395*	1	1920-38	£930-£1060	$1995-$2275
HN 396*	1	1920-38	£930-£1060	$1995-$2275
HN 421*	1	1920-38	£750-£940	$1610-$2015
HN 468*	1	1921-38	£930-£1060	$1995-$2275
HN 572*	1	1923-38	£930-£1060	$1995-$2275
HN 685*	1	1924-38	£930-£1060	$1995-$2275
HN 686*	1	1924-38	£750-£940	$1610-$2015
HN 1323*	1	1929-38	£750-£940	$1610-$2015

COOKIE
Designer: Peggy Davies

HN 2218	1	1958-75	£100-£120	$215-$255

COPPELIA
Designer: Peggy Davies

HN 2115	1	1953-59	£370-£440	$795-$945

COQUETTE, The
Designer: William White

HN 20*	1	1913-38	£1120-£1380	$2405-$2960
HN 37*	1	1914-38	£1120-£1380	$2405-$2960

CORALIE
Designer: Peggy Davies

HN 2307	1	1964-88	£120-£140	$255-$300

CORINTHIAN, The
Designer: Harry Fenton

HN 1973	1	1941-49	£1000-£1200	$2145-$2575

HN No *Ver* *Prod Dates* *Market Values*

CORPORAL, 1st NEW HAMPSHIRE REGIMENT 1778
Designer: Eric J Griffiths. Ltd Ed: 350
HN 2780 1 1975-76 £450-£550 $965-$1180

COUNTESS OF HARRINGTON
Reynolds Ladies Series
Designer: Peter Gee. Ltd Ed: 5000
HN 3317 1 1992-95 £200-£250 $430-$535

COUNTESS SPENCER
Reynolds Ladies Series
Designer: Peter Gee. Ltd Ed: 5000
HN 3320 1 1992-95 £200-£250 $430-$535

COUNTRY GIRL
Reflections Series
Designer: Adrian Hughes
HN 3051 1 1987-92 £100-£130 $215-$280
Elegance Collection Series
Designer: Tim Potts
HN 3856 2 1996 RRP RRP

COUNTRY LASS
Designer: Leslie Harradine
HN 1991 1 1975-81 £125-£160 $270-$345
Renamed version of Market Day

COUNTRY LOVE
Designer: John Bromley. Ltd Ed: 12500
HN 2418 1 1990 RRP RRP

COUNTRY MAID
Designer: Adrian Hughes
HN 3163 1 1988-91 £100-£120 $215-$255

COUNTRY ROSE
Designer: Peggy Davies
HN 3221 1 1989 RRP RRP

COURT SHOEMAKER, The
Designer: Leslie Harradine
HN 1755 1 1936-49 £800-£850 $1715-$1825

COURTIER, The
Designer: Leslie Harradine
HN 1338* 1 1929-38 £750-£880 $1610-$1890

COVENT GARDEN
Designer: Leslie Harradine
HN 1339 1 1929-38 £600-£650 $1285-$1395
Reflections Series
Designer: William K Harper
HN 2857 2 1988-90 £100-£120 $215-$255

CRADLE SONG
Designer: Peggy Davies
HN 2246 1 1959-62 £270-£330 $580-$710

CRAFTSMAN, The
Designer: Mary Nicoll
HN 2284* 1 1961-65 £370-£440 $795-$945

CRICKETER
Designer: Alan Maslankowski
HN 3814 1 1996 RRP RRP
Resin

CRINOLINE LADY
Miniature Series
Designer: Unknown
HN 650* 1 1924-38 £310-£410 $665-$880
HN 651* 1 1924-38 £310-£410 $665-$880
HN 652* 1 1924-38 £310-£410 $665-$880
HN 653* 1 1924-38 £310-£410 $665-$880
HN 654* 1 1924-38 £310-£410 $665-$880
HN 655* 1 1924-38 £310-£410 $665-$880

CRINOLINE, The
Designer: George Lambert
HN 8 1 1913-38 £680-£810 $1460-$1740
HN 9 1 1913-38 £680-£810 $1460-$1740
HN 9A 1 1913-38 £680-£810 $1460-$1740
HN 21 1 1913-38 £680-£810 $1460-$1740
HN 21A 1 1913-38 £680-£810 $1460-$1740
HN 413 1 1920-38 £750-£880 $1610-$1890
HN 566 1 1923-38 £680-£810 $1460-$1740
HN 628 1 1924-38 £680-£810 $1460-$1740

CROQUET
British Sporting Heritage Series
Designer: Valerie Annand. Ltd Ed: 5000
HN 3470 1 1996 RRP RRP

CROUCHING NUDE
Designer: Unknown
HN 457* 1 1921-38 £750-£880 $1610-$1890

CUP OF TEA, The
Designer: Mary Nicoll
HN 2322 1 1964-83 £120-£150 $255-$320

CURLY KNOB
Designer: Leslie Harradine
HN 1627 1 1934-49 £350-£400 $750-$860

CURLY LOCKS
Designer: Peggy Davies
HN 2049 1 1949-53 £150-£200 $320-$430

CURTSEY, The
Designer: Ernest W Light
HN 57 1 1916-38 £1000-£1200 $2145-$2575
HN 57B 1 1916-38 £1000-£1200 $2145-$2575
HN 66A 1 1916-38 £1000-£1200 $2145-$2575
HN 327 1 1918-38 £1000-£1200 $2145-$2575
HN 334 1 1918-38 £1000-£1200 $2145-$2575
HN 363 1 1919-38 £1000-£1200 $2145-$2575
HN 371 1 1920-38 £1000-£1200 $2145-$2575
HN 518 1 1921-38 £1000-£1200 $2145-$2575
HN 547 1 1922-38 £1000-£1200 $2145-$2575
HN 629 1 1924-38 £1000-£1200 $2145-$2575
HN 670 1 1924-38 £1000-£1200 $2145-$2575

CYMBALS
Lady Musicians Series
Designer: Peggy Davies. Ltd Ed: 750
HN 2699 1 1974 £450-£500 $965-$1075

HN No	Ver	Prod Dates	Market Values	

CYNTHIA

Designer: Leslie Harradine

HN 1685	1	1935-49	£500-£550	$1075-$1180
HN 1686	1	1935-49	£500-£550	$1075-$1180

Designer: Peggy Davies

HN 2440	2	1984-92	£100-£130	$215-$280

CYRANO DE BERGERAC

Designer: David Biggs

HN 3751	1	1995	RRP	RRP

Resin

D'ARTAGNAN

Designer: Robert Tabbenor

HN 3638	1	1993	RRP	RRP

Resin

DADDY'S GIRL

Designer: Alan Maslankowski

HN 3435	1	1993	RRP	RRP

DADDY'S JOY

Designer: Adrian Hughes. Ltd Ed: 12500

HN 3294	1	1990	RRP	RRP

DAFFY DOWN DILLY

Designer: Leslie Harradine

HN 1712	1	1935-75	£200-£250	$430-$535
HN 1713	1	1935-49	£400-£450	$860-$965

DAINTY MAY

Designer: Leslie Harradine

HN 1639	1	1934-49	£250-£310	$535-$665
HN 1656	1	1934-49	£220-£280	$470-$600
M 67	1	1935-49	£250-£300	$535-$645
M 73	1	1936-49	£250-£300	$535-$645

DAISY

Designer: Leslie Harradine

HN 1575	1	1933-49	£250-£310	$535-$665
HN 1961	1	1941-49	£280-£350	$600-$750

Charleston Series

Designer: Alan Maslankowski

HN 3802	2	1996	RRP	RRP

Green version

HN 3803	2	1996	RRP	RRP

Blue version

HN 3804	2	1996	RRP	RRP

Pink version

HN 3805	2	1996	RRP	RRP

Ivory version

DAMARIS

Designer: Peggy Davies

HN 2079*	1	1951-52	£1000-£1200	$2145-$2575

DANCING DELIGHT

Reflections Series

Designer: Adrian Hughes

HN 3078	1	1986-89	£110-£130	$235-$280

DANCING EYES AND SUNNY HAIR

Designer: Unknown

HN 1543	1	1933-49	£150-£190	$320-$405

DANCING FIGURE

Designer: Unknown

HN 311*	1	1918-38	£1250-£1300	$2680-$2790

DANCING YEARS

Designer: Peggy Davies

HN 2235	1	1965-71	£200-£220	$430-$470

DANDY, The

Designer: Leslie Harradine

HN 753	1	1925-38	£620-£750	$1330-$1610

DANIELLE

Elegance Series

Designer: Adrian Hughes

HN 3056	1	1984	£180-£200	$385-$430

This figure was test marketed but not put into full production

Vanity Fair Series

Designer: Peter Gee

HN 3001	2	1990-95	RRP	RRP

See also Spring Song

DAPHNE

Designer: Peggy Davies

HN 2268	1	1963-75	£160-£180	$345-$385

DAPPLE GREY

Designer: William M Chance

HN 2521	1	1938-60	£180-£240	$385-$515

DARBY

Designer: Leslie Harradine

HN 1427	1	1930-49	£180-£220	$385-$470
HN 2024	1	1949-59	£180-£220	$385-$470

DARLING

Designer: Charles Vyse

HN 1	1	1913-28	£370-£440	$795-$945
HN 1319	1	1929-59	£120-£150	$255-$320
HN 1371	1	1930-38	£100-£140	$215-$300
HN 1372	1	1930-38	£100-£140	$215-$300
HN 1985	2	1946	RRP	RRP
HN 3613	2	1993only	£40-£60	$85-$130

Peter Jones exclusive

DAVID COPPERFIELD

Dickens Series

Designer: Leslie Harradine

M 88	1	1949-83	£40-£60	$85-$130

DAWN (with headdress)

Designer: Leslie Harradine

HN 1858A	1	1938	£1000-£1200	$2145-$2575

DAWN

Designer: Leslie Harradine

HN 1858	1	1938-49	£800-£1000	$1715-$2145

Designer: Douglas V Tootle

HN 3258	2	1990-92	£130-£150	$280-$320

Vanity Fair Series

Designer: Nada Pedley

HN 3600	3	1993	RRP	RRP

HN No	Ver	Prod Dates		Market Values

DAYBREAK
Reflections Series
Designer: Robert Jefferson
HN 3107 1 1986-89 RRP RRP

DAYDREAMS
Designer: Leslie Harradine
HN 1731 1 1935 RRP RRP
Early versions have a large rose bouquet
HN 1732 1 1935-49 £170-£230 $365-$495
HN 1944 1 1940-49 £220-£260 $470-$555

DEAUVILLE
Sweet & Twenties Series
Designer: Peggy Davies. Ltd Ed: 1500
HN 2344 1 1982 £150-£180 $320-$385

DEBBIE (Memory Lane)
Designer: Peggy Davies
HN 3746 1 1996 RRP RRP
Colourway for The Bay, Canada

DEBBIE (Tranquility)
Designer: Peggy Davies
HN 3747 1 1996 RRP RRP
Colourway for The Bay, Canada

DEBBIE
Designer: Peggy Davies
HN 2385 1 1969-82 £80-£100 $170-$215
HN 2400 1 1983-95 £60-£80 $130-$170

DEBORAH
Ladies of Covent Garden Series
Designer: Peggy Davies
HN 2701 1 1983-84 £120-£130 $255-$280
Commissioned by American Express
Figure of the Year Series
Designer: Nada Pedley
HN 3644 2 1995 £130-£150 $280-$320

DEBUT
Reflections Series
Designer: Pauline Parsons
HN 3046 1 1985-89 £110-£130 $235-$280

DEBUTANTE
Designer: Peggy Davies
HN 2210 1 1963-67 £160-£190 $345-$405
Reflection Series
Designer: Eric J Griffiths
HN 3188 2 1988 £100-£130 $215-$280
Commissioned by Home Shopping Network

DECEMBER
Figure of the Month Series
Designer: Peggy Davies
HN 2696 1 1987 £140-£160 $300-$345
For Home Shopping Network, USA
Designer: Robert Tabbenor
HN 3329 2 1990 £100-£130 $215-$280
Colourway of Amanda. USA only
Wild Flower of the Month Series
Designer: Peggy Davis
HN 3412 3 1991 £130-£150 $280-$320
Colourway of Beartrice for Sears of Canada

DEIDRE
Designer: Leslie Harradine
HN 2020 1 1949-55 £180-£240 $385-$515

DELICIA
Designer: Leslie Harradine
HN 1662 1 1934-38 £500-£550 $1075-$1180
HN 1663 1 1934-38 £500-£550 $1075-$1180
HN 1681 1 1935-38 £550-£600 $1180-$1285

DELIGHT
Designer: Leslie Harradine
HN 1772 1 1936-67 £130-£160 $280-$345
HN 1773 1 1936-49 £180-£230 $385-$495

DELPHINE
Designer: Peggy Davies
HN 2136 1 1954-67 £170-£210 $365-$450

DEMURE
Reflections Series
Designer: Pauline Parsons
HN 3045 1 1985-89 £110-£130 $235-$280

DENISE
Designer: Unknown†
M 34 1 1933-45 £300-£350 $645-$750
M 35 1 1933-45 £300-£350 $645-$750
†Although it is not certain, it is thought that these figures were designed by Leslie Harradine
Designer: Peggy Davies
HN 2273 2 1964-71 £150-£190 $320-$405
Vanity Fair Series
HN 2477 3 1987-96 £100-£120 $215-$255
See also Summer Rose (2nd version)

DERRICK
Designer: Leslie Harradine
HN 1398 1 1930-38 £310-£380 $665-$815

DESDEMONA
Shakespeares Ladies Series
Designer: Pauline Parsons
HN 3676 1 1995 RRP RRP
Lawleys by Post

DESPAIR
Designer: Charles J Noke
HN 596* 1 1924-38 £620-£750 $1330-$1610

DETECTIVE, The
Designer: Eric J Griffiths
HN 2359 1 1977-83 £140-£160 $300-$345

DEVOTION
Reflections Series
Designer: Pauline Parsons
HN 3228 1 1989-95 £100-£130 $215-$280

HN No Ver Prod Dates Market Values

DIANA
Designer: Leslie Harradine
HN 1716 1 1935-49 £170-£200 $365-$430
HN 1717 1 1935-49 £170-£200 $365-$430
HN 1986 1 1946-75 £150-£170 $320-$365
Designer: Peggy Davies
HN 2468 2 1986 RRP RRP
Michael Doulton Exclusive Series
HN 3266 2 1990 £100-£120 $215-$255
Miniature Series
HN 3310 2 1991-95 RRP RRP

DIANA THE HUNTRESS
Myths and Maidens Series
Designer: Robert Jefferson. Ltd Ed: 300
HN 2829 1 1986 £450-£550 $965-$1180

DIANE
Designer: Nada Pedley
HN 3604 1 1994only £130-£150 $280-$320
For RDICC

DICK SWIVELLER
Dickens Series
Designer: Unknown
M 90 1 1949-81 £40-£60 $85-$130

DICK TURPIN
Designer: Graham Tongue. Ltd Ed: 5000
HN 3272 1 1989-95 RRP RRP
Designer: Robert Tabbenor
HN 3637 2 1993 RRP RRP
Resin

DIGGER (Australian)
Designer: Ernest W Light
HN 322* 1 1918-38 £800-£850 $1715-$1825
HN 353* 1 1919-38 £800-£850 $1715-$1825

DIGGER (New Zealand)
Designer: Ernest W Light
HN 321* 1 1918-38 £800-£850 $1715-$1825

DILIGENT SCHOLAR, The
Designer: William White
HN 26* 1 1913-38 £1000-£1200 $2145-$2575

DIMITY
Designer: Leslie Harradine
HN 2169 1 1956-59 £160-£190 $345-$405

DINKY DO
Designer: Leslie Harradine
HN 3618 1 1994 £60-£80 $130-$170

DINKY DOO
Designer: Leslie Harradine
HN 1678 1 1934-96 £50-£70 $105-$150
HN 2120 1 1983-96 £50-£70 $105-$150

DINNERTIME
Designer: Alan Maslankowski
HN 3726 1 1995 RRP RRP

DISCOVERY
RDICC Exclusive Series
Designer: Angela Munslow
HN 3428 1 1992 £200-£250 $430-$535

"DO YOU WONDER WHERE . . ."
Designer: Unknown
HN 1544 1 1933-49 £150-£180 $320-$385

DOCTOR, The
Designer: William K Harper
HN 2858 1 1979-92 £110-£140 $235-$300

DOLLY
Designer: Charles J Noke
HN 355* 1 1919-38 £750-£850 $1610-$1825
Designer: Harry Tittensor
HN 389*† 2 1920-38 £750-£850 $1610-$1825
HN 390*† 2 1920-38 £750-£850 $1610-$1825
HN 469*† 2 1921-38 £750-£850 $1610-$1825
†Also known as Little Mother

DOLLY VARDON
Designer: Leslie Harradine
HN 1514 1 1932-38 £450-£500 $965-$1075
HN 1515 1 1932-49 £450-£500 $965-$1075

DOMINIQUE
Elegance Series
Designer: Adrian Hughes
HN 3054 1 1984 £180-£200 $385-$430
This figure was test marketed but not put into full production

DONNA
Vanity Fair Series
Designer: Peter Gee
HN 2939 1 1986-94 £90-£110 $195-$235

DORCAS
Designer: Leslie Harradine
HN 1490 1 1932-38 £240-£280 $515-$600
HN 1491 1 1932-38 £240-£280 $515-$600
HN 1558 1 1933-52 £180-£220 $385-$470

DOREEN
Designer: Leslie Harradine
HN 1363 1 1929-38 £500-£550 $1075-$1180
HN 1389 1 1930-38 £500-£550 $1075-$1180
HN 1390 1 1929-38 £500-£550 $1075-$1180

DORIS KEENE as Cavallini
Designer: Charles J Noke
HN 90* 1 1918-36 £1000-£1200 $2145-$2575
HN 96* 1 1918-38 £1000-£1200 $2145-$2575
HN 345* 1 1919-49 £870-£1060 $1865-$2275
HN 467* 1 1921-36 £870-£1060 $1865-$2275

DOROTHY
Designer: Pauline Parsons
HN 3098 1 1987-90 £130-£150 $280-$320

DOUBLE JESTER
Designer: Charles J Noke
HN 365* 1 1920-38 £1250-£1500 $2680-$3220
An example has been discovered entitled 'Two Heads are Better than One'

HN No *Ver* *Prod Dates* *Market Values*

DREAMING
Reflections Series
Designer: Pauline Parsons
HN 3133 1 1987-95 £100-£120 $215-$255

DREAMLAND
Designer: Leslie Harradine
HN 1473 1 1931-38 £870-£1130 $1865-$2425
HN 1481 1 1931-38 £870-£1130 $1865-$2425

DREAMWEAVER
Designer: Mary Nicoll
HN 2283 1 1972-76 £120-£150 $255-$320

DRESSING UP
Childhood Days Series
Designer: Pauline Parsons
HN 2964 1 1982-85 £100-£130 $215-$280
Designer: Adrian Hughes. Ltd Ed: 9500
HN 3300 2 1991 RRP RRP

DRUMMER BOY
Designer: Mary Nicoll
HN 2679 1 1976-81 £300-£350 $645-$750

DRYAD OF THE PINES
Designer: Richard Garbe
HN 1869* 1 1938-49 £1870-£2190 $4015-$4700

DUCHESS OF YORK
Designer: Eric J Griffiths. Ltd Ed: 1500
HN 3086 1 1986 £350-£400 $750-$860

DUKE OF EDINBURGH
Designer: Peggy Davies. Ltd Ed: 1500
HN 2386 1 1981 £175-£250 $375-$535

DUKE OF WELLINGTON
Designer: Alan Maslankowski. Ltd Ed: 1500
HN 3432 1 1993 RRP RRP

DULCIE
Designer: Peggy Davies
HN 2305 1 1981-84 £120-£150 $255-$320

DULCIMER
Lady Musicians Series
Designer: Peggy Davies. Ltd Ed: 750
HN 2798 1 1975 £400-£450 $860-$965

DULCINEA
Designer: Leslie Harradine
HN 1343 1 1929-38 £900-£1100 $1930-$2360
HN 1419 1 1930-38 £900-£1100 $1930-$2360

DUNCE
Designer: Charles J Noke
HN 6* 1 1913-38 £870-£1130 $1865-$2425
HN 310* 1 1918-38 £870-£1130 $1865-$2425
HN 357* 1 1919-38 £870-£1130 $1865-$2425

EASTER DAY
Designer: Leslie Harradine
HN 1976 1 1945-51 £250-£310 $535-$665
HN 2039 1 1949-69 £220-£250 $470-$535

EASTERN GRACE
Reflections Series
HN 3138 1 1988-89 £90-£110 $195-$235
This figure was re-issued in flambé glaze in 1996
Flambé Series
Designer: Pauline Parsons. Ltd Ed: 2500
HN 3683 1 1996 RRP RRP
This is the last flambé figure to be issued

EDITH
Kate Greenaway Series
Designer: Peggy Davies
HN 2957 1 1982-85 £140-£180 $300-$385

ELAINE
Designer: Peggy Davies
HN 2791 1 1980 RRP RRP
HN 3307 1 1990 RRP RRP
Miniatures Series
HN 3214 1 1988 RRP RRP
Michael Doulton Series
HN 3247 1 1989 RRP RRP

ELEANOR OF PROVENCE
Designer: Peggy Davies
HN 2009 1 1948-53 £310-£380 $665-$815

ELEANORE
Designer: Leslie Harradine
HN 1753 1 1936-49 £500-£550 $1075-$1180
HN 1754 1 1936-49 £500-£550 $1075-$1180

ELEGANCE
Designer: Peggy Davies
HN 2264 1 1961-85 £130-£150 $280-$320

ELFREDA
Designer: Leslie Harradine
HN 2078 1 1951-55 £430-£530 $920-$1135

ELIZA
Haute Ensemble Series
Designer: Eric J Griffiths
HN 2543 1 1974-79 £200-£220 $430-$470
Designer: Douglas V Tootle
HN 3179 2 1988-92 £80-£100 $170-$215
Charleston Series
Designer: Alan Maslankowski
HN 3798 3 1996 RRP RRP
Green version
HN 3799 3 1996 RRP RRP
Blue version
HN 3800 3 1996 RRP RRP
Pink version
HN 3801 3 1996 RRP RRP
Ivory version

ELIZA FARREN (Countess of Derby)
RDICC Series
Designer: Peter Gee. Ltd Ed: 5000
HN 3442 1 1992-93 £150-£180 $320-$385

HN No Ver Prod Dates Market Values

ELIZABETH
Designer: B Franks
HN 2946 1 1982-86 £140-£160 $300-$345
Designer: John Bromley
HN 2465 2 1990 RRP RRP

ELIZABETH FRY
Designer: Charles Vyse
HN 2* 1 1913-38 £1120-£1500 $2405-$3220
HN 2A* 1 1913-38 £1120-£1500 $2405-$3220

ELLEN
Kate Greenaway Series
Designer: Pauline Parsons
HN 3020 1 1984-87 £140-£180 $300-$385

ELLEN TERRY
Famous Actresses Series
Designer: Douglas V Tootle. Ltd Ed: 5000
HN 3826 1 1996 RRP RRP
Lawleys by Post

ELLEN TERRY as Queen Catherine
Designer: Charles J Noke
HN 379* 1 1920-49 £620-£880 $1330-$1890

ELSIE MAYNARD
Designer: Charles J Noke
HN 639 1 1924-49 £250-£300 $535-$645
Gilbert and Sullivan Series
Designer: William K Harper
HN 2902 2 1982-85 £310-£340 $665-$730

ELYSE
Designer: Peggy Davies
HN 2429 1 1972-95 £120-£150 $255-$320
HN 2474 1 1986 RRP RRP

EMBROIDERING
Designer: William K Harper
HN 2855 1 1980-90 £120-£160 $255-$345

EMILY (in Autumn)
Four Seasons Series
Designer: Peter Gee
HN 3004 1 1986 £150-£180 $320-$385
Commissioned by Danbury Mint

EMILY
Vanity Fair Series
Designer: Adrian Hughes.
HN 3204 2 1989-93 £100-£120 $215-$255
Designer: Nada Pedley
HN 3688 3 1995only £110-£130 $235-$280
For RDICC
Charleston Series
Designer: Alan Maslankowski
HN 3806 4 1996 RRP RRP
Green version
HN 3807 4 1996 RRP RRP
Blue version
HN 3808 4 1996 RRP RRP
Pink version
HN 3809 4 1996 RRP RRP
Ivory version

EMIR
Later models known as *Ibraham*
Designer: Charles J Noke
HN 1604 1 1933-49 £380-£420 $815-$900
HN 1605 1 1933-49 £380-£420 $815-$900

EMMA
Kate Greenaway Series
Designer: Peggy Davies.
HN 2834 1 1977-81 £140-£180 $300-$385
Designer: Adrian Hughes
HN 3208 2 1990 RRP RRP
Miniature version of Louise

ENCHANTING EVENING
Reflections Series
Designer: Robert Jefferson
HN 3108 1 1986-92 £90-£110 $195-$235

ENCHANTMENT
Designer: Peggy Davies
HN 2178 1 1957-82 £120-£140 $255-$300

ENCORE
Reflections Series
Designer: Douglas V Tootle
HN 2751 1 1988-89 £130-£160 $280-$345

ENGLAND
Ladies of the British Isles Series
Designer: Valerie Annand
HN 3627 1 1996 RRP RRP

ENIGMA
Reflections Series
Designer: Robert Jefferson
HN 3110 1 1986-95 £90-£110 $195-$235

ENTRANCED
Reflections Series
Designer: Eric J Griffiths
HN 3186 1 1988-89 £90-£120 $195-$255

ERMINE COAT, The
Designer: Leslie Harradine
HN 1981 1 1945-67 £160-£190 $345-$405

ERMINIE
Designer: Unknown
M 40 1 1933-45 £250-£300 $535-$645

ESMERALDA
Designer: Peggy Davies
HN 2168 1 1956-59 £160-£200 $345-$430

ESTELLE
Designer: Leslie Harradine
HN 1566 1 1933-38 £500-£630 $1075-$1350
HN 1802 1 1937-49 £550-£650 $1180-$1395

ETÉ
Les Saisons Series
Designer: Robert Jefferson. Ltd Ed: 300
HN 3067 1 1989 £400-£450 $860-$965

HN No *Ver* *Prod Dates* *Market Values*

EUGENE

Designer: Leslie Harradine

HN No	Ver	Prod Dates	Market Values	
HN 1520	1	1932-38	£600-£650	$1285-$1395
HN 1521	1	1932-38	£600-£650	$1285-$1395

EUROPA AND THE BULL

Designer: Harry Tittensor

HN No	Ver	Prod Dates	Market Values	
HN 95*	1	1918-38	£1000-£1250	$2145-$2680

Myths and Maidens Series

Designer: Robert Jefferson. Ltd Ed: 300

HN No	Ver	Prod Dates	Market Values	
HN 2828	2	1985	£600-£900	$1285-$1930

EVE

Les Femmes Fatales Series

Designer: Peggy Davies. Ltd Ed: 750

HN No	Ver	Prod Dates	Market Values	
HN 2466	1	1984	£450-£500	$965-$1075

EVELYN

Designer: Leslie Harradine

HN No	Ver	Prod Dates	Market Values	
HN 1622*	1	1934-49	£550-£600	$1180-$1285
HN 1637*	1	1934-38	£550-£600	$1180-$1285

EVENTIDE

Designer: William K Harper

HN No	Ver	Prod Dates	Market Values	
HN 2814	1	1977-91	£130-£150	$280-$320

FAGIN

Dickens Series

Designer: Leslie Harradine

HN No	Ver	Prod Dates	Market Values	
HN 534	1	1922-32	£55-£60	$120-$130
M 49	1	1932-83	£40-£60	$85-$130

Designer: Arthur Dobson

HN No	Ver	Prod Dates	Market Values	
HN 3752	2	1995	RRP	RRP

Resin

FAIR LADY

Designer: Peggy Davies

HN No	Ver	Prod Dates	Market Values	
HN 2193†	1	1963-96	£110-£130	$235-$280
HN 2832†	1	1977-96	£110-£130	$235-$280
HN 2835†	1	1977-96	£110-£130	$235-$280

†See also Kay

Miniatures Series

HN No	Ver	Prod Dates	Market Values	
HN 3216	1	1988	RRP	RRP

Michael Doulton Miniature Series

HN No	Ver	Prod Dates	Market Values	
HN 3336	1	1991	RRP	RRP

FAIR MAIDEN

Designer: Peggy Davies

HN No	Ver	Prod Dates	Market Values	
HN 2211	1	1967-94	£60-£80	$130-$170
HN 2434	1	1983-94	£60-£80	$130-$170

FAIRY

Designer: Leslie Harradine

HN No	Ver	Prod Dates	Market Values	
HN 1324	1	1929-38	£600-£800	$1285-$1715
HN 1374	2	1930-38	£600-£800	$1285-$1715
HN 1376	2	1930-38	£600-£800	$1285-$1715
HN 1380	2	1930-38	£600-£800	$1285-$1715
HN 1532	2	1932-38	£600-£800	$1285-$1715
HN 1375	3	1930-38	£600-£800	$1285-$1715
HN 1395	3	1930-38	£600-£800	$1285-$1715
HN 1533	3	1932-38	£600-£800	$1285-$1715
HN 1536	3	1932-38	£600-£800	$1285-$1715
HN 1378	4	1930-38	£600-£800	$1285-$1715
HN 1396	4	1930-38	£600-£800	$1285-$1715
HN 1535	4	1932-38	£600-£800	$1285-$1715
HN 1379	5	1930-38	£600-£800	$1285-$1715
HN 1394	5	1930-38	£600-£800	$1285-$1715
HN 1534	5	1932-38	£600-£800	$1285-$1715
HN 1393	6	1930-38	£400-£600	$860-$1285
HN 1377	7	1930-38	£400-£600	$860-$1285

FAIRYSPELL

Enchantment Series

Designer: Adrian Hughes

HN No	Ver	Prod Dates	Market Values	
HN 2979	1	1983-86	£100-£130	$215-$280

FAITH

Designer: Eric J Griffiths. Ltd Ed: 9500

HN No	Ver	Prod Dates	Market Values	
HN 3082	1	1986	£120-£150	$255-$320

FAITHFUL FRIEND

Designer: Nada Pedley

HN No	Ver	Prod Dates	Market Values	
HN 3696	1	1995	RRP	RRP

FALSTAFF

Designer: Charles J Noke

HN No	Ver	Prod Dates	Market Values	
HN 571	1	1923-38	£600-£650	$1285-$1395
HN 575	1	1923-38	£600-£650	$1285-$1395
HN 608	1	1924-38	£600-£650	$1285-$1395
HN 609	1	1924-38	£600-£650	$1285-$1395
HN 619	1	1924-38	£600-£650	$1285-$1395
HN 638	1	1924-38	£600-£650	$1285-$1395
HN 1216	1	1926-49	£600-£650	$1285-$1395
HN 1606	1	1933-49	£600-£650	$1285-$1395
HN 618	2	1924-38	£600-£650	$1285-$1395
HN 2054	2	1950-92	£110-£130	$235-$280

Miniature Series

HN No	Ver	Prod Dates	Market Values	
HN 3236	2	1989-90	£60-£80	$130-$170

FAMILY

Images Series

Designer: Eric J Griffiths

HN No	Ver	Prod Dates	Market Values	
HN 2720	1	1981	RRP	RRP
HN 2721	1	1981-92	£80-£100	$170-$215

FAMILY ALBUM

Designer: Mary Nicoll

HN No	Ver	Prod Dates	Market Values	
HN 2321	1	1966-73	£180-£220	$385-$470

FANTASY

Reflections Series

Designer: Adrian Hughes

HN No	Ver	Prod Dates	Market Values	
HN 3296	1	1990-92	£100-£130	$215-$280

FARAWAY

Designer: Peggy Davies

HN No	Ver	Prod Dates	Market Values	
HN 2133	1	1958-62	£200-£250	$430-$535

FARMER

Designer: Adrian Hughes

HN No	Ver	Prod Dates	Market Values	
HN 3195	1	1988-91	£120-£140	$255-$300

FARMER'S BOY

Designer: William M Chance

HN No	Ver	Prod Dates	Market Values	
HN 2520	1	1938-60	£700-£750	$1500-$1610

HN No Ver Prod Dates Market Values

FARMER'S WIFE
Designer: Leslie Harradine
HN 2069 1 1951-55 £300-£375 $645-$805
Designer: Adrian Hughes
HN 3164 2 1988-91 £120-£140 $255-$300

FAT BOY The
Dickens Series
Designer: Leslie Harradine
HN 530 1 1922-32 £55-£60 $120-$130
M 44 1 1932-83 £40-£60 $85-$130
HN 555 2 1923-39 £200-£240 $430-$515
HN 1893 2 1938-52 £180-£230 $385-$495
HN 2096 3 1952-67 £180-£230 $385-$495

FATHER CHRISTMAS
Designer: Robert Tabbenor
HN 3399 1 1992 RRP RRP

FAVOURITE, The
Designer: Mary Nicoll
HN 2249 1 1960-90 £120-£150 $255-$320

FEBRUARY
Figure of the Month Series
Designer: Peggy Davies
HN 2703 1 1987 £140-£160 $300-$345
For Home Shopping Network, USA
Designer: Robert Tabbenor
HN 3331 2 1990 £100-£130 $215-$280
Colourway of Amanda. USA only
Wild Flower of the Month Series
Designer: Peggy Davies
HN 3342 3 1991 £130-£150 $280-$320
Colourway of Beartrice for Sears of Canada

FEEDING TIME
Age of Innocence Series
Designer: Nada Pedley. Ltd Ed: 9500
HN 3373 1 1991-94 £120-£150 $255-$320

FEMALE STUDY
Designer: Leslie Harradine
HN 604A 1 1924-38 £200-£250 $430-$535
HN 604B 1 1924-38 £200-£250 $430-$535

FIDDLER, The
Designer: Mary Nicoll
HN 2171 1 1956-62 £400-£450 $860-$965

FIELD MARSHALL MONTGOMERY
Designer: Robert Tabbenor. Ltd Ed: 1994
HN 3405 1 1994 RRP RRP

FIONA
Designer: Leslie Harradine.
HN 1924 1 1940-49 £600-£650 $1285-$1395
HN 1925 1 1940-49 £600-£650 $1285-$1395
HN 1933 1 1940-49 £600-£650 $1285-$1395
Designer: Peggy Davies
HN 2694 2 1974-81 £120-£140 $255-$300
Designer: Douglas V Tootle
HN 3252 3 1989-92 £120-£140 $255-$300
Designer: Peggy Davies
HN 3748 4 1996 RRP RRP
Colourway of Adrienne for Scotland

FIRST DANCE
Designer: Peggy Davies
HN 2803 1 1977-92 £120-£140 $255-$300
See also Samantha (2nd version)

FIRST LOVE
Images Series
Designer: Douglas V Tootle
HN 2747 1 1988 RRP RRP

FIRST OUTING
Age of Innocence Series
Designer: Nada Pedley. Ltd Ed: 9500
HN 3377 1 1992-94 £120-£150 $255-$320

FIRST PERFORMANCE
Designer: Nada Pedley
HN 3605 1 1994 RRP RRP

FIRST RECITAL
Designer: Nada Pedley
HN 3652 1 1994 RRP RRP

FIRST STEPS
Designer: Peggy Davies
HN 2242 1 1959-65 £200-£245 $430-$525
Image Series
Designer: Robert Tabbenor
HN 3282 2 1991 RRP RRP
Little Cherubs Series
Designer: Valerie Annand
HN 3361 3 1992 RRP RRP

FIRST VIOLIN
Edwardian String Quartet Series
Designer: Valerie Annand. Ltd Ed: 1500
HN 3704 1 1995 RRP RRP
Lawleys by Post

FIRST WALTZ
Designer: Peggy Davies
HN 2862 1 1979-83 £125-£150 $270-$320

FISHERWOMAN
Designer: Unknown
HN 80* 1 1917-38 £2000-£2500 $4290-$5365
HN 349* 1 1919-68 £2000-£2500 $4290-$5365
HN 359* 1 1919-38 £2000-£2500 $4290-$5365
HN 631* 1 1924-38 £2000-£2500 $4290-$5365

FLEUR
Designer: John Bromley
HN 2368 1 1968-95 £100-£120 $215-$255
HN 2369 1 1983-86 £100-£120 $215-$255
See also Flower of Love

FLEURETTE
Designer: Leslie Harradine
HN 1587 1 1933-49 £300-£350 $645-$750

FLIRTATION
Reflections Series
Designer: Adrian Hughes
HN 3071 1 1985-95 £100-£120 $215-$255

HN No Ver Prod Dates Market Values

FLORA
Designer: Mary Nicoll
HN 2349 1 1966-73 £150-£200 $320-$430

FLORENCE
Designer: Douglas V Tootle
HN 2745 1 1988-92 £100-£120 $215-$255

FLORENCE NIGHTINGALE
Designer: Pauline Parsons. Ltd Ed: 5000
HN 3144 1 1988 £350-£400 $750-$860

FLOUNCED SKIRT, The
Designer: Ernest W Light
HN 57A* 1 1916-38 £680-£810 $1460-$1740
HN 66* 1 1916-38 £680-£810 $1460-$1740
HN 77* 1 1917-38 £680-£810 $1460-$1740
HN 78* 1 1917-38 £680-£810 $1460-$1740
HN 333* 1 1918-38 £680-£810 $1460-$1740

FLOWER ARRANGING
Gentle Arts Series
Designer: Don Brindley. Ltd Ed: 750
HN 3040 1 1988 £450-£500 $965-$1075

FLOWER OF LOVE
Vanity Fair Series
Designer: John Bromley
HN 2460 1 1991 RRP RRP
Colourway of Fleur

FLOWER SELLER, The
Designer: Leslie Harradine
HN 789 1 1926-38 £400-£450 $860-$965

FLOWER SELLER'S CHILDREN, The
Designer: Leslie Harradine
HN 525 1 1921-49 £375-£450 $805-$965
HN 551 1 1922-49 £375-£450 $805-$965
HN 1206 1 1926-49 £375-£450 $805-$965
HN 1342 1 1929-93 £200-£250 $430-$535
HN 1406 1 1930-38 £400-£475 $860-$1020

FLOWERGIRL
Designer: Valerie Annand
HN 3479 1 1994 RRP RRP
Same model as Bridesmaid (3476). Canada only
Designer: Nada Pedley
HN 3602 2 1993 RRP RRP
North America only

FLOWERS FOR MOTHER
Designer: Pauline Parsons
HN 3454 1 1994 RRP RRP

FLUTE
Lady Musicians Series
Designer: Peggy Davies. Ltd Ed: 750
HN 2483 1 1973 £500-£550 $1075-$1180

FOAMING QUART, The
Designer: Peggy Davies
HN 2162 1 1955-92 £125-£150 $270-$320

FOLLY
Designer: Leslie Harradine
HN 1335 1 1929-38 £950-£1100 $2040-$2360
HN 1750 1 1936-49 £850-£950 $1825-$2040

FOR YOU
Name Your Own Figure Series
Designer: Tim Potts
HN 3754 1 1995 RRP RRP
Customer can add special name on brass plate on base

FORGET-ME-NOT
Designer: Leslie Harradine
HN 1812 1 1937-49 £250-£300 $535-$645
HN 1813 1 1937-49 £250-£300 $535-$645
Sentiments Series
Designer: Alan Maslankowski
HN 3388 2 1991 RRP RRP

FORGET-ME-NOTS
Flowers of Love Series
Designer: Valerie Annand
HN 3700 1 1995 RRP RRP

FORTUNE TELLER
Designer: Leslie Harradine
HN 2159 1 1955-67 £225-£275 $480-$590

FORTY WINKS
Designer: Harry Fenton
HN 1974 1 1945-73 £120 £150 $255-$320

FOUR O'CLOCK
Designer: Leslie Harradine
HN 1760 1 1936-49 £450-£500 $965-$1075

FRAGRANCE
Designer: Peggy Davies
HN 2334 1 1966-95 £100-£120 $215-$255
Miniatures Series
HN 3220 1 1988-92 £60-£80 $130-$170
Michael Doulton Miniature Series
HN 3250 1 1991 RRP RRP
Michael Doulton Series
HN 3311 1 1991 £110-£130 $235-$280

FRANCINE
Designer: John Bromley
HN 2422 1 1972-81 £90-£110 $195-$235

FRANCOISE
Elegance Series
Designer: William K Harper
HN 2897 1 1984 £180-£200 $385-$430
This figure was test marketed but not put into full production

FRANGCON
Designer: Leslie Harradine
HN 1720 1 1935-49 £600-£650 $1285-$1395
HN 1721 1 1935-49 £600-£650 $1285-$1395

FREE AS THE WIND
Reflections Series
Designer: Pauline Parsons
HN 3139 1 1989-95 £100-£130 $215-$280

HN No	Ver	Prod Dates	Market Values	

FREE SPIRIT
Images Series
Designer: Adrian Hughes

HN 3157	1	1988-92	£100-£120	$215-$255
HN 3159	1	1988-92	£100-£120	$215-$255

Elegance Series
Designer: Alan Maslankowski

HN 3728	2	1996	RRP	RRP

FRENCH HORN
Lady Musicians Series
Designer: Peggy Davies. Ltd Ed: 750

HN 2795	1	1976	£450-£500	$965-$1075

FRENCH PEASANT
Designer: Leslie Harradine

HN 2075	1	1951-55	£250-£300	$535-$645

FRIAR TUCK
Designer: Peggy Davies

HN 2143	1	1954-65	£300-£350	$645-$750

FRIENDSHIP
Sentiments Series
Designer: Alan Maslankowski

HN 3491	1	1994	RRP	RRP

FRODO
Tolkien Series
Designer: David Lyttleton

HN 2912	1	1980-84	£60-£90	$130-$195

FRUIT GATHERING
Designer: Leslie Harradine

HN 449	1	1921-38	£930-£1060	$1995-$2275
HN 476	1	1921-38	£930-£1060	$1995-$2275
HN 503	1	1921-38	£930-£1060	$1995-$2275
HN 561	1	1923-38	£930-£1060	$1995-$2275
HN 562	1	1923-38	£930-£1060	$1995-$2275
HN 706	1	1925-38	£930-£1060	$1995-$2275
HN 707	1	1925-38	£930-£1060	$1995-$2275

GAFFER, The
Designer: Leslie Harradine

HN 2053	1	1950-59	£220-£280	$470-$600

GAIETY
Reflections Series
Designer: Pauline Parsons

HN 3140	1	1988-90	£100-£130	$215-$280

USA only

GAIL
Designer: Peter Gee

HN 2937	1	1986	RRP	RRP

Miniature Series

HN 3321	1	1992	RRP	RRP

GAINSBOROUGH HAT, The
Designer: Harry Tittensor

HN 46*	1	1915-38	£620-£690	$1330-$1480
HN 46A*	1	1915-38	£620-£690	$1330-$1480
HN 47*	1	1915-38	£620-£690	$1330-$1480
HN 329*	1	1918-38	£620-£690	$1330-$1480
HN 352*	1	1919-38	£850-£910	$1825-$1950
HN 383*	1	1920-38	£620-£690	$1330-$1480
HN 453*	1	1921-38	£620-£690	$1330-$1480
HN 675*	1	1924-38	£750-£810	$1610-$1740
HN 705*	1			

GALADRIEL
Tolkien Series
Designer: David Lyttleton

HN 2915	1	1981-84	£80-£100	$170-$215

GAMEKEEPER , The
Designer: Eric J Griffiths

HN 2879	1	1984-92	£100-£120	$215-$255

GANDALF
Tolkien Series
Designer: David Lyttleton

HN 2911	1	1980-84	£100-£140	$215-$300

GARDENER, The
Reflections Series
Designer: Adrian Hughes

HN 3161	1	1989-91	£100-£130	$215-$280

GARDENING TIME
Designer: Robert Tabbenor

HN 3401	1	1992-94	£100-£120	$215-$255

GAY MORNING
Designer: Peggy Davies

HN 2135	1	1954-67	£170-£210	$365-$450

GEISHA, A
Designer: Harry Tittensor

HN 354*	1	1919-38	£430-£560	$920-$1200
HN 376*	1	1920-38	£1000-£1250	$2145-$2680
HN 376A*	1	1920-38	£800-£1000	$1715-$2145
HN 387*	1	1920-38	£430-£500	$920-$1075
HN 634*	1	1924-38	£430-£500	$920-$1075
HN 741*	1	1925-38	£430-£500	$920-$1075
HN 779*	1	1926-38	£430-£500	$920-$1075
HN 1321*	1	1929-38	£1000-£1250	$2145-$2680
HN 1322*	1	1929-38	£1000-£1250	$2145-$2680

Designer: Charles J. Noke

HN 1223*	2	1927-38	£620-£880	$1330-$1890
HN 1234*	2	1927-38	£620-£880	$1330-$1890
HN 1292*	2	1928-38	£620-£880	$1330-$1890
HN 1310*	2	1929-38	£620-£880	$1330-$1890

Flambé Series
Designer: Pauline Parsons

HN 3229*	3	1989	£120-£150	$255-$320

RDICC Exclusive

GEMMA
Designer: Nada Pedley

HN 3661	1	1995	RRP	RRP

HN No	*Ver*	*Prod Dates*	*Market Values*	

GENERAL ROBERT E LEE
Designer: Robert Tabbenor. Ltd Ed: 5000
HN 3404 1 1993-95 £450-£550 $965-$1180
USA only

GENEVIEVE
Designer: Leslie Harradine
HN 1962 1 1941-75 £150-£200 $320-$430

GENIE, The
Flambé Series
Designer: Robert Tabbenor
HN 2999 1 1990-95 £150-£180 $320-$385
HN 2989 1 1983-90 £120-£140 $255-$300

GENTLEMAN FROM WILLIAMSBURG
Designer: Peggy Davies
HN 2227 1 1960-83 £120-£140 $255-$300

GENTLEWOMAN, A
Designer: Leslie Harradine
HN 1632 1 1934-49 £310-£380 $665-$815

GEOFF BOYCOTT OBE
Designer: Robert Tabbenor. Ltd Ed: 8114
HN 3890 1 1996 RRP RRP
Limited edition size corresponds to the number of runs Boycott made in his Test Match career

GEORGE WASHINGTON AT PRAYER
Designer: Laszlo Ispanky. Ltd Ed: 750
HN 2861 1 1977-78 £450 £550 $965-$1180

GEORGIANA
Designer: Peggy Davies
HN 2093 1 1952-55 £600-£650 $1285-$1395

GEORGINA
Kate Greenaway Series
Designer: Peggy Davies
HN 2377 1 1981-86 £120-£140 $255-$300

GERALDINE
Designer: Peggy Davies
HN 2348 1 1972-76 £0-£150 $150-$210

GIFT OF FREEDOM
Images Series
Designer: Peter Gee
HN 3443 1 1993 RRP RRP

GIFT OF LOVE
Designer: Nada Pedley
HN 3427 1 1993 RRP RRP

GILLIAN
Designer: Leslie Harradine
HN 1670* 1 1934-49 £450-£500 $965-$1075
Designer: Pauline Parsons
HN 3042 2 1984-91 £110-£130 $235-$280
Designer: Unknown
HN 3742 3 RRP RRP
Colourway for Great Universal Stores. Details unavailable

GIMLI
Tolkien Series
Designer: David Lyttleton
HN 2922 1 1981-84 £80-£100 $170-$215

GIRL EVACUEE, The
Children of the Blitz Series
Designer: Adrian Hughes. Ltd Ed: 9500
HN 3203 1 1989 £225-£275 $480-$590

GIRL WITH YELLOW FROCK
Designer: Unknown
HN 588* 1 1923-28 £650-£850 $1395-$1825
Now known as Spring (2nd version)

GISELLE
Designer: Peggy Davies
HN 2139 1 1954-69 £260-£280 $555-$600

GISELLE, The FOREST GLADE
Designer: Peggy Davies
HN 2140 1 1954-65 £260-£280 $555-$600

GLADYS
Designer: Leslie Harradine
HN 1740 1 1935-49 £400-£450 $860-$965
HN 1741 1 1935-38 £400-£450 $860-$965

GLEANER
Designer: Unknown
HN 1302* 1 1928-38 £870-£1130 $1865-$2425
Previously known as Gypsy Girl with Flowers. Inspired by Augustus John

GLORIA
Designer: Leslie Harradine
HN 1488* 1 1932-38 £800-£850 $1715-$1825
HN 1700* 1 1935-38 £850-£900 $1825-$1930
Designer: Adrian Hughes
HN 3200* 2 1989-90 £110-£130 $235-$280

GNOME, A
Designer: Harry Tittensor
HN 319 1 1918-38 £500-£600 $1075-$1285
HN 380 1 1920-38 £500-£600 $1075-$1285
HN 381 1 1920-38 £500-£600 $1075-$1285

GOD BLESS YOU
Images Series
Designer: Robert Tabbenor
HN 3400 1 1992 RRP RRP

GOLDEN DAYS
Designer: Peggy Davies
HN 2274 1 1964-73 £100-£120 $215-$255

GOLFER
Reflections Series
Designer: Robert Tabbenor
HN 2992 1 1989-91 £100-£130 $215-$280

GOLLUM
Tolkien Series
Designer: David Lyttleton
HN 2913 1 1980-84 £90-£120 $195-$255

HN No	Ver	Prod Dates	Market Values	

GOLLYWOG
Designer: Leslie Harradine

HN 1979	1	1945-59	£200-£250	$430-$535
HN 2040	1	1949-59	£175-£225	$375-$480

GOOD CATCH, A
Designer: Mary Nicoll

HN 2258	1	1966-86	£130-£150	$280-$320

GOOD COMPANION
Designer: Nada Pedley

HN 3608	1	1994	RRP	RRP

GOOD DAY SIR
Designer: William K Harper

HN 2896	1	1986-89	£120-£150	$255-$320

GOOD FRIENDS
Designer: William K Harper

HN 2783	1	1985-90	£100-£120	$215-$255

GOOD KING WENCESLAS
Designer: Peggy Davies

HN 2118	1	1953-76	£180-£200	$385-$430
HN 3262 *Miniature*	1	1989-92	£65-£85	$140-$180

GOOD MORNING
Designer: Mary Nicoll

HN 2671	1	1974-76	£120-£140	$255-$300

GOOD PALS
Reflections Series
Designer: Pauline Parsons

HN 3132	1	1987-92	£100-£120	$215-$255

GOODY TWO SHOES
Designer: Leslie Harradine

HN 1889	1	1938-49	£150-£180	$320-$385
HN 1905	1	1939-49	£150-£180	$320-$385
HN 2037	1	1949-89	£90-£110	$195-$235
M 80	1	1939-49	£350-£400	$750-$860
M 81	1	1939-49	£350-£400	$750-$860

GOOSEGIRL, The
Designer: Leslie Harradine

HN 425*	1	1921-38	£1370-£1880	$2940-$4035
HN 436*	1	1921-38	£1370-£1880	$2940-$4035
HN 437*	1	1921-38	£1370-£1880	$2940-$4035
HN 448*	1	1921-38	£1370-£1880	$2940-$4035
HN 559*	1	1923-38	£1370-£1880	$2940-$4035
HN 560*	1	1923-38	£1370-£1880	$2940-$4035

Designer: John Bromley. Ltd Ed: 12500

HN 2419*	2	1990	RRP	RRP

GOSSIPS, The
Designer: Leslie Harradine

HN 1426	1	1930-49	£275-£325	$590-$695
HN 1429	1	1930-49	£275-£325	$590-$695
HN 2025	1	1949-67	£250-£300	$535-$645

GRACE
Designer: Mary Nicoll

HN 2318	1	1966-81	£130-£150	$280-$320

Designer: Nada Pedley

HN 3699	2	1996	RRP	RRP

GRACE DARLING
Designer: Eric J Griffiths. Ltd Ed: 9500

HN 3089	1	1987	£125-£140	$270-$300

GRADUATE
Designer: Pauline Parsons

HN 3016 *Female*	1	1984-92	£100-£130	$215-$280
HN 3017 *Male*	1	1984-92	£100-£130	$215-$280

GRAND MANNER
Designer: William K Harper

HN 2723	1	1975-81	£110-£130	$235-$280

GRANDMA
Designer: Leslie Harradine

HN 2052	1	1950-59	£200-£220	$430-$470

GRANDPA'S STORY
Designer: Pauline Parsons

HN 3456	1	1994	RRP	RRP

GRANNY
Designer: Leslie Harradine

HN 1804	1	1937-49	£600-£650	$1285-$1395
HN 1832	1	1937-49	£600-£650	$1285-$1395

GRANNY'S HERITAGE
Designer: Leslie Harradine

HN 1873	1	1938-49	£300-£350	$645-$750
HN 1874	1	1938-49	£300-£350	$645-$750
HN 2031	1	1949-69	£220-£260	$470-$555

GRANNY'S SHAWL
Designer: Leslie Harradine

HN 1642	1	1934-49	£220-£250	$470-$535
HN 1647	1	1934-49	£200-£230	$430-$495

GRETA
Designer: Leslie Harradine

HN 1485	1	1931-53	£180-£200	$385-$430

GRETCHEN
Designer: Leslie Harradine

HN 1397	1	1930-38	£400-£450	$860-$965
HN 1562	1	1933-38	£400-£450	$860-$965

GRIEF
Designer: Charles J Noke

HN 595	1	1924-38	£470-£540	$1010-$1160

GRISELDA
Designer: Leslie Harradine

HN 1993	1	1947-53	£400-£450	$860-$965

GRIZEL
Designer: Leslie Harradine

HN 1629*	1	1934-38	£600-£650	$1285-$1395

HN No Ver Prod Dates Market Values

GROSSMITH'S 'TSANG IHANG' PERFUME OF TIBET
Designer: Unknown
HN 582 1 1923? £310-£350 $665-$750

GROUCHO MARX
Designer: William K Harper. Ltd Ed: 9500
HN 2777 1 1991 £150-£180 $320-$385

GUARDSMAN
Designer: William K Harper
HN 2784 1 1992-95 £110-£130 $235-$280

GULLIVER
Designer: David Biggs
HN 3750 1 1995 RRP RRP
Resin

GUY FAWKES
Designer: Charles J Noke
HN 98 1 1918-49 £800-£850 $1715-$1825
HN 347 1 1919-38 £900-£960 $1930-$2060
HN 445 1 1921-38 £900-£950 $1930-$2040
Miniature Series
HN 3271 1 1989-91 £60-£80 $130-$170

GWENDOLEN
Designer: Leslie Harradine
HN 1494* 1 1932-38 £420-£500 $900-$1075
HN 1503* 1 1932-49 £420-£500 $900-$1075
HN 1570* 1 1933-49 £420-£500 $900-$1075

GWYNNETH
Designer: Leslie Harradine
HN 1980 1 1945-52 £220-£250 $470-$535

GYPSY DANCE, A
Designer: Peggy Davies
HN 2157 1 1955-57 £200-£250 $430-$535
HN 2230 2 1959-71 £160-£200 $345-$430

HANNAH
Designer: Nada Pedley
HN 3369 1 1990 RRP RRP
HN 3649 1 1994 RRP RRP
Miniature
HN 3655 1 1995 only RRP RRP
Colourway

HAPPY ANNIVERSARY
Designer: Pauline Parsons
HN 3097 1 1987-93 £110-£130 $235-$280
Images Series
Designer: Douglas V Tootle
HN 3254 2 1989 RRP RRP

HAPPY BIRTHDAY
Designer: Pauline Parsons
HN 3095 1 1987-94 £110-£130 $235-$280
Designer: Nada Pedley
HN 3660 2 1995 RRP RRP

"HAPPY JOY, BABY BOY"
Designer: Unknown
HN 1541 1 1933-49 £150-£180 $320-$385

HARLEQUIN
Designer: Peggy Davies
HN 2186 1 1957-69 £140-£180 $300-$385
Prestige Series
Designer: Douglas V Tootle
HN 3287 1 1993 RRP RRP
HN 2737 2 1982 RRP RRP

HARLEQUINADE
Designer: Leslie Harradine
HN 585 1 1923-38 £400-£450 $860-$965
HN 635 1 1924-38 £400-£450 $860-$965
HN 711 1 1925-38 £400-£450 $860-$965
HN 780 1 1926-38 £400-£450 $860-$965

HARLEQUINADE MASKED
Designer: Leslie Harradine
HN 768* 1 1925-38 £1000-£1200 $2145-$2575
HN 769* 1 1925-38 £1000-£1200 $2145-$2575
HN 1274* 1 1928-38 £1000-£1200 $2145-$2575
HN 1304* 1 1928-38 £1000-£1200 $2145-$2575

HARMONY
Designer: Robert Jefferson
HN 2824 1 1978-84 £150-£170 $320-$365

HARP
Lady Musicians Series
Designer: Peggy Davies. Ltd Ed: 750
HN 2482 1 1973 £550-£600 $1180-$1285

HARRIET
Designer: Douglas V Tootle
HN 3177 1 1988-91 £100-£130 $215-$280
Charleston Series
Designer: Alan Maslankowski
HN 3794 2 1996 RRP RRP
Green version
HN 3795 2 1996 RRP RRP
Blue version
HN 3796 2 1996 RRP RRP
Pink version
HN 3797 2 1996 RRP RRP
Ivory version

HARVESTIME
Reflections Series
Designer: Eric J Griffiths
HN 3084 1 1988-90 £100-£130 $215-$280

HAZEL
Designer: Leslie Harradine
HN 1796 1 1936-49 £250-£310 $535-$665
HN 1797 1 1936-49 £250-£310 $535-$665
Designer: Peggy Davies
HN 3167 2 1988-91 £100-£120 $215-$255

HE LOVES ME
Designer: Leslie Harradine
HN 2046 1 1949-62 £130-£150 $280-$320

HEART TO HEART
Designer: Peggy Davies
HN 2276 1 1961-71 £200-£250 $430-$535

HN No Ver Prod Dates Market Values

HEATHER
Vanity Fair Series
Designer: Pauline Parsons
HN 2956 1 1982 RRP RRP
See also Marie (3rd version)

HEIDI
Children's Literature Series
Designer: Adrian Hughes
HN 2975 1 1983-85 £100-£120 $215-$255

HELEN
Designer: Leslie Harradine
HN 1508 1 1932-38 £370-£500 $795-$1075
HN 1509 1 1932-38 £370-£500 $795-$1075
HN 1572 1 1933-38 £430-£500 $920-$1075
Vanity Fair Children Series
Designer: Robert Tabbenor
HN 2994 2 1985-87 £60-£80 $130-$170
Designer: Nada Pedley
HN 3687 3 1996 RRP RRP
Colourway for Canada
HN 3687 3 1995 RRP RRP
Colourway for UK Express Gifts

HELEN OF TROY
Les Femmes Fatales Series
Designer: Peggy Davies. Ltd Ed: 750
HN 2387 1 1981 £600-£650 $1285-$1395

HELLO DADDY
Designer: Nada Pedley
HN 3651 1 1994 RRP RRP

HELMSMAN
Designer: Mary Nicoll
HN 2499 1 1974-86 £130-£150 $280-$320

HENLEY
British Sporting Heritage Series
Designer: Valerie Annand. Ltd Ed: 5000
HN 3367 1 1993 RRP RRP

HENRIETTA MARIA
Designer: Peggy Davies
HN 2005 1 1948-53 £350-£400 $750-$860

HENRY IRVING as CARDINAL WOLSEY
Designer: Charles J Noke
HN 344* 1 1919-49 £1250-£1500 $2680-$3220

HENRY LYTTON as JACK POINT
Designer: Charles J Noke
HN 610 1 1924-49 £310-£440 $665-$945

HENRY VIII
Designer: Charles J Noke
HN 370* 1 1920-38 £1000-£1130 $2145-$2425
HN 673* 1 1924-38 £1000 $2145
Ltd Ed: 200
HN 1792* 2 1933 £1000 $2145
Designer: Pauline Parsons. Ltd Ed: 1991
HN 3350 3 1991 £600-£800 $1285-$1715
Lawleys by Post
Ltd Ed: 9500
HN 3458 4 1994 RRP RRP
Lawleys by Post

HER LADYSHIP
Designer: Leslie Harradine
HN 1977 1 1945-59 £200-£240 $430-$515

"HERE A LITTLE CHILD I STAND"
Designer: Unknown
HN 1546* 1 1933-49 £180-£230 $385-$495

HERMINIA
Designer: Leslie Harradine
HN 1644 1 1934-38 £500-£550 $1075-$1180
HN 1646 1 1934-38 £500-£550 $1075-$1180
HN 1704 1 1935-38 £500-£550 $1075-$1180

HERMIONE
Designer: Peggy Davies
HN 2058* 1 1950-52 £850-£1100 $1825-$2360

HIBERNIA
Ships Figureheads Series
Designer: Sharon Keenan. Ltd Ed: 950
HN 2932 1 1983 £200-£250 $430-$535

HIGHWAYMAN The
Beggar's Opera Series
Designer: Leslie Harradine
HN 527 1 1921-49 £350-£400 $750-$860
HN 592 1 1924-49 £350-£400 $750-$860
HN 1257 1 1927-49 £320-£380 $685-$815

HILARY
Designer: Peggy Davies
HN 2335 1 1967-81 £120-£140 $255-$300

HINGED PARASOL, The
Designer: Leslie Harradine
HN 1578 1 1933-49 £250-£350 $535-$750
HN 1579 1 1933-49 £250-£350 $535-$750

HIVER
Les Saisons Series
Designer: Robert Jefferson. Ltd Ed: 300
HN 3069 1 1988 £400-£450 $860-$965

HMS AJAX
Ships Figureheads Series
Designer: Sharon Keenan. Ltd Ed: 950
HN 2908 1 1980 £200-£250 $430-$535

HOLD TIGHT
Designer: Adrian Hughes
HN 3298 1 1990-95 £180-£220 $385-$470

HOLLY
Designer: Nada Pedley
HN 3647 1 1994 RRP RRP

HOME AGAIN
Designer: Peggy Davies
HN 2167 1 1956-95 £60-£80 $130-$170

HN No	Ver	Prod Dates	Market Values	

HOME AT LAST
Designer: Nada Pedley
HN 3697 1 1995 RRP RRP

HOMECOMING, The
Children of the Blitz Series
Designer: Adrian Hughes. Ltd Ed: 9500
HN 3295 1 1990-95 £150-£170 $320-$365

HOMETIME
Designer: Nada Pedley
HN 3685 1 1995 RRP RRP

HON FRANCES DUNCOMBE
Gainsborough Ladies Series
Designer: Peter Gee. Ltd Ed: 5000
HN 3009 1 1991-94 £200-£250 $430-$535

HONEY
Designer: Leslie Harradine
HN 1909 1 1939-49 £290-£350 $620-$750
HN 1910 1 1939-49 £290-£350 $620-$750
HN 1963 1 1941-49 £290-£350 $620-$750

HOPE
Designer: Sheila Mitchell. Ltd Ed: 9500
HN 3061 1 1984 £180-£200 $385-$430

HORNPIPE, The
Designer: Mary Nicoll
HN 2161 1 1955-62 £280-£340 $600-$730

HOSTESS OF WILLIAMSBURG
Designer: Peggy Davies
HN 2209 1 1960-83 £120-£140 $255-$300

HUCKLEBERRY FINN
Children's Literature Series
Designer: David Lyttleton
HN 2927 1 1982-85 £100-£120 $215-$255

HUNTING SQUIRE
Designer: Unknown
HN 1409* 1 1930-38 £1000-£1250 $2145-$2680
Later models known as The Squire
HN 1814* 1 1930-38 £750-£850 $1610-$1825

HUNTS LADY
Designer: Leslie Harradine
HN 1201* 1 1926-38 £1000-£1250 $2145-$2680

HUNTSMAN, The
Designer: Leslie Harradine
HN 1226 1 1927-38 £1000-£1250 $2145-$2680
HN 1815 2 1937-49 £1000-£1250 $2145-$2680
Also see John Peel
Designer: Mary Nicoll
HN 2492 3 1974-79 £140-£160 $300-$345

HURDY GURDY
Lady Musicians Series
Designer: Peggy Davies. Ltd Ed: 750
HN 2796 1 1975 £400-£450 $860-$965

IBRAHIM
Designer: Charles J Noke
HN 2095 1 1952-55 £310-£380 $665-$815
Early models known as Emir

IDLE HOURS
Reflections Series
Designer: Alan Maslankowski
HN 3115 1 1986-89 £110-£130 $235-$280

IN GRANDMA'S DAYS
Same model as *A Lilac Shawl* and *The Poke Bonnet*
Designer: Charles J Noke
HN 339 1 1919-38 £450-£600 $965-$1285
HN 340 1 1919-38 £450-£600 $965-$1285
HN 362 1 1919-38 £450-£600 $965-$1285
HN 388 1 1920-38 £450-£600 $965-$1285
HN 442 1 1921-38 £450-£600 $965-$1285

IN THE STOCKS
Designer: Leslie Harradine
HN 1474† 1 1931-38 £870-£940 $1865-$2015
HN 1475† 1 1931-38 £870-£940 $1865-$2015
†Also known as Love in the Stocks and Love Locked In
Designer: Mary Nicoll
HN 2163 2 1955-59 £400-£450 $860-$965

INDIAN BRAVE
Designer: Peggy Davies. Ltd Ed: 500
HN 2376 1 1967-78 £2800-£3000 $6010 $6440

INDIAN MAIDEN
Reflections Series
Designer: Alan Maslankowski
HN 3117 1 1988-90 £100-£130 $215-$280

INDIAN TEMPLE DANCER
Dancers of the World Series
Designer: Peggy Davies. Ltd Ed: 750
HN 2830 1 1977 £400-£450 $860-$965

INNOCENCE
Designer: Eric J Griffiths
HN 2842 1 1979-83 £100-£120 $215-$255
Designer: Pauline Parsons. Ltd Ed: 9500
HN 3226 2 1991 RRP RRP
Designer: Alan Maslankowski
HN 3730 3 1996 RRP RRP

INVITATION
Designer: Peggy Davies
HN 2170 1 1956-75 £120-£140 $255-$300

IONA
Designer: Leslie Harradine
HN 1346* 1 1929-38 £1000-£1380 $2145-$2960

IRELAND
Ladies of British Isles Series
Designer: Valerie Annand
HN 3628 1 1996 RRP RRP

HN No Ver Prod Dates Market Values

IRENE
Designer: Leslie Harradine
HN 1621 1 1934-51 £270-£300 $580-$645
HN 1697 1 1935-49 £320-£380 $685-$815
HN 1952 1 1940-50 £320-£380 $685-$815

IRISH COLLEEN
Designer: Leslie Harradine
HN 766* 1 1925-38 £800-£1000 $1715-$2145
HN 767* 1 1925-38 £750-£810 $1610-$1740

IRISHMAN, An
Designer: Harry Fenton
HN 1307 1 1928-38 £520-£590 $1115-$1265

ISABELLA, COUNTESS OF SEFTON
Gainsborough Ladies Series
Designer: Peter Gee. Ltd Ed: 5000
HN 3010 1 1991-94 £200-£250 $430-$535

ISADORA
Designer: Peter Gee
HN 2938 1 1986-92 £130-£150 $280-$320
See also Celeste (2nd version)

IT WON'T HURT
Childhood Days Series
Designer: Pauline Parsons
HN 2963 1 1982-85 £100-£120 $215-$255

IVY
Designer: Leslie Harradine
HN 1768 1 1936-79 £70-£100 $150-$215
HN 1769 1 1936-38 £160-£200 $345-$430

I'M NEARLY READY
Childhood Days Series
Designer: Adrian Hughes
HN 2976 1 1983-85 £100-£130 $215-$280

JACK
Designer: Leslie Harradine
HN 2060 1 1950-71 £100-£120 $215-$255

JACK POINT
Designer: Charles J Noke
HN 85* 1 1918-38 £1120-£1750 $2405-$3755
HN 91 1 1918-38 £870-£1250 $1865-$2680
HN 99 1 1918-38 £870-£1250 $1865-$2680
Prestige Figure Series
HN 2080 1 1952 RRP RRP
Prestige Series
Designer: Charles Noke. Ltd Ed: 250
HN 3920 1 1996 RRP RRP

JACQUELINE
Designer: Leslie Harradine
HN 2000 1 1947-51 £340-£410 $730-$880
HN 2001 1 1947-51 £340-£410 $730-$880
Designer: Peggy Davies
HN 2333 2 1983-91 £100-£130 $215-$280
Designer: Nada Pedley
HN 3689 3 1995 RRP RRP
Royal Doulton Roadshow exclusive

JAMES
Kate Greenaway Series
Designer: Pauline Parsons
HN 3013 1 1983-87 £200-£250 $430-$535

JAMES I
Stuart Kings Series
Designer: Douglas V Tootle. Ltd Ed: 1500
HN 3822 1 1996 RRP RRP
Lawleys by Post

JANE
Designer: Leslie Harradine
HN 2014 1 1948-51 £300-£350 $645-$750
Designer: Peggy Davies
HN 2806 2 1983-86 £120-£140 $255-$300
Designer: Douglas V Tootle
HN 3260 3 1990-95 £100-£130 $215-$280

JANE SEYMOUR
King Henry VIII's Wives Series
Designer: Pauline Parsons. Ltd Ed: 9500
HN 3349 1 1991 RRP RRP

JANET
Designer: Leslie Harradine
HN 1537 1 1932-95 £100-£120 $215-$255
HN 1538 1 1932-49 £150-£200 $320-$430
HN 1652 1 1934-49 £150-£200 $320-$430
HN 1737 1 1935-49 £150-£200 $320-$430
M 69 1 1936-49 £250-£300 $535-$645
M 75 1 1936-49 £250-£300 $535-$645
HN 1916 2 1939-49 £170-£230 $365-$495
HN 1964 2 1941-49 £170-£230 $365-$495

JANETTE
Designer: Peggy Davies
HN 3415 1 1992 £100-£130 $215-$280
Colourway of Kirsty for Great Universal Stores.

JANICE
Designer: Peggy Davies
HN 2022 1 1949-55 £325-£375 $695-$805
HN 2165 1 1955-65 £300-£350 $645-$750
Designer: Valerie Annand
HN 3624 2 RRP RRP
See also Lady Eaton for Great Universal Stores

JANINE
Designer: John Bromley
HN 2461 1 1971-95 £100-£130 $215-$280

JANUARY
Figure of the Month Series
Designer: Peggy Davies
HN 2697 1 1987 £140-£160 $300-$345
For Home Shopping Network, USA
Designer: Robert Tabbenor
HN 3330 2 1990 £100-£130 $215-$280
Colourway of Amanda. USA only
WIld Flower of the Month Series
Designer: Peggy Davies
HN 3341 3 1991 £130-£150 $280-$320
Colourway of Beatrice for Sears of Canada

HN No — Ver — Prod Dates — Market Values

JAPANESE FAN

Designer: Harry Tittensor

HN No	Ver	Prod Dates	Market Values	
HN 399	1	1920-38	£600-£650	$1285-$1395
HN 405	1	1920-38	£600-£650	$1285-$1395
HN 439	1	1921-38	£600-£650	$1285-$1395
HN 440	1	1921-38	£600-£650	$1285-$1395

JASMINE

Designer: Leslie Harradine

HN No	Ver	Prod Dates	Market Values	
HN 1862	1	1938-49	£400-£450	$860-$965
HN 1863	1	1938-49	£400-£450	$860-$965
HN 1876	1	1938-49	£400-£450	$860-$965

JEAN

Designer: Leslie Harradine

HN No	Ver	Prod Dates	Market Values	
HN 1877	1	1938-49	£280-£340	$600-$730
HN 1878	1	1938-49	£280-£340	$600-$730
HN 2032	1	1949-59	£280-£340	$600-$730

Vanity Fair Children Series

Designer: Peggy Davies

HN No	Ver	Prod Dates	Market Values	
HN 2710	2	1983-86	£70-£100	$150-$215

Designer: Tim Potts

HN No	Ver	Prod Dates	Market Values	
HN 3757	3	1996	RRP	RRP

Colourway for Great Universal Stores

JEMMA

Designer: Peggy Davies

HN No	Ver	Prod Dates	Market Values	
HN 3168	1	1988-91	£100-£130	$215-$280

JENNIFER

Designer: Leslie Harradine

HN No	Ver	Prod Dates	Market Values	
HN 1484	1	1931-49	£270-£350	$580-$750

Designer: Peggy Davies

HN No	Ver	Prod Dates	Market Values	
HN 2392	2	1982-92	£120-£150	$255-$320

Figure of the Year Series

Designer: Peter Gee

HN No	Ver	Prod Dates	Market Values	
HN 3447	3	1994	£130-£150	$280-$320

JERSEY MILKMAID, The

Designer: Leslie Harradine

HN No	Ver	Prod Dates	Market Values	
HN 2057	1	1950-59	£150-£180	$320-$385

Also see The Milkmaid

JESSICA

Vanity Fair Series

Designer: Peggy Davies

HN No	Ver	Prod Dates	Market Values	
HN 3169	1	1988-95	£100-£130	$215-$280

JESTER, A

Designer: Charles J Noke

HN No	Ver	Prod Dates	Market Values	
HN 45	1	1915-38	£800-£1200	$1715-$2575
HN 71	1	1917-38	£800-£1200	$1715-$2575
HN 320	1	1918-38	£1000-£1200	$2145-$2575
HN 367	1	1920-38	£800-£1200	$1715-$2575
HN 412	1	1920-38	£1000-£1200	$2145-$2575
HN 426	1	1921-38	£1000-£1200	$2145-$2575
HN 446	1	1921-38	£1000-£1200	$2145-$2575
HN 552	1	1922-38	£1000-£1200	$2145-$2575
HN 616	1	1924-38	£1200-£1500	$2575-$3220
HN 627	1	1924-38	£1200-£1500	$2575-$3220
HN 1295	1	1928-49	£1200-£1500	$2575-$3220
HN 1702	1	1935-49	£600-£800	$1285-$1715
HN 2016	1	1949	RRP	RRP
HN 45A	2	1915-38	£1200-£1500	$2575-$3220
HN 45B	2	1915-38	£1200-£1500	$2575-$3220
HN 55	2	1916-38	£1200-£1500	$2575-$3220
HN 308	2	1918-38	£1200-£1500	$2575-$3220
HN 630	2	1924-38	£1200-£1500	$2575-$3220
HN 1333	2	1929-49	£1200-£1500	$2575-$3220

Miniature Series

HN No	Ver	Prod Dates	Market Values	
HN 3335	1	1990only	£80-£100	$170-$215

RDICC Exclusive

JESUS

Holy Family Series

Designer: Alan Maslankowski

HN No	Ver	Prod Dates	Market Values	
HN 3484	1	1993	RRP	RRP
HN 3487	1	1993	RRP	RRP

JILL

Designer: Leslie Harradine

HN No	Ver	Prod Dates	Market Values	
HN 2061	1	1950-71	£100-£120	$215-$255

JOAN

Designer: Leslie Harradine

HN No	Ver	Prod Dates	Market Values	
HN 1422	1	1930-49	£220-£250	$470-$535
HN 2023	1	1949-59	£160-£200	$345-$430

Designer: Peggy Davies. Ltd Ed: 2000

HN No	Ver	Prod Dates	Market Values	
HN 3217	2	1988	£120-£150	$255-$320

Commissioned by Joan's Gift Shop. Colourway of Adrienne

JOAN OF ARC

Designer: Pauline Parsons

HN No	Ver	Prod Dates	Market Values	
HN 3681	1	1996	RRP	RRP

JOANNE

Vanity Fair Series

Designer: John Bromley

HN No	Ver	Prod Dates	Market Values	
HN 2373	1	1983-88	£120-£140	$255-$300

Designer: Nada Pedley

HN No	Ver	Prod Dates	Market Values	
HN 3422	2	1993	RRP	RRP

JOHN PEEL

Designer: Unknown

HN No	Ver	Prod Dates	Market Values	
HN 1408*	1	1930-37	£870-£1130	$1865-$2425

Later models known as The Huntsman

JOKER, The

Reflections Series

Designer: Adrian Hughes

HN No	Ver	Prod Dates	Market Values	
HN 3196	1	1988-90	£120-£140	$255-$300

Designer: Mary Nicoll

HN No	Ver	Prod Dates	Market Values	
HN 2252	2	1990-92	£120-£140	$255-$300

JOLLY SAILOR

Designer: Mary Nicoll

HN No	Ver	Prod Dates	Market Values	
HN 2172	1	1956-65	£450-£600	$965-$1285

JOSEPH

Holy Family Series

Designer: Alan Maslankowski

HN No	Ver	Prod Dates	Market Values	
HN 3438	1	1993	RRP	RRP
HN 3486	1	1993	RRP	RRP

JOVIAL MONK, The

Designer: Peggy Davies

HN No	Ver	Prod Dates	Market Values	
HN 2144	1	1954-76	£175-£200	$375-$430

HN No	Ver	Prod Dates	Market Values	

JOY
Reflections Series
Designer: Douglas V Tootle
HN 3184 1 1988-90 £100-£130 $215-$280

JUDGE AND JURY
Designer: J G Hughes
HN 1264* 1 1927-38 £1870-£2500 $4015-$5365

JUDGE, The
Designer: Mary Nicoll
HN 2443 1 1972-76 £150-£180 $320-$385
Matt finish
HN 2443 1 1976-92 £130-£150 $280-$320
Gloss finish

JUDITH
Designer: Leslie Harradine
HN 2089 1 1952-59 £190-£250 $405-$535
Designer: Mary Nicoll
HN 2278 2 1986-89 £0-£150 $180-$220
. Ltd Ed: 1000
HN 2313 2 1988 £100-£130 $215-$280
Commissioned by the Guild of Specialist China and Glass Retailers

JULIA
Designer: Peggy Davies
HN 2705 1 1975-90 £120-£140 $255-$300
HN 2706 1 1985-93 £120-£140 $255-$300

JULIE
Designer: Robert Tabbenor
HN 3407 1 1993 RRP RRP
USA only
Vanity Fair Series
HN 2995 1 1985-95 £50-£70 $105-$150

JULIET
Ladies of Covent Garden Series
Designer: Pauline Parsons
HN 2968 1 1983-84 £160-£200 $345-$430
Shakespeare's Ladies Series
HN 3453 2 1994 RRP RRP
Lawleys by Post

JULY
Figure of the Month Series
Designer: Peggy Davies
HN 2794 1 1987 £140-£160 $300-$345
For Home Shopping Network, USA
Designer: Robert Tabbenor
HN 3324 2 1990 £100-£130 $215-$280
Colorway of Amanda. USA only
Wild Flower of the Month Series
Designer: Peggy Davies
HN 3347 3 1991 £130-£150 $280-$320
Colourway of Beatrice for Sears of Canada

JUNE
Designer: Leslie Harradine
HN 1690 1 1935-49 £400-£450 $860-$965
HN 1691 1 1935-49 £350-£400 $750-$860
HN 2027 1 1949-52 £300-£350 $645-$750
M 65 1 1935-49 £300-£350 $645-$750
M 71 1 1936-49 £300-£350 $645-$750
Designer: Robert Tabbenor
HN 1947 1 1940-49 £400-£450 $860-$965
Figure of the Month Series
Designer: Peggy Davies
HN 2790 2 1987 £140-£160 $300-$345
For Home Shopping Network, USA
Designer: Robert Tabbenor
HN 2991 3 1988-94 £120-£140 $255-$300
Figure of the Month Series
HN 3323 4 1990 £100-£130 $215-$280
Colourway of Amanda. USA only
Wild Flower of the Month Series
Designer: Peggy Davies
HN 3346 5 1991 £130-£150 $280-$320
Colourway of Beatrice for Sears of Canada

JUNO AND THE PEACOCK
Myths and Maidens Series
Designer: Robert Jefferson. Ltd Ed: 300
HN 2827 1 1984 £400-£450 $860-$965

JUST FOR YOU
Designer: Pauline Parsons
HN 3355 1 1992 RRP RRP

JUST ONE MORE
Childhood Days Series
Designer: Adrian Hughes
HN 2980 1 1983-85 £100-£120 $215-$255

KAREN
Designer: Leslie Harradine
HN 1994 1 1947-55 £220-£275 $470-$590
Designer: Peggy Davies
HN 2388 2 1982 RRP RRP
Michael Doulton Miniature Series
HN 3338 2 1991 RRP RRP
Miniature Series
HN 3270 2 1990-95 RRP RRP

KATE
Designer: Peggy Davies
HN 2789 1 1978-87 £120-£140 $255-$300
Designer: Nada Pedley
HN 3765 2 1996 RRP RRP
Colourway for Great Universal Stores

KATE HANNIGAN
Designer: Eric J Griffiths. Ltd Ed: 9500
HN 3088 1 1987 £120-£150 $255-$320

HN No Ver Prod Dates Market Values

KATE HARDCASTLE
Designer: Leslie Harradine
HN 1718 1 1935-49 £310-£380 $665-$815
HN 1719 1 1935-49 £310-£380 $665-$815
HN 1734 1 1935-49 £310-£380 $665-$815
HN 1861 1 1938-49 £370-£440 $795-$945
HN 1919 1 1939-49 £370-£440 $795-$945
HN 2028 1 1949-52 £310-£380 $665-$815

KATHERINE (LADY DOULTON)
Michael Doulton Exclusive Series
Designer: Valerie Annand
HN 3708 2 1996 RRP RRP

KATHERINE
Designer: Charles J Noke
HN 61* 1 1916-38 £500-£750 $1075-$1610
HN 74* 1 1917-38 £500-£750 $1075-$1610
HN 341* 1 1919-38 £500-£750 $1075-$1610
HN 471* 1 1921-38 £500-£750 $1075-$1610
HN 615* 1 1924-38 £500-£750 $1075-$1610
HN 793* 1 1926-38 £500-£750 $1075-$1610

KATHLEEN
Designer: Leslie Harradine
HN 1252* 1 1927-38 £370-£440 $795-$945
HN 1253* 1 1927-38 £400-£500 $860-$1075
HN 1275* 1 1928-38 £400-£500 $860-$1075
HN 1279* 1 1928-38 £400-£500 $860-$1075
HN 1291* 1 1928-38 £400-£500 $860-$1075
HN 1357* 1 1929-38 £400-£500 $860-$1075
HN 1512* 1 1932-38 £400-£500 $860-$1075
Designer: Sharon Keenan
HN 2933 2 1984-87 £140-£170 $300-$365
Michael Doulton Series
HN 3100 2 1986 £150-£180 $320-$385
Designer: Nada Pedley
HN 3609 3 1994 RRP RRP

KATHY
Kate Greenaway Series
Designer: Peggy Davies
HN 2346 1 1981-87 £100-£130 $215-$280
HN 3305 2 1990-96 £110-£130 $235-$280
Colourway of Lynne

KATIE
Designer: Valerie Annand
HN 3360 1 1992 RRP RRP

KATRINA
Designer: Peggy Davies
HN 2327 1 1965-69 £160-£190 $345-$405

KAY
Designer: Peggy Davies
HN 3340 1 1991 £130-£150 $280-$320
Colourway of Fair Lady for Kays catolouge

KELLY
Designer: Peggy Davies
HN 2478 1 1985-92 £100-£120 $215-$255
HN 3222 1 1989 £100-£120 $215-$255
Commissioned by Kay's Catalogue

KERRY
Vanity Fair Children Series
Designer: Adrian Hughes
HN 3036 1 1986-92 £60-£80 $130-$170

KIMBERLEY
Ladies of Covent Garden Series
Designer: Pauline Parsons
HN 2969 1 1983-84 £160-£180 $345-$385
Vanity Fair Series
Designer: Tim Potts
HN 3379 2 1992 RRP RRP

HN 3382 2 1993 RRP RRP
Colourway forUSA only

KING CHARLES
Designer: Charles J Noke and Harry Tittensor
HN 404* 1 1920-51 £750-£1000 $1610-$2145
Prestige Series
HN 2084* 1 1952-92 £700-£900 $1500-$1930

KING CHARLES I
Designer: Charles J Noke and Harry Tittensor. Ltd Ed: 350
HN 3459 1 1992 RRP RRP

KIRSTY
Designer: Peggy Davies
HN 2381 1 1971 RRP RRP
See also Jeanette
Michael Doulton Miniature Series
HN 3213 1 1988 RRP RRP
HN 3246 1 1989 RRP RRP
Miniature Series
Designer: Peggy Davis
HN 3743 2 1995 RRP RRP
Colourway for Great Universal Stores

KITTY
Designer: Unknown
HN 1367* 1 1930-38 £460-£560 $985-$1200

KO-KO
Designer: Leslie Harradine
HN 1266 1 1928-49 £400-£450 $860-$965
HN 1286 1 1938-49 £400-£450 $860-$965
Gilbert and Sullivan Series
Designer: William K Harper
HN 2898 2 1980-85 £250-£310 $535-$665

KURDISH DANCER
Dancers of the World Series
Designer: Peggy Davies. Ltd Ed: 750
HN 2867 1 1979 £320-£380 $685-$815

L'AMBITEUSE
RDICC Series
Designer: Valerie Annand. Ltd Ed: 5000
HN 3359 1 1991 £180-£220 $385-$470
RDICC

LA LOGE
Designer: Valerie Annand. Ltd Ed: 7500
HN 3472 1 1992-95 £180-£200 $385-$430
Lawleys by Post

HN No Ver Prod Dates Market Values

LA SYLPHIDE
Designer: Peggy Davies

HN No	Ver	Prod Dates	Market Values	
HN 2138	1	1954-65	£260-£280	$555-$600

LADY AND BLACKAMOOR
Designer: Harry Tittensor

HN No	Ver	Prod Dates	Market Values	
HN 374*	1	1920-38	£1120-£1500	$2405-$3220
HN 375*	1	1920-38	£1120-£1500	$2405-$3220
HN 377*	1	1920-38	£1120-£1500	$2405-$3220
HN 470*	1	1921-38	£1120-£1500	$2405-$3220

LADY AND THE UNICORN
Myths and Maidens Series
Designer: Robert Jefferson. Ltd Ed: 300

HN No	Ver	Prod Dates	Market Values	
HN 2825	1	1982	£400-£450	$860-$965

LADY ANNE NEVILL, The
Designer: Peggy Davies

HN No	Ver	Prod Dates	Market Values	
HN 2006	1	1948-53	£370-£440	$795-$945

LADY ANNE, The
Designer: Ernest W Light

HN No	Ver	Prod Dates	Market Values	
HN 83*	1	1918-38	£870-£1130	$1865-$2425
HN 87*	1	1918-38	£870-£1130	$1865-$2425
HN 93*	1	1918-38	£870-£1134	$1865-$2435

LADY APRIL
Designer: Leslie Harradine

HN No	Ver	Prod Dates	Market Values	
HN 1958	1	1940-59	£150-£200	$320-$430
HN 1965	1	1941-49	£200-£250	$430-$535

LADY BETTY
Designer: Leslie Harradine

HN No	Ver	Prod Dates	Market Values	
HN 1967	1	1941-51	£200-£250	$430-$535

LADY CHARMIAN
Designer: Leslie Harradine

HN No	Ver	Prod Dates	Market Values	
HN 1948	1	1940-73	£150-£180	$320-$385
HN 1949	1	1940-75	£150-£180	$320-$385

LADY CLARE
Designer: Leslie Harradine

HN No	Ver	Prod Dates	Market Values	
HN 1465*	1	1931-38	£500-£630	$1075-$1350

LADY DIANA SPENCER
Designer: Eric J Griffiths. Ltd Ed: 1500

HN No	Ver	Prod Dates	Market Values	
HN 2885	1	1982	£300-£350	$645-$750

LADY EATON
Designer: Valerie Annand. Ltd Ed: 2500

HN No	Ver	Prod Dates	Market Values	
HN 3623	1	1994	RRP	RRP

For Thomas Eaton of Canada. See also Janice (2nd version)

LADY ERMINE
Designer: Charles J Noke

HN No	Ver	Prod Dates	Market Values	
HN 54*	1	1916-38	£600-£800	$1285-$1715
HN 332*	1	1918-38	£600-£800	$1285-$1715
HN 671*	1	1924-38	£600-£800	$1285-$1715

Also known as Ermine Muff and Lady with Ermine Muff

LADY FAYRE
Designer: Leslie Harradine

HN No	Ver	Prod Dates	Market Values	
HN 1265	1	1928-38	£400-£450	$860-$965
HN 1557	1	1933-38	£500-£600	$1075-$1285

LADY FROM WILLIAMSBURG
Designer: Peggy Davies

HN No	Ver	Prod Dates	Market Values	
HN 2228	1	1960-83	£120-£150	$255-$320

LADY JANE GREY
TudorRoses Series
Designer: Pauline Parsons

HN No	Ver	Prod Dates	Market Values	
HN 3680	1	1995	RRP	RRP

Lawleys by Post

LADY JESTER
Designer: Leslie Harradine

HN No	Ver	Prod Dates	Market Values	
HN 1221*	1	1927-38	£800-£1000	$1715-$2145
HN 1222*	1	1927-38	£800-£1000	$1715-$2145
HN 1332*	1	1929-38	£800-£1000	$1715-$2145
HN 1284*	2	1928-38	£750-£900	$1610-$1930
HN 1285*	2	1928-38	£750-£900	$1610-$1930

LADY OF THE ELIZABETHAN PERIOD
Designer: Ernest W Light

HN No	Ver	Prod Dates	Market Values	
HN 40*	1	1914-38	£810-£1060	$1740-$2275
HN 40A*	1	1914-38	£810-£1060	$1740-$2275
HN 73*	1	1917-38	£810-£1060	$1740-$2275
HN 309*	1	1918-38	£810-£1060	$1740-$2275
HN 411*	1	1920-38	£810-£1060	$1740-$2275

LADY OF THE FAN
Designer: Ernest W Light

HN No	Ver	Prod Dates	Market Values	
HN 48*	1	1916-38	£780-£910	$1675-$1950
HN 52*	1	1916-38	£780-£910	$1675-$1950
HN 53*	1	1916-38	£780-£910	$1675-$1950
HN 53A*	1	1916-38	£780-£910	$1675-$1950
HN 335*	1	1919-38	£780-£910	$1675-$1950
HN 509*	1	1921-38	£780-£910	$1675-$1950

LADY OF THE GEORGIAN PERIOD
Designer: Ernest W Light

HN No	Ver	Prod Dates	Market Values	
HN 41*	1	1914-38	£750-£1000	$1610-$2145
HN 331*	1	1918-38	£750-£1000	$1610-$2145
HN 444*	1	1921-38	£750-£1000	$1610-$2145
HN 690*	1	1925-38	£750-£1000	$1610-$2145
HN 702*	1	1925-38	£750-£1000	$1610-$2145

LADY OF THE SNOWS
Designer: Richard Garbe. Ltd Ed: 50

HN No	Ver	Prod Dates	Market Values	
HN 1780*	1	1933-39	£1120-£1630	$2405-$3495

. Ltd Ed: 50

HN No	Ver	Prod Dates	Market Values	
HN 1830*	1	1937-49	£1120-£1630	$2405-$3495

LADY PAMELA
Designer: Douglas V Tootle

HN No	Ver	Prod Dates	Market Values	
HN 2718	1	1974-80	£130-£150	$280-$320

LADY WITH ROSE
Designer: Ernest W Light

HN No	Ver	Prod Dates	Market Values	
HN 48A*	1	1916-38	£780-£880	$1675-$1890
HN 52A*	1	1916-38	£780-£880	$1675-$1890
HN 68*	1	1916-38	£780-£880	$1675-$1890
HN 304*	1	1918-38	£780-£880	$1675-$1890
HN 336*	1	1919-38	£780-£880	$1675-$1890
HN 515*	1	1921-38	£780-£880	$1675-$1890
HN 517*	1	1921-38	£780-£880	$1675-$1890
HN 584*	1	1923-38	£780-£880	$1675-$1890
HN 624*	1	1924-38	£780-£880	$1675-$1890

HN No *Ver* *Prod Dates* *Market Values*

LADY WITH SHAWL
Designer: Leslie Harradine
HN 447* 1 1921-38 £870-£1130 $1865-$2425
HN 458* 1 1921-38 £870-£1130 $1865-$2425
HN 626* 1 1924-38 £870-£1130 $1865-$2425
HN 678* 1 1924-38 £870-£1130 $1865-$2425
HN 679* 1 1924-38 £870-£1130 $1865-$2425

LADY WITHOUT BOUQUET
Now known as *Necklace*
Designer: George Lambert
HN 393* 1 1920-38 £1000-£1100 $2145-$2360
HN 394* 1 1920-38 £1000-£1100 $2145-$2360

LADY WORSLEY
Reynolds Ladies Series
Designer: Peter Gee. Ltd Ed: 5000
HN 3318 1 1991-95 £250-£275 $535-$590

LADYBIRD
Designer: Leslie Harradine
HN 1638 1 1934-49 £800-£1000 $1715-$2145
HN 1640 1 1934-38 £800-£1000 $1715-$2145

LAIRD, The
Designer: Mary Nicoll
HN 2361 1 1969 RRP RRP

LALLA ROOKH
Ships Figureheads Series
Designer: Sharon Keenan. Ltd Ed: 950
HN 2910 1 1981 £200-£250 $430-$535

LAMBETH WALK, The
Designer: Leslie Harradine
HN 1880* 1 1938-49 £800-£1000 $1715-$2145
HN 1881* 1 1938-49 £800-£1000 $1715-$2145

LAMBING TIME
Designer: Leslie Harradine
HN 1890 1 1938-81 £120-£160 $255-$345
Elegance Collection Series
Designer: Tim Potts
HN 3855 2 1996 RRP RRP

LAMP SELLER
Flambé Series
Designer: Robert Tabbenor
HN 3278 1 1990-95 £160-£190 $345-$405

LANCELOT & GUINEVERE
Great Lovers Collection Series
Designer: Robert Jefferson. Ltd Ed: 150
HN 3112 1 1996 RRP RRP

LAND OF NOD, The
Designer: Harry Tittensor
HN 56* 1 1916-38 £1870-£2500 $4015-$5365
HN 56A* 1 1916-38 £1870-£2500 $4015-$5365
HN 56B* 1 1916-38 £1870-£2500 $4015-$5365

LAST WALTZ
Designer: Mary Nicoll
HN 2315 1 1967-93 £100-£130 $215-$280
Ltd Ed: 2000
HN 2316 1 1987only £100-£130 $215-$280
For Royal Doulton

LAURA
Designer: Pauline Parsons
HN 2960 1 1983-94 £100-£130 $215-$280
Michael Doulton Exclusive Series
HN 3136 1 1988 £140-£160 $300-$345
Designer: Nada Pedley
HN 3760 2 1996 RRP RRP

LAUREN
Designer: Douglas Tootle
HN 3290 1 1922 RRP RRP
Colourway of Ann (2nd version) for Great Universal Stores.

LAURIANNE
Designer: Douglas V Tootle
HN 2719 1 1974-79 £130-£150 $280-$320

LAVENDER ROSE
Designer: Peggy Davies
HN 3481 1 1993 RRP RRP
Colourway of Debbie

LAVENDER WOMAN, The
Designer: Phoebe Stabler
HN 22 1 1913-38 £810-£1060 $1740-$2275
HN 23 1 1913-38 £810-£1060 $1740-$2275
HN 23A 1 1913-38 £810-£1060 $1740-$2275
HN 342 1 1919-38 £810-£1060 $1740-$2275
HN 569 1 1924-38 £620-£750 $1330-$1610
HN 744 1 1925-38 £810-£1060 $1740-$2275

LAVINIA
Designer: Leslie Harradine
HN 1955 1 1940-79 £100-£120 $215-$255

LAWYER, The
Designer: Pauline Parsons
HN 3041 1 1985-95 £100-£130 $215-$280

LE BAL
Designer: Valerie Annand. Ltd Ed: 5000
HN 3702 1 1995-96 £150-£180 $320-$385
For RDICC

LEADING LADY
Designer: Peggy Davies
HN 2269 1 1965-76 £120-£150 $255-$320

LEDA AND THE SWAN
Myths and Maidens Series
Designer: Robert Jefferson. Ltd Ed: 300
HN 2826 1 1983 £400-£450 $860-$965

LEGOLAS
Tolkien Series
Designer: D Lyttleton
HN 2917 1 1981-84 £90-£100 $195-$215

HN No	Ver	Prod Dates	Market Values	

LEISURE HOUR, The
Designer: Peggy Davis
HN 2055 1 1950-65 £250-£280 $535-$600

LES PARAPLUIES
Designer: Valerie Annand. Ltd Ed: 7500
HN 3473 1 1993-95 £180-£220 $385-$470
Lawleys by Post

LESLEY
Designer: Mary Nicoll
HN 2410 1 1986-90 £100-£140 $215-$300

LET'S PLAY
Vanity Fair Series
Designer: Alan Maslankowski
HN 3397 1 1992 RRP RRP

LIBERTY
Designer: Adrian Hughes
HN 3201 1 1989-90 £100-£130 $215-$280

LIDO LADY
Designer: Leslie Harradine
HN 1220* 1 1927-38 £600-£800 $1285-$1715
HN 1229* 1 1927-38 £600-£800 $1285-$1715

LIFEBOAT MAN
Designer: William K Harper
HN 2764 1 1987-91 £130-£150 $280-$320

LIFEGUARD
Designer: William K Harper
HN 2781 1 1992-95 £120-£150 $255-$320

LIGHTS OUT
Designer: Peggy Davies
HN 2262 1 1965-69 £140-£175 $300-$375

LILAC SHAWL, A
Same model as *The Poke Bonnet* and *In Grandma's Days*
Designer: Charles J Noke
HN 44 1 1915-38 £750-£880 $1610-$1890
HN 44A 1 1915-38 £750-£880 $1610-$1890

LILAC TIME
Designer: Peggy Davies
HN 2137 1 1954-69 £160-£200 $345-$430

LILIAN (in Summer)
Four Seasons Series
Designer: Peter Gee
HN 3003 1 1985 £100-£120 $215-$255
Commissioned by Danbury Mint

LILLIE LANGTRY
Famous Actresses Series
Designer: Douglas V Tootle
HN 3820 1 1996 RRP RRP
Lawleys by Post

LILY (LADY DOULTON)
Michael Doulton Exclusive Series
Designer: Valerie Annand
HN 3626 2 1995only £150-£180 $320-$385

LILY
Designer: Leslie Harradine
HN 1798 1 1936-71 £115-£130 $245-$280
HN 1799 1 1936-49 £180-£250 $385-$535

LINDA
Designer: Leslie Harradine
HN 2106 1 1953-76 £100-£130 $215-$280
Vanity Fair Children Series
Designer: Eric J Griffiths
HN 2758 2 1984-88 £80-£100 $170-$215
Designer: Nada Pedley
HN 3374 3 1991-95 £120-£150 $255-$320

LINDSEY
Designer: Nada Pedley
HN 3645 1 1994 RRP RRP

LISA
Designer: Peggy Davies
HN 2310 1 1969-82 £130-£160 $280-$345
HN 2394 1 1983-91 £100-£130 $215-$280
HN 3265 1 1989-95 £100-£130 $215-$280

LISE
Renoir Ladies Series
Designer: Valerie Annand. Ltd Ed: 7500
HN 3474 1 1994 RRP RRP
Lawleys by Post

LISETTE
Designer: Leslie Harradine
HN 1523* 1 1932-38 £500-£600 $1075-$1285
HN 1524* 1 1932-38 £500-£600 $1075-$1285
HN 1684* 1 1935-38 £500-£600 $1075-$1285

LITTLE BALLERINA
Designer: Alan Maslankowski. Ltd Ed: 2000
HN 3431 1 1993 RRP RRP
For USA
Vanity Fair Series
HN 3395 1 1992 RRP RRP

LITTLE BO PEEP
Nursery Rhymes Series
Designer: Adrian Hughes
HN 3030 1 1984-87 £100-£120 $215-$255

LITTLE BOY BLUE
Nursery Rhymes Series
Designer: Leslie Harradine
HN 2062 1 1950-73 £100-£130 $215-$280
Designer: Adrian Hughes
HN 3035 2 1984-87 £90-£110 $195-$235

"LITTLE CHILD SO RARE AND SWEET"
Designer: Unknown
HN 1540 1 1933-49 £140-£190 $300-$405
HN 1542 2 1933-49 £140-£190 $300-$405

HN No Ver Prod Dates Market Values

LITTLE JACK HORNER
Nursery Rhymes Series
Designer: Leslie Harradine
HN 2063 1 1950-53 £270-£340 $580-$730
Designer: Adrian Hughes
HN 3034 2 1984-87 £90-£110 $195-$235

LITTLE LADY MAKE BELIEVE
Designer: Leslie Harradine
HN 1870* 1 1938-49 £240-£290 $515-$620

LITTLE LAND, The
Designer: Harry Tittensor
HN 63* 1 1916-38 £1250-£1750 $2680-$3755
HN 67* 1 1916-38 £1000-£1250 $2145-$2680

LITTLE LORD FAUNTLEROY
Children's Literature Series
Designer: Adrian Hughes
HN 2972 1 1982-85 £90-£110 $195-$235

LITTLE MISS MUFFET
Nursery Rhymes Series
Designer: William K Harper
HN 2727 1 1984-87 £90-£110 $195-$235

LITTLE MISTRESS, The
Designer: Leslie Harradine
HN 1449* 1 1931-49 £250-£300 $535-$645

LITTLE MOTHER, The
Also known as *Dolly*
Designer: Harry Tittensor
HN 389* 1 1920-38 £1000-£1250 $2145-$2680
HN 390* 1 1920-38 £1000-£1250 $2145-$2680
HN 469* 1 1921-38 £870-£1190 $1865-$2555
Also known as *The Young Widow*
Designer: Leslie Harradine
HN 1418* 2 1930-38 £800-£1000 $1715-$2145
HN 1641* 2 1934-49 £800-£1000 $1715-$2145

LITTLE NELL
Dickens Series
Designer: Leslie Harradine
HN 540 1 1922-32 £55-£65 $120-$140
M 51 1 1932-83 £40-£65 $85-$140

LIZANA
Designer: Leslie Harradine
HN 1756 1 1936-49 £600-£800 $1285-$1715
HN 1761 1 1936-38 £600-£800 $1285-$1715

LIZZIE
Designer: Douglas V Tootle
HN 2749 1 1988-91 £110-£130 $235-$280

LOBSTER MAN, The
Designer: Mary Nicoll
HN 2317 1 1964-94 £120-£140 $255-$300
HN 2323 1 1987-95 £120-£140 $255-$300

LONDON CRY, STRAWBERRIES
Designer: Leslie Harradine
HN 749 1 1925-38 £600-£800 $1285-$1715
HN 772 1 1925-38 £600-£800 $1285-$1715

LONDON CRY, TURNIPS AND CARROTS
Designer: Leslie Harradine
HN 752* 1 1925-38 £600-£800 $1285-$1715
HN 771* 1 1925-38 £600-£800 $1285-$1715

LONG JOHN SILVER
Designer: Mary Nicoll
HN 2204 1 1957-65 £225-£275 $480-$590
Designer: Alan Maslankowski
HN 3719 2 1993 RRP RRP
Resin

LORD OLIVIER as RICHARD III
Designer: Eric J Griffiths. Ltd Ed: 750
HN 2881 1 1985 £250-£300 $535-$645

LORETTA
Designer: Peggy Davies
HN 2337 1 1966-81 £120-£140 $255-$300

LORI
Kate Greenaway Series
Designer: Peggy Davies
HN 2801 1 1976-87 £100-£130 $215-$280

LORNA
Designer: Peggy Davies
HN 2311 1 1965-85 £120-£150 $255-$320

LORRAINE
Designer: Alan Maslankowski
HN 3118 1 1988-95 £110-£130 $235-$280

LOUISE
Kate Greenaway Series
Designer: Peggy Davies
HN 2869 1 1979-86 £130-£150 $280-$320
Designer: Adrian Hughes
HN 3207 2 1990-96 £140-£160 $300-$345
Miniature version known as Emma

LOVE LETTER
Designer: Peggy Davies
HN 2149 1 1958-76 £200-£250 $430-$535
Reflections Series
Designer: Robert Jefferson
HN 3105 2 1986-89 £100-£120 $215-$255

LOVERS
Designer: Douglas V Tootle
HN 2762 1 1981 RRP RRP
Images Series
HN 2763 1 1981-92 £100-£120 $215-$255

LOVING YOU
Sentiments Series
Designer: Alan Maslankowski
HN 3389 1 1991 RRP RRP

LOYAL FRIEND
Designer: Valerie Annand
HN 3358 1 1991-95 £120-£150 $255-$320

HN No Ver Prod Dates Market Values

LT GENERAL ULYSSES S GRANT
Designer: Robert Tabbenor. Ltd Ed: 5000
HN 3403 1 1993-95 £400-£500 $860-$1075
USA only

LUCREZIA BORGIA
Les Femmes Fatales Series
Designer: Peggy Davies. Ltd Ed: 750
HN 2342 1 1984 £550-£600 $1180-$1285

LUCY
Kate Greenaway Series
Designer: Peggy Davies
HN 2863 1 1980-84 £130-£150 $280-$320
HN 3653 2 1994 £100-£120 $215-$255
Colourway of Beatrice for Great Universal Stores

LUCY ANN
Designer: Leslie Harradine
HN 1502 1 1932-51 £130-£180 $280-$385
HN 1565 1 1933-38 £180-£220 $385-$470

LUCY LOCKETT
Beggar's Opera Series
Designer: Leslie Harradine
HN 485 1 1921-49 £330-£390 $710-$835
HN 524 2 1921-49 £330-£390 $710-$835
HN 695 3 1925-49 £330-£390 $710-$835
HN 696 3 1925-49 £330-£390 $710-$835

LUNCHTIME
Designer: Mary Nicoll
HN 2485 1 1973-81 £150-£180 $320-$385

LUTE
Lady Musicians Series
Designer: Peggy Davies. Ltd Ed: 750
HN 2431 1 1972 £400-£450 $860-$965

LYDIA
Designer: Leslie Harradine
HN 1906 1 1939-49 £220-£280 $470-$600
HN 1907 1 1939-49 £220-£280 $470-$600
HN 1908 1 1939-95 £90-£110 $195-$235

LYNNE
Designer: Peggy Davies
HN 2329 1 1971-96 £110-£130 $235-$280
See also Kathy (2nd version)
HN 3740 1 1995 RRP RRP
Royal Doulton roadshow exclusive

LYNSEY
Vanity Fair Children Series
Designer: Pauline Parsons
HN 3043 1 1985-95 £50-£70 $105-$150

LYRIC
Enchantment Series
Designer: Eric J Griffiths
HN 2757 1 1983-85 £100-£130 $215-$280

L'AMBITIEUSE
Exclusive Series
Designer: Valerie Annand. Ltd Ed: 5000
HN 3359 1 1991-93 £180-£200 $385-$430

MACAW
Designer: Richard Garbe
HN 1779 1 1933-49 £1000-£1400 $2145-$3005
HN 1829 1 1933-49 £1000-£1400 $2145-$3005

MADELAINE
Designer: Doulgas V Tootle
HN 3255 1 1989-92 £110-£130 $235-$280

MADONNA OF THE SQUARE
Designer: Phoebe Stabler
HN 10* 1 1913-38 £620-£750 $1330-$1610
HN 10A* 1 1913-38 £620-£750 $1330-$1610
HN 11* 1 1913-38 £620-£750 $1330-$1610
HN 14* 1 1913-38 £620-£750 $1330-$1610
HN 27* 1 1913-38 £620-£750 $1330-$1610
HN 326* 1 1918-38 £620-£750 $1330-$1610
HN 573* 1 1923-38 £620-£750 $1330-$1610
HN 576* 1 1923-38 £560-£690 $1200-$1480
HN 594* 1 1924-38 £560-£690 $1200-$1480
HN 613* 1 1924-38 £560-£690 $1200-$1480
HN 764* 1 1925-38 £560-£690 $1200-$1480
HN 1968* 1 1941-49 £430-£500 $920-$1075
HN 1969* 1 1941-49 £430-£500 $920-$1075
HN 2034* 1 1949-51 £430-£630 $920-$1350

MAGIC DRAGON
Enchantment Series
Designer: Adrian Hughes
HN 2977 1 1983-86 £150-£175 $320-$375

MAGPIE RING, The
Enchantment Series
Designer: Adrian Hughes
HN 2978 1 1983-86 £140-£160 $300-$345

MAISIE
Designer: Leslie Harradine
HN 1618 1 1934-49 £350-£450 $750-$965
HN 1619 1 1934-49 £325-£400 $695-$860

MAJOR, 3rd NEW JERSEY REGIMENT, 1776
Designer: Eric J Griffiths. Ltd Ed: 350
HN 2752 1 1975-76 £450-£550 $965-$1180

MAKE BELIEVE
Designer: Mary Nicoll
HN 2224 1 1984-88 £90-£110 $195-$235
HN 2225 1 1962-88 £110-£130 $235-$280

MAKING FRIENDS
Age of Innocence Series
Designer: Nada Pedley. Ltd Ed: 9500
HN 3372 1 1991-94 £130-£150 $280-$320

MAM'SELLE
Designer: Leslie Harradine
HN 658* 1 1924-38 £650-£850 $1395-$1825
HN 659* 1 1924-38 £650-£850 $1395-$1825
HN 724* 1 1925-38 £650-£850 $1395-$1825
HN 786* 1 1926-38 £650-£850 $1395-$1825

MAN IN TUDOR COSTUME
Designer: Unknown
HN 563* 1 1923-38 £750-£810 $1610-$1740

HN No Ver Prod Dates Market Values

MANDARIN, A
Designer: Charles J Noke

HN 84*	1	1918-38	£750-£1000	$1610-$2145
HN 316*	1	1918-38	£750-£1000	$1610-$2145
HN 318*	1	1918-38	£750-£1000	$1610-$2145
HN 382*	1	1920-38	£1000-£1250	$2145-$2680
HN 611*	1	1924-38	£750-£1000	$1610-$2145
HN 746*	1	1925-38	£750-£1000	$1610-$2145
HN 787*	1	1926-38	£750-£1000	$1610-$2145
HN 791*	1	1926-38	£750-£1000	$1610-$2145
HN 366*	2	1920-38	£500-£630	$1075-$1350
HN 455*	2	1921-38	£750-£880	$1610-$1890
HN 641*	2	1924-38	£500-£630	$1075-$1350
HN 601*	3	1924-38	£750-£1000	$1610-$2145

MANDY
Designer: Peggy Davies
HN 2476 1 1982-92 £60-£80 $130-$170

MANTILLA
Designer: Eric J Griffiths
HN 3192 1 1992 £200-£250 $430-$535
Made for Expo 92 in Seville
Haute Ensemble Series
HN 2712 1 1974-79 £150-£200 $320-$430

MARCH
Figure of the Month Series
Designer: Peggy Davies
HN 2707 1 1989 £140-£160 $300-$345
For Home Shopping Network, USA
Designer: Robert Tabbenor
HN 3332 2 1990 £100-£130 $215-$280
Colourway of Amanda. USA only
Wild Flowers of the Month Series
Designer: Peggy Davies
HN 3343 3 1991 £130-£150 $280-$320
Colourway of Beartrice for Sears of Canada

MARGARET
Designer: Leslie Harradine
HN 1989 1 1947-59 £220-£280 $470-$600
Vanity Fair Series
Designer: Peggy Davies
HN 2397 2 1982 RRP RRP
HN 3496 2 1993 RRP RRP
USA only

MARGARET OF ANJOU
Designer: Peggy Davies
HN 2012 1 1948-53 £350-£400 $750-$860

MARGERY
Designer: Leslie Harradine
HN 1413 1 1930-49 £210-£260 $450-$555

MARGOT
Designer: Leslie Harradine

HN 1628	1	1934-38	£350-£400	$750-$860
HN 1636	1	1934-38	£350-£400	$750-$860
HN 1653	1	1934-38	£350-£400	$750-$860

MARGRET THATCHER
Designer: Eric J Griffiths
HN 2886 1 1983 £80-£100 $170-$215
A bust

MARGUERITE
Designer: Leslie Harradine

HN 1928	1	1940-59	£160-£240	$345-$515
HN 1929	1	1940-49	£350-£400	$750-$860
HN 1930	1	1940-49	£350-£400	$750-$860
HN 1946	1	1940-49	£350-£400	$750-$860

MARIA
Designer: Tim Potts
HN 3381 1 1993 RRP RRP

MARIANNE
Designer: Leslie Harradine
HN 2074 1 1951-53 £400-£450 $860-$965

MARIE
Designer: Leslie Harradine

HN 401*	1	1920-38	£1000-£1250	$2145-$2680
HN 434*	1	1921-38	£1000-£1250	$2145-$2680
HN 502*	1	1921-38	£1000-£1250	$2145-$2680
HN 504*	1	1921-38	£1000-£1250	$2145-$2680
HN 505*	1	1921-38	£1000-£1250	$2145-$2680
HN 506*	1	1921-38	£1000-£1250	$2145-$2680
HN 1531	1	1932-38	£90-£130	$195-$280
HN 1635	1	1934-49	£90-£130	$195-$280
HN 1655	1	1934-38	£90-£130	$195-$280
HN 1370	2	1930-88	£80-£100	$170-$215
HN 1388	2	1930-38	£100-£150	$215-$320
HN 1417	2	1930-49	£100-£150	$215-$320
HN 1489	2	1932-49	£100-£150	$215-$320

Designer: Pauline Parsons
HN 3357 1 1992 RRP RRP
Colourway of Heather for Great Universal Stores

MARIETTA
Designer: Leslie Harradine

HN 1341	1	1929-49	£400-£500	$860-$1075
HN 1446*	1	1931-49	£450-£600	$965-$1285
HN 1699*	1	1935-49	£500-£700	$1075-$1500

MARIGOLD
Designer: Leslie Harradine

HN 1447	1	1931-49	£310-£380	$665-$815
HN 1451	1	1931-38	£310-£380	$665-$815
HN 1555	1	1933-49	£310-£380	$665-$815

MARILYN
Designer: Peter Gee
HN 3002 1 1985-95 £100-£130 $215-$280

MARION
Designer: Leslie Harradine

HN 1582*	1	1933-38	£600-£800	$1285-$1715
HN 1583*	1	1933-38	£600-£800	$1285-$1715

MARIQUITA
Designer: Leslie Harradine
HN 1837 1 1938-49 £680-£750 $1460-$1610

MARJORIE
Designer: Peggy Davies
HN 2788 1 1980-84 £150-£180 $320-$385

HN No Ver Prod Dates Market Values

MARKET DAY
Designer: Leslie Harradine
HN 1991 1 1947-55 £180-£220 $385-$470
See also Country Lass

MARRIAGE OF ART AND INDUSTRY
Designer: Peggy Davies. Ltd Ed: 12
HN 2261 1 1958 £0 $0
This figure was never sold to the public. Value impossible to determine

MARTINE
Elegance Series
Designer: Adrian Hughes
HN 3053 1 1984 £130-£150 $280-$320
This figure was test marketed but not put into full production

MARY
Vanity Fair Series
Designer: John Bromley
HN 2374 1 1984-86 £60-£80 $130-$170
Figure of the Year Series
Designer: Nada Pedley
HN 3375 2 1992 £160-£200 $345-$430
Holy Family Series
Designer: Alan Maslankowski
HN 3437 3 1993 RRP RRP
HN 3485 3 1993 RRP RRP

MARY HAD A LITTLE LAMB
Designer: Peggy Davies
HN 2048 1 1949-88 £100-£120 $215-$255

MARY JANE
Designer: Leslie Harradine
HN 1990* 1 1947-52 £200-£250 $430-$535

MARY MARY
Designer: Leslie Harradine
HN 2044 1 1949-73 £100-£9120 $215-$19570

MARY TUDOR
Tudor Roses Series
Designer: Pauline Parsons. Ltd Ed: 5000
HN 3834 1 1996 RRP RRP
Lawleys by Post

MARY, COUNTESS HOWE
Gainsborough Ladies Series
Designer: Peter Gee. Ltd Ed: 5000
HN 3007 1 1990-94 £200-£250 $430-$535

MARY, QUEEN OF SCOTS
Queens of the Realm Series
Designer: Pauline Parsons. Ltd Ed: 5000
HN 3142 1 1990-93 £350-£400 $750-$860
Ships Figureheads Series
Designer: Sharon Keenan. Ltd Ed: 950
HN 2931 1 1983 £300-£350 $645-$750

MASK SELLER
Designer: Leslie Harradine
HN 1361 1 1929-38 £600-£800 $1285-$1715
HN 2103 1 1953-95 £120-£130 $255-$280

MASK, The
Designer: Leslie Harradine
HN 656* 1 1924-38 £800-£1000 $1715-$2145
HN 657* 1 1924-38 £800-£1000 $1715-$2145
HN 729* 1 1925-38 £800-£1000 $1715-$2145
HN 733* 1 1925-38 £800-£1000 $1715-$2145
HN 785* 1 1926-38 £800-£1000 $1715-$2145
HN 1271* 1 1928-38 £800-£1000 $1715-$2145

MASQUE
Designer: Douglas V Tootle
HN 2554 1 1973-74 £200-£250 $430-$535
Hand out
HN 2554 2 1974-82 £160-£180 $345-$385
Remodlelled hand

MASQUERADE (Female)
Designer: Leslie Harradine
HN 600 1 1924-49 £310-£380 $665-$815
HN 637 1 1924-38 £530-£560 $1135-$1200
HN 674 1 1924-38 £500-£600 $1075-$1285

MASQUERADE (Male)
Designer: Leslie Harradine
HN 599 1 1924-49 £310-£380 $665-$815
HN 636 1 1924-38 £530-£560 $1135-$1200
HN 683 1 1924-38 £500-£600 $1075-$1285

MASQUERADE
Designer: Peggy Davies
HN 2251 2 1960-65 £180-£200 $385-$430
HN 2259 2 1960-65 £180-£200 $385-$430

MASTER SWEEP
Designer: Mary Nicoll
HN 2205 1 1957-62 £300-£400 $645-$860

MASTER, The
Designer: Peggy Davies
HN 2325 1 1967-92 £130-£150 $280-$320

MATADOR AND BULL
Designer: Peggy Davies
HN 2324 1 1964 RRP RRP
Prestige

MATILDA
Designer: Peggy Davies
HN 2011 1 1948-53 £430-£480 $920-$1030

MAUREEN
Designer: Leslie Harradine
HN 1770 1 1936-59 £200-£250 $430-$535
HN 1771 1 1936-49 £250-£300 $535-$645
M 84 1 1939-49 £400-£450 $860-$965
M 85 1 1939-49 £400-£450 $860-$965
Vanity Fair Series
Designer: Peggy Davies
HN 2481 2 1987-92 £100-£130 $215-$280

MAXINE
Designer: Adrian Hughes
HN 3199 1 1989-90 £130-£150 $280-$320

HN No — Ver — Prod Dates — Market Values

MAY
Designer: Douglas V Tootle. Ltd Ed: 2000
HN 2746 1 1987-92 £130-£150 $280-$320
HN 3251 1 1989 £160-£200 $345-$430
Commissioned by Royal Doulton USA
Figure of the Month Series
Designer: Peggy Davies
HN 2711 2 1987 £130-£150 $280-$320
For Home Shopping Network, USA
Designer: Robert Tabbenor
HN 3334 3 1990 £100-£130 $215-$280
Colourway of Amanda. USA only
Wildflower of the Month Series
Designer: Peggy Davies
HN 3345 4 1991 £130-£150 $280-$320
Colourway of Beatrice for Sears of Canada

MAYOR, The
Designer: Mary Nicoll
HN 2280 1 1963-71 £200-£250 $430-$535

MAYTIME
Designer: Leslie Harradine
HN 2113 1 1953-67 £180-£225 $385-$480

MEDITATION
Designer: Peggy Davies
HN 2330 1 1971-83 £160-£180 $345-$385

MEG
Designer: Douglas V Tootle
HN 2743 1 1988-91 £100-£130 $215-$280

MEGAN
Vanity Fair Children Series
Designer: Peggy Davies
HN 3306 1 1991-94 £60-£80 $130-$170

MELANIE
Designer: Peggy Davies
HN 2271 1 1965-81 £120-£140 $255-$300

MELISSA
Designer: Peggy Davies
HN 2467 1 1981-94 £100-£130 $215-$280

MELODY
Designer: Peggy Davies
HN 2202 1 1957-62 £150-£180 $320-$385

MEMORIES
Designer: Leslie Harradine
HN 1855 1 1938-49 £250-£300 $535-$645
HN 1856 1 1938-49 £250-£300 $535-$645
HN 1857 1 1938-49 £250-£300 $535-$645
HN 2030 1 1949-59 £200-£250 $430-$535

MENDICANT, The
Designer: Leslie Harradine
HN 1355 1 1929-38 £200-£250 $430-$535
HN 1365 1 1929-69 £160-£190 $345-$405

MEPHISTO
Designer: Leslie Harradine
HN 722* 1 1925-38 £750-£1000 $1610-$2145
HN 723* 1 1925-38 £750-£1000 $1610-$2145

MEPHISTOPHELES AND MARGUERITE
Designer: Charles J Noke
HN 755 1 1925-49 £750-£880 $1610-$1890
HN 775 1 1925-49 £750-£880 $1610-$1890

MERIEL
Designer: Leslie Harradine
HN 1931* 1 1940-49 £600-£800 $1285-$1715
HN 1932* 1 1940-49 £600-£800 $1285-$1715

MERMAID, The
Designer: Harry Tittensor
HN 97 1 1918-36 £350-£400 $750-$860
HN 300 1 1918-36 £350-£400 $750-$860

MERRY CHRISTMAS
Designer: Pauline Parsons
HN 3096 1 1987-92 £130-£180 $280-$385

MERYLL
Designer: Leslie Harradine
HN 1917* 1 1939-40 £800-£1000 $1715-$2145
Renamed Toinette and re-issued as HN 1940

MEXICAN DANCER
Dancers of the World Series
Designer: Peggy Davies. Ltd Ed: 750
HN 2866 1 1979 £300-£350 $645-$750

MICHELE
Designer: Peggy Davies
HN 2234 1 1967-94 £100-£130 $215-$280
See also Autumn Attraction

MIDINETTE
Designer: Leslie Harradine
HN 1289* 1 1928-38 £700-£900 $1500-$1930
HN 1306* 1 1928-38 £700-£900 $1500-$1930
HN 2090* 2 1952-65 £180-£220 $385-$470

MIDSUMMER NOON
Designer: Leslie Harradine
HN 1899 1 1939-49 £350-£400 $750-$860
HN 1900 1 1939-49 £350-£400 $750-$860
HN 2033 1 1949-55 £350-£400 $750-$860

MILADY
Designer: Leslie Harradine
HN 1970 1 1941-49 £500-£700 $1075-$1500

MILESTONE
Designer: Adrian Hughes
HN 3297 1 1990-94 £150-£180 $320-$385

MILKING TIME
Designer: Phoebe Stabler
HN 3* 1 1913-38 £1370-£1630 $2940-$3495
HN 306* 1 1913-38 £1370-£1630 $2940-$3495

MILKMAID, The
Designer: Leslie Harradine
HN 2057 1 1975-81 £120-£160 $255-$345
See also Jersey Milkmaid

HN No	Ver	Prod Dates	Market Values	

MILLICENT
Designer: Leslie Harradine

HN 1714*	1	1935-49	£600-£800	$1285-$1715
HN 1715*	1	1935-49	£600-£800	$1285-$1715
HN 1860*	1	1938-49	£600-£800	$1285-$1715

MINUET
Designer: Peggy Davies

HN 2019*	1	1949-71	£180-£220	$385-$470
HN 2066*	1	1950-55	£320-£380	$685-$815

MIRABEL
Designer: Leslie Harradine

HN 1743	1	1935-49	£400-£450	$860-$965
HN 1744	1	1935-49	£400-£450	$860-$965
M 68	1	1936-49	£300-£350	$645-$750
M 74	1	1936-49	£300-£350	$645-$750

MIRANDA
Designer: Leslie Harradine

HN 1818	1	1937-49	£450-£550	$965-$1180
HN 1819	1	1937-49	£450-£550	$965-$1180

Designer: Adrian Hughes

HN 3037	2	1987-90	£130-£150	$280-$320

MIRROR, The
Designer: Leslie Harradine

HN 1852*	1	1938-49	£600-£800	$1285-$1715
HN 1853*	1	1938-49	£600-£800	$1285-$1715

MISS 1926
Designer: Leslie Harradine

HN 1205*	1	1926-38	£900-£1250	$1930-$2680
HN 1207*	1	1926-38	£870-£1250	$1865-$2680

This figure was named for different years, i.e. 1928, 1929 etc.

MISS DEMURE
Designer: Leslie Harradine

HN 1402	1	1930-75	£130-£180	$280-$385
HN 1440	1	1930-49	£250-£350	$535-$750
HN 1463	1	1931-49	£250-£350	$535-$750
HN 1499	1	1932-38	£250-£350	$535-$750
HN 1560	1	1933-49	£250-£350	$535-$750

MISS FORTUNE
Designer: Leslie Harradine

HN 1897	1	1938-49	£600-£800	$1285-$1715
HN 1898	1	1938-49	£600-£800	$1285-$1715

MISS KAY
Designer: Nada Pedley

HN 3659	1	1994	RRP	RRP

Colourway of Helen for Kays Catalogue

MISS MUFFET
Designer: Leslie Harradine

HN 1936	1	1940-67	£125-£175	$270-$375
HN 1937	1	1940-52	£150-£195	$320-$420

MISS WINSOME
Designer: Leslie Harradine

HN 1665	1	1934-49	£320-£380	$685-$815
HN 1666	1	1934-38	£350-£400	$750-$860

MODENA
Designer: Leslie Harradine

HN 1845	1	1938-49	£650-£850	$1395-$1825
HN 1846	1	1938-49	£650-£850	$1395-$1825

MODERN PIPER, The
Designer: Leslie Harradine

HN 756*	1	1925-38	£800-£1000	$1715-$2145

MODESTY
Designer: Douglas V Tootle

HN 2744	1	1988-91	£100-£130	$215-$280

MOIRA
Designer: Leslie Harradine

HN 1347*	1	1929-38	£870-£1250	$1865-$2680

MOLLY MALONE
Designer: Leslie Harradine

HN 1455*	1	1931-38	£750-£1130	$1610-$2425

MONICA
Designer: Leslie Harradine

HN 1458	1	1931-49	£120-£150	$255-$320
HN 1459	1	1931-49	£150-£180	$320-$385
HN 1467	1	1931-95	£60-£90	$130-$195
HN 3617	1	1993	RRP	RRP
M 66	1	1935-49	£300-£350	$645-$750
M 72	1	1936-49	£300-£350	$645-$750

MONIQUE
Elegance Series
Designer: Eric J Griifiths

HN 2880	1	1984	£130-£150	$280-$320

This figure was test marketed but not put into full production

MONTE CARLO
Sweet and Twenties Series
Designer: Peggy Davies. Ltd Ed: 1500

HN 2332	1	1982	£180-£220	$385-$470

MOONDANCER
Reflections Series
Designer: Douglas V Tootle

HN 3181	1	1988-90	£100-£130	$215-$280

US only

MOONLIGHT ROSES
Designer: Peggy Davies

HN 3483	1	1993	RRP	RRP

Colourway of Debbie

MOOR
Flambé Series
Designer: Charles J Noke

HN 3642	1	1994-96	RRP	RRP

HN No Ver Prod Dates Market Values

MOOR, The
See also *The Arab*
Designer: Charles J Noke

HN No	Ver	Prod Dates	Market Values	
HN 1308	1	1929-38	£620-£750	$1330-$1610
HN 1366	1	1930-49	£620-£750	$1330-$1610
HN 1425	1	1930-49	£620-£750	$1330-$1610
HN 1657	1	1934-49	£620-£750	$1330-$1610

Prestige Series

HN 2082	1	1952	RRP	RRP

MOORISH MINSTREL
Designer: Charles J Noke

HN 34*	1	1913-38	£750-£1000	$1610-$2145
HN 364*	1	1920-38	£750-£1000	$1610-$2145
HN 415*	1	1920-38	£750-£1000	$1610-$2145
HN 797*	1	1926-49	£750-£1000	$1610-$2145

MOORISH PIPER MINSTREL
Designer: Charles J Noke

HN 301*	1	1918-38	£750-£1000	$1610-$2145
HN 328*	1	1918-38	£750-£1000	$1610-$2145
HN 416*	1	1920-38	£750-£1000	$1610-$2145

MOOTHERHOOD
Designer: Unknown

HN 462*	2	1921-28	£800-£1000	$1715-$2145

MORNING BREEZE
Designer: Peter Gee

HN 3313	1	1990-94	£110-£130	$235-$280

MORNING GLORY
Reflections Series
Designer: Pauline Parsons

HN 3093	1	1986-89	£100-£130	$215-$280

MORNING MA'AM
Designer: William K Harper

HN 2895	1	1986-89	£130-£150	$280-$320

MOTHER AND CHILD
Designer: Pauline Parsons

HN 3235	1	1991-93	£130-£150	$280-$320
HN 3348	1	1991-93	£130-£150	$280-$320
HN 3353	1	1992	RRP	RRP

Canada only

MOTHER AND DAUGHTER
Images Series
Designer: Eric J Griffiths

HN 2841	1	1980	RRP	RRP
HN 2843	1	1981-92	£100-£130	$215-$280

MOTHERHOOD
Designer: P Stabler

HN 28*	1	1913-28	£1000-£1250	$2145-$2680
HN 30*	1	1913-38	£1120-£1630	$2405-$3495
HN 303*	1	1918-38	£1120-£1630	$2405-$3495

Designer: Unknown

HN 570*	2	1923-38	£800-£1000	$1715-$2145
HN 703*	2	1925-38	£800-£1000	$1715-$2145
HN 743*	2	1925-38	£800-£1000	$1715-$2145

MOTHERS HELPER
Designer: Nada Pedley

HN 3650	1	1994	RRP	RRP

MOTHER'S HELP
Designer: Peggy Davies

HN 2151	1	1962-69	£120-£140	$255-$300

MOUNTIE 1873
Designer: Douglas V Tootle. Ltd Ed: 1500

HN 2555	1	1973	£200-£250	$430-$535

MOUNTIE 1973
Designer: Douglas V Tootle. Ltd Ed: 1500

HN 2547	1	1973	£200-£250	$430-$535

MR MICAWBER
Dickens Series
Designer: Leslie Harradine

HN 532	1	1922-32	£55-£60	$120-$130
M 42	1	1932-83	£40-£60	$85-$130
HN 557	2	1923-39	£180-£220	$385-$470
HN 1895	2	1938-52	£150-£220	$320-$470
HN 2097	3	1952-67	£160-£180	$345-$385

MR PICKWICK
Dickens Series
Designer: Leslie Harradine

HN 529	1	1922-32	£55-£60	$120-$130
M 41	1	1932-83	£40-£60	$85-$130
HN 556	2	1923-39	£180-£220	$385-$470
HN 1894	2	1938-52	£180-£220	$385-$470
HN 2099	3	1952-67	£160-£180	$345-$385

MRS BARDELL
Dickens Series
Designer: Leslie Harradine

M 86	1	1949-82	£40-£65	$85-$140

MRS FITZHERBERT
Designer: Peggy Davies

HN 2007	1	1948-53	£370-£500	$795-$1075

MRS HUGH BONFOY
Reynolds Ladies Series
Designer: Peter Gee. Ltd Ed: 5000

HN 3319	1	1992-95	£200-£250	$430-$535

MRS SISLEY
Renoir Ladies Series
Designer: Valerie Annand. Ltd Ed: 7500

HN 3475	1	1994	£0	$0

Lawleys by Post

MUSICALE
Enchantment Series
Designer: Eric J Griffiths

HN 2756	1	1983-85	£130-£150	$280-$320

MY BEST FRIEND
Designer: Peter Gee

HN 3011	1	1990	RRP	RRP

HN No	Ver	Prod Dates	Market Values	

MY FIRST FIGURINE
Designer: Nada Pedley

HN 3424	1	1993	RRP	RRP

MY FIRST PET
Vanity Fair Children Series
Designer: Alan Maslankowski

HN 2460	1	1991	RRP	RRP

MY LOVE
Designer: Peggy Davies

HN 2339	1	1969	RRP	RRP

MY PET
Designer: Peggy Davies

HN 2238	1	1962-75	£100-£125	$215-$270

MY PRETTY MAID
Designer: Leslie Harradine

HN 2064	1	1950-54	£170-£230	$365-$495

MY TEDDY
Designer: Peggy Davies

HN 2177	1	1962-67	£300-£350	$645-$750

M'LADY'S MAID
Designer: Leslie Harradine

HN 1795*	1	1936-49	£650-£850	$1395-$1825
HN 1822	1	1937-49	£650-£850	$1395-$1825

NADINE
Designer: Leslie Harradine

HN 1885*	1	1938-49	£600-£800	$1285-$1715
HN 1886*	1	1938-49	£600-£800	$1285-$1715

NANA
Designer: Leslie Harradine

HN 1766	1	1936-49	£175-£225	$375-$480
HN 1767	1	1936-49	£175-£225	$375-$480

NANCY
Vanity Fair Series
Designer: Pauline Parsons

HN 2955	1	1982-94	£60-£80	$130-$170

NANNY
Designer: Mary Nicoll

HN 2221	1	1958-91	£130-£150	$280-$320

NAPOLEON AT WATERLOO
Designer: Alan Maslankowski. Ltd Ed: 1500

HN 3429	1	1992-95	£800-£900	$1715-$1930

NATALIE
Vanity Fair Series
Designer: Peggy Davies

HN 3173	1	1988-96	£100-£120	$215-$255
HN 3498	1	1993	RRP	RRP

USA only

NECKLACE
Previously known as *Lady Without Bouquet*
Designer: George Lambert

HN 393*	1	1920-36	£750-£850	$1610-$1825
HN 394*	1	1920-36	£750-£850	$1610-$1825

NEGLIGEE
Designer: Leslie Harradine

HN 1219	1	1927-38	£600-£800	$1285-$1715
HN 1228	1	1927-38	£600-£800	$1285-$1715
HN 1272	1	1928-38	£600-£800	$1285-$1715
HN 1273	1	1928-38	£600-£800	$1285-$1715
HN 1454	1	1931-38	£600-£800	$1285-$1715

NELL
Kate Greenaway Series
Designer: Pauline Parsons

HN 3014	1	1982-87	£120-£150	$255-$320

NELL GWYNN
Designer: Leslie Harradine

HN 1882	1	1938-49	£600-£800	$1285-$1715
HN 1887	1	1938-49	£600-£800	$1285-$1715

NELSON
Ships Figureheads Series
Designer: Sharon Keenan. Ltd Ed: 950

HN 2928	1	1981	£200-£250	$430-$535

NEW BONNET, The
Designer: Leslie Harradine

HN 1728	1	1935-49	£400-£600	$860-$1285
HN 1957	1	1940-49	£400-£600	$860-$1285

NEW COMPANIONS
Designer: William K Harper

HN 2770	1	1982-85	£130-£170	$280-$365

NEWHAVEN FISHWIFE
Designer: Harry Fenton

HN 1480*	1	1931-38	£600-£800	$1285-$1715

NEWS VENDOR
Designer: William K Harper. Ltd Ed: 2500

HN 2891	1	1986	£140-£160	$300-$345

NEWSBOY
Designer: Mary Nicoll

HN 2244	1	1959-65	£260-£310	$555-$665

NICOLA
Designer: Peggy Davies

HN 2839	1	1978-95	£150-£180	$320-$385

Michael Doulton Series

HN 2804	1	1987	£150-£180	$320-$385

NICOLE
Designer: Nada Pedley

HN 3421	1	1993	RRP	RRP

NINA
Designer: Peggy Davies

HN 2347	1	1969-76	£130-£150	$280-$320

NINETTE
Designer: Peggy Davies

HN 2379	1	1971	RRP	RRP

See also Olivia (2nd version)

HN 3215	1	1988	RRP	RRP

Miniature

HN 3417	1	1992-94	£130-£180	$280-$385

Roadshow Special Gold edition

HN No Ver Prod Dates Market Values

Michael Doulton Series
HN 3248 1 1989 RRP RRP

NOELLE
Designer: Peggy Davies
HN 2179 1 1957-67 £180-£240 $385-$515

NORMA
Designer: Unknown
M 36 1 1933-45 £300-£350 $645-$750
M 37 1 1933-45 £300-£2350 $645-$5045

NORTH AMERICAN INDIAN DANCER
Dancers of the World Series
Designer: Peggy Davies
HN 2809 1 1982 £350-£400 $750-$860

NOVEMBER
Figure of the Month Series
Designer: Peggy Davies
HN 2695 1 1987 £130-£150 $280-$320
For Home Shopping Network, USA
Designer: Robert Tabbenor
HN 3328 2 1990 £100-£130 $215-$280
Colourway of Amanda. USA only
Wild Flower of the Month Series
Designer: Peggy Davies
HN 3411 3 1991 £130-£150 $280-$320
Colourway of Beatrice for Sears of Canada

NUDE ON ROCK
Designer: Unknown
HN 593 1 1924-38 £450-£500 $965-$1075

OCTOBER
Figure of the Month Series
Designer: Peggy Davies
HN 2693 1 1987 £130-£150 $280-$320
For Home Shopping Network, USA
Designer: Robert Tabbenor
HN 3327 2 1990 £100-£130 $215-$280
Colourway of Amanda. USA only
Wild Flower of the Month Series
Designer: Peggy Davies
HN 3410 3 1991 £130-£150 $280-$320
Colourway of Beatrice for Sears of Canada

ODDS AND ENDS
Designer: Leslie Harradine
HN 1844* 1 1938-49 £600-£800 $1285-$1715

OFF TO SCHOOL
Designer: Nada Pedley
HN 3768 1 1996 RRP RRP

OFFICER OF THE LINE
Designer: William K Harper
HN 2733 1 1983-86 £150-£180 $320-$385

OLD BALLOON SELLER
Designer: Leslie Harradine
HN 1315 1 1929 RRP RRP
Miniature Series
HN 2129 1 1989-91 £130-£150 $280-$320

OLD BALLOON SELLER AND BULLDOG
Designer: Leslie Harradine
HN 1791* 1 1932-38 £600-£650 $1285-$1395
HN 1912* 1 1939-49 £650-£710 $1395-$1525
It is not clear exactly how these two versions differ

OLD BEN
Designer: Eric J Griffiths. Ltd Ed: 1500
HN 3190 1 1990 £80-£90 $170-$195
Commissioned by the Newsvendors Benevolent Association

OLD COUNTRY ROSES
Designer: Nada Pedley
HN 3692 1 1995 RRP RRP

OLD FATHER THAMES
Designer: Robert Tabbenor
HN 2993 1 1988 £80-£100 $170-$215
Commissioned by Thames Water

OLD KING COLE
Designer: Peggy Davies
HN 2217 1 1963-67 £320-£350 $685-$750

OLD KING, An
Designer: Charles J Noke
HN 358* 1 1919-38 £600-£650 $1285-$1395
HN 623* 1 1924-38 £620-£690 $1330-$1480
HN 1801* 1 1937-54 £560-£630 $1200-$1350
HN 2134 1 1954-92 £300-£400 $645-$860

OLD LAVENDER SELLER
Designer: Leslie Harradine
HN 1492 1 1932-49 £350-£450 $750-$965
HN 1571 1 1933-49 £350-£450 $750-$965

OLD MAN, An
Designer: Unknown
HN 451* 1 1921-38 £1250-£1500 $2680-$3220

OLD MEG
Designer: Mary Nicoll
HN 2494 1 1974-76 £150-£190 $320-$405

OLD MOTHER HUBBARD
Designer: Mary Nicoll
HN 2314 1 1964-75 £225-£275 $480-$590

OLGA
Designer: John Bromley
HN 2463 1 1972-75 £150-£170 $320-$365

OLIVER HARDY
Famous Movie Comedians Series
Designer: William K Harper
HN 2775 1 1990 RRP RRP
Commissioned by Lawleys by Post

OLIVER TWIST
Dickens Series
Designer: Leslie Harradine
M 89 1 1949-83 £40-£60 $85-$130

OLIVER TWIST AND ARTFUL DODGER
Designer: Arthur Dobson
HN 3786 1 1996 RRP RRP
Resin

HN No *Ver* *Prod Dates* *Market Values*

OLIVIA

Designer: Leslie Harradine

HN No	Ver	Prod Dates	Market Values	
HN 1995	1	1947-51	£300-£350	$645-$750

Designer: Peggy Davies

HN No	Ver	Prod Dates	Market Values	
HN 3339	2	1992	RRP	RRP

Colourway of Ninette for Great Universal Stores

OMAR KHAYYAM

Designer: Charles J Noke

HN No	Ver	Prod Dates	Market Values	
HN 408*	1	1920-38	£1000-£1250	$2145-$2680
HN 409*	1	1920-38	£1000-£1250	$2145-$2680

Designer: Mary Nicoll

HN No	Ver	Prod Dates	Market Values	
HN 2247*	2	1965-83	£150-£170	$320-$365

OMAR KHAYYAM AND THE BELOVED

Designer: Charles J Noke

HN No	Ver	Prod Dates	Market Values	
HN 407*	1	1920-38	£870-£1130	$1865-$2425
HN 419*	1	1920-38	£870-£1130	$1865-$2425
HN 459*	1	1921-38	£870-£1130	$1865-$2425
HN 598*	1	1924-38	£870-£1130	$1865-$2425

ONCE UPON A TIME

Designer: Leslie Harradine

HN No	Ver	Prod Dates	Market Values	
HN 2047	1	1949-55	£150-£230	$320-$495

ONE OF THE FORTY

Designer: Harry Tittensor

HN No	Ver	Prod Dates	Market Values	
HN 417	1	1920-38	£560-£880	$1200-$1890
HN 418	1	1920-38	£560-£880	$1200-$1890
HN 423	1	1921-38	£370-£560	$795-$1200
HN 427	1	1921-38	£560-£880	$1200-$1890
HN 480	1	1921-38	£560-£880	$1200-$1890
HN 481	1	1921-38	£560-£880	$1200-$1890
HN 482	1	1921-38	£560-£880	$1200-$1890
HN 483	1	1921-38	£560-£880	$1200-$1890
HN 484	1	1921-38	£560-£880	$1200-$1890
HN 490	1	1921-38	£560-£880	$1200-$1890
HN 491	1	1921-38	£560-£880	$1200-$1890
HN 492	1	1921-38	£560-£880	$1200-$1890
HN 493	1	1921-38	£560-£880	$1200-$1890
HN 494	1	1921-38	£560-£880	$1200-$1890
HN 495	1	1921-38	£620-£940	$1330-$2015
HN 496	1	1921-38	£620-£940	$1330-$2015
HN 497	1	1921-38	£930-£1250	$1995-$2680
HN 498	1	1921-38	£620-£940	$1330-$2015
HN 499	1	1921-38	£620-£940	$1330-$2015
HN 500	1	1921-38	£620-£940	$1330-$2015
HN 501	1	1921-38	£620-£940	$1330-$2015
HN 528	1	1921-38	£620-£940	$1330-$2015
HN 645	1	1924-38	£620-£940	$1330-$2015
HN 646	1	1924-38	£620-£940	$1330-$2015
HN 647	1	1924-38	£620-£940	$1330-$2015
HN 648	1	1924-38	£620-£940	$1330-$2015
HN 649	1	1924-38	£620-£940	$1330-$2015
HN 663	1	1924-38	£620-£940	$1330-$2015
HN 664	1	1924-38	£620-£940	$1330-$2015
HN 665	1	1924-38	£620-£940	$1330-$2015
HN 666	1	1924-38	£620-£940	$1330-$2015
HN 667	1	1924-38	£620-£940	$1330-$2015
HN 677	1	1924-38	£620-£940	$1330-$2015
HN 704	1	1925-38	£620-£940	$1330-$2015
HN 712	1	1925-38	£620-£940	$1330-$2015
HN 713	1	1925-38	£620-£940	$1330-$2015
HN 714	1	1925-38	£620-£940	$1330-$2015
HN 1336	1	1929-38	£620-£940	$1330-$2015
HN 1350	1	1929-49	£620-£940	$1330-$2015
HN 1351	1	1920-49	£620-£940	$1330-$2015
HN 1352	1	1929-49	£620-£940	$1330-$2015
HN 1353	1	1929-49	£810-£1060	$1740-$2275
HN 1354	1	1929-49	£620-£940	$1330-$2015

ONE THAT GOT AWAY, The

Designer: Peggy Davies

HN No	Ver	Prod Dates	Market Values	
HN 2153	1	1955-59	£170-£190	$365-$405

ORANGE LADY, The

Designer: Leslie Harradine

HN No	Ver	Prod Dates	Market Values	
HN 1759	1	1936-75	£150-£180	$320-$385
HN 1953	1	1940-75	£150-£180	$320-$385

ORANGE SELLER, The

Designer: Leslie Harradine

HN No	Ver	Prod Dates	Market Values	
HN 1325	1	1929-49	£450-£500	$965-$1075

ORANGE VENDOR, An

Designer: Charles J Noke

HN No	Ver	Prod Dates	Market Values	
HN 72	1	1917-38	£375-£425	$805-$910
HN 508	1	1921-38	£375-£425	$805-$910
HN 521	1	1921-38	£375-£425	$805-$910
HN 1966	1	1941-49	£375-£425	$805-$910

ORGAN GRINDER, The

Designer: Mary Nicoll

HN No	Ver	Prod Dates	Market Values	
HN 2173	1	1956-65	£375-£425	$805-$910

OUR FIRST CHRISTMAS

Images Series

Designer: Pauline Parsons

HN No	Ver	Prod Dates	Market Values	
HN 3452	1	1993	RRP	RRP

OUT FOR A WALK

Designer: Harry Tittensor

HN No	Ver	Prod Dates	Market Values	
HN 86*	1	1918-36	£870-£1130	$1865-$2425
HN 443*	1	1921-36	£870-£1130	$1865-$2425
HN 748*	1	1925-36	£870-£1130	$1865-$2425

OVER THE THRESHOLD

Images Series

Designer: Robert Tabbenor

HN No	Ver	Prod Dates	Market Values	
HN 3274	1	1989	RRP	RRP

OWD WILLUM

Designer: Leslie Harradine

HN No	Ver	Prod Dates	Market Values	
HN 2042	1	1949-73	£140-£180	$300-$385

PAINTING

Gentle Arts Series

Designer: Pauline Parsons. Ltd Ed: 750

HN No	Ver	Prod Dates	Market Values	
HN 3012	1	1987	£450-£500	$965-$1075

HN No	Ver	Prod Dates	Market Values	

PAISLEY SHAWL
Designer: Leslie Harradine

HN 1392	1	1930-49	£175-£225	$375-$480
HN 1460	1	1931-49	£200-£250	$430-$535
HN 1707	1	1935-49	£200-£250	$430-$535
HN 1739	1	1935-49	£200-£250	$430-$535
HN 1987	1	1946-59	£175-£225	$375-$480
M 3	1	1932-38	£200-£250	$430-$535
M 4	1	1932-45	£180-£200	$385-$430
M 26	1	1932-45	£180-£200	$385-$430
HN 1914	2	1939-49	£175-£225	$375-$480
HN 1988	2	1946-75	£150-£175	$320-$375

PALIO, The
Designer: Peggy Davies. Ltd Ed: 500

HN 2428	1	1971-75	£2500-£3000	$5365-$6440

PAMELA
Designer: Leslie Harradine

HN 1468	1	1931-38	£325-£400	$695-$860
Ltd Ed: 25				
HN 1469	1	1931-38	£275-£325	$590-$695
HN 1564	1	1933-38	£325-£400	$695-$860
Designer: Peggy Davies				
HN 2479	2	1986-94	£100-£130	$215-$280
HN 3223	2	1989only	£130-£150	$280-$320
For Michael Doulton events				
Designer: Tim Potts				
HN 3756	3	1996	RRP	RRP
For RDICC				

PAN ON ROCK
Designer: Unknown

HN 621	1	1924-38	£250-£310	$535-$665
HN 622	1	1924-38	£250-£310	$535-$665

PANORAMA
Reflections Series
Designer: Robert Jefferson

HN 3028	1	1985-89	£100-£130	$215-$280

PANTALETTES
Designer: Leslie Harradine

HN 1362	1	1929-38	£250-£300	$535-$645
HN 1412	1	1930-49	£250-£300	$535-$645
HN 1507	1	1932-49	£350-£450	$750-$965
HN 1709	1	1935-38	£450-£500	$965-$1075
M 15	1	1932-45	£200-£250	$430-$535
M 16	1	1932-45	£200-£250	$430-$535
M 31	1	1932-45	£200-£250	$430-$535

PARADISE
Reflections Series
Designer: Adrian Hughes

HN 3074	1	1985-92	£100-£130	$215-$280

PARISIAN
Designer: Mary Nicoll

HN 2445	1	1972-75	£130-£150	$280-$320

PARK PARADE
Reflections Series
Designer: Alan Maslankowski

HN 3116	1	1988-94	£120-£140	$255-$300

PARSON'S DAUGHTER
Designer: Harry Tittensor

HN 337	1	1919-38	£310-£380	$665-$815
HN 338	1	1919-38	£310-£380	$665-$815
HN 441	1	1921-38	£310-£380	$665-$815
HN 564	1	1923-49	£180-£200	$385-$430
HN 790	1	1926-38	£250-£300	$535-$645
HN 1242	1	1927-38	£250-£300	$535-$645
HN 1356	1	1929-38	£250-£300	$535-$645
HN 2018	1	1949-53	£180-£200	$385-$430

PARTNERS
Designer: Alan Maslankowski

HN 3119	1	1990-92	£130-£150	$280-$320

PAST GLORY
Designer: Mary Nicoll

HN 2484	1	1973-79	£190-£250	$405-$535

PATCHWORK QUILT, The
Designer: Leslie Harradine

HN 1984	1	1945-59	£180-£250	$385-$535

PATRICIA
Designer: Leslie Harradine

HN 1414	1	1930-49	£250-£350	$535-$750
HN 1431	1	1930-49	£300-£400	$645-$860
HN 1462	1	1931-38	£350-£450	$750-$965
HN 1567	1	1933-49	£350-£450	$750-$965
M 7	1	1932-45	£200-£250	$430-$535
M 8	1	1932-38	£250-£300	$535-$645
M 28	1	1932-45	£200-£250	$430-$535
Vanity Fair Series				
Designer: Peggy Davies				
HN 2715	1	1982-85	£130-£150	$280-$320
Figure of the Year Series				
Designer: Valerie Annand				
HN 3365	1	1993	£150-£180	$320-$385

PAULA
Designer: Pauline Parsons

HN 2906	1	1980-86	£130-£150	$280-$320
Vanity Fair Series				
HN 3234	2	1990-96	£130-£150	$280-$320

Versions 1 and 2 are very similar. In fact they both have the same model number, however Royal Doulton specify there are two versions

PAULINE
Designer: Leslie Harradine

HN 1444	1	1931-48	£200-£240	$430-$515
Designer: Peggy Davies				
HN 2441	2	1984-89	£130-£150	$280-$320
Designer: Nada Pedley				
HN 3643	3	1994	RRP	RRP
Made for Littlewoods				
HN 3656	3	1994	RRP	RRP
Made for RDICC Canada (same as 3643)				

PAVLOVA
Designer: Charles J Noke

HN 487*	1	1921-38	£800-£1000	$1715-$2145
HN 676*	1	1924-38	£800-£1000	$1715-$2145

HN No Ver Prod Dates Market Values

PEACE
Images Series
Designer: Peggy Davies
HN 2433 1 1981 RRP RRP
HN 2470 1 1981 RRP RRP

PEARLY BOY
Designer: Leslie Harradine
HN 1482 1 1931-49 £150-£200 $320-$430
HN 1547 1 1933-49 £150-£200 $320-$430
HN 2035 1 1949-59 £125-£150 $270-$320
Designer: William K Harper
HN 2767 2 1988-92 £130-£150 $280-$320

PEARLY GIRL
Designer: Leslie Harradine
HN 1483 1 1931-49 £150-£200 $320-$430
HN 1548 1 1933-49 £150-£200 $320-$430
HN 2036 1 1949-59 £125-£150 $270-$320
Designer: William K Harper
HN 2769 2 1989-92 £100-£130 $215-$280

PECKSNIFF
Dickens Series
Designer: Leslie Harradine
HN 535 1 1922-32 £40-£60 $85-$130
M 43 1 1932-82 £30-£50 $65-$105
HN 553 2 1923-39 £170-£210 $365-$450
HN 1891 2 1938-52 £170-£210 $365-$450
HN 2098 3 1952-67 £170-£180 $365-$385

PEDLAR WOLF
Designer: Charles J Noke
HN 7* 1 1913-38 £750-£1000 $1610-$2145

PEEK A BOO
Little Cherubs Series
Designer: Valerie Annand
HN 3363 1 1992 RRP RRP

PEGGY
Designer: Leslie Harradine
HN 1941 1 1940-49 £150-£200 $320-$430
HN 2038 1 1949-79 £80-£100 $170-$215

PENELOPE
Designer: Leslie Harradine
HN 1901 1 1939-75 £180-£250 $385-$535
HN 1902 1 1939-49 £310-£380 $665-$815

PENNY
Designer: Peggy Davies
HN 2338 1 1968-95 £50-£70 $105-$150
HN 2424 1 1983-92 £50-£70 $105-$150

PENNY'S WORTH, A
Designer: Mary Nicoll
HN 2408 1 1986-90 £120-£140 $255-$300

PENSIVE
Reflections Series
Designer: Robert Jefferson
HN 3109 1 1986-89 £80-£100 $170-$215

PENSIVE MOMENTS
Designer: Peggy Davies
HN 2704 1 1975-81 £130-£150 $280-$320

PERFECT PAIR
Designer: Leslie Harradine
HN 581 1 1923-38 £450-£525 $965-$1125

PHILIPPA OF HAINAULT
Designer: Peggy Davies
HN 2008 1 1948-53 £380-£450 $815-$965

PHILIPPINE DANCER
Dancers of the World Series
Designer: Peggy Davies. Ltd Ed: 750
HN 2439 1 1978 £350-£425 $750-$910

PHYLLIS
Designer: Leslie Harradine
HN 1420 1 1930-49 £280-£350 $600-$750
HN 1430 1 1930-38 £350-£400 $750-$860
HN 1486 1 1931-49 £350-£400 $750-$860
HN 1698 1 1935-49 £350-£400 $750-$860
Designer: Douglas V Tootle
HN 3180 2 1988-91 £130-£150 $280-$320

PICARDY PEASANT
Designer: Phoebe Stabler
HN 4* 1 1913-38 £620-£750 $1330-$1610
Female
HN 5* 1 1913-38 £620-£750 $1330-$1610
Female
HN 13* 1 1913-38 £620-£750 $1330-$1610
Male
HN 17A* 1 1913-38 £620-£750 $1330-$1610
Female
HN 17* 1 1913-38 £620-£750 $1330-$1610
Male
HN 19* 1 1913-38 £620-£750 $1330-$1610
Male
HN 351* 1 1919-38 £620-£750 $1330-$1610
Female
HN 513* 1 1921-38 £620-£750 $1330-$1610
Male

PICNIC
Designer: Peggy Davies
HN 2308 1 1965-88 £110-£130 $235-$280

PIED PIPER, The
Designer: Leslie Harradine
HN 1215 1 1926-38 £500-£630 $1075-$1350
HN 2102 1 1953-76 £160-£200 $345-$430
Designer: Alan Maslankowski
HN 3721 2 1993 RRP RRP
Resin

HN No	Ver	Prod Dates	Market Values	

PIERRETTE
Designer: Leslie Harradine

HN 642*	1	1924-38	£650-£750	$1395-$1610
HN 643*	1	1924-38	£650-£750	$1395-$1610
HN 644*	1	1924-38	£650-£750	$1395-$1610
HN 691*	1	1925-38	£650-£750	$1395-$1610
HN 721*	1	1925-38	£650-£750	$1395-$1610
HN 731*	1	1925-38	£650-£750	$1395-$1610
HN 732*	1	1925-38	£650-£750	$1395-$1610
HN 784*	1	1926-38	£650-£750	$1395-$1610
HN 1391*	3	1930-38	£750-£850	$1610-$1825
HN 1749*	3	1936-49	£750-£850	$1610-$1825
Miniature Series				
HN 795*	2	1926-38	£750-£850	$1610-$1825
HN 796*	2	1926-38	£750-£850	$1610-$1825

PILLOW FIGHT
Designer: Peggy Davies

HN 2270	1	1965-69	£170-£200	$365-$430

PINKIE
Designer: Leslie Harradine

HN 1552	1	1933-38	£350-£450	$750-$965
HN 1553	1	1933-38	£350-£450	$750-$965

PIPER, The
Designer: Michael Abbirley

HN 2907	1	1980-92	£130-£150	$280-$320

Designer: Peter Gee

HN 3444	2	1993-95	£130-£150	$280-$320

PIRATE KING
Gilbert & Sullivan Series
Designer: William K Harper

HN 2901	1	1981-85	£310-£340	$665-$730

PIROUETTE
Designer: Peggy Davies

HN 2216	1	1959-67	£120-£160	$255-$345

PLAYMATES
Reflection Series
Designer: Pauline Parsons

HN 3127	1	1988-92	£80-£100	$170-$215

PLEASE KEEP STILL
Childhood Days Series
Designer: Pauline Parsons

HN 2967	1	1982-85	£130-£150	$280-$320

PLEASE SIR
Designer: Adrian Hughes

HN 3302	1	1992	RRP	RRP

POACHER, The
Designer: Leslie Harradine

HN 2043	1	1949-59	£150-£200	$320-$430

POCAHONTAS
Ships Figureheads Series
Designer: Sharon Keenan. Ltd Ed: 950

HN 2930	1	1982	£200-£250	$430-$535

POKE BONNET
Same model as *A Lilac Shawl* and *In Grandma's Days*
Designer: Charles J Noke

HN 612	1	1924-38	£750-£880	$1610-$1890
HN 765	1	1925-38	£750-£880	$1610-$1890

POLISH DANCER
Dancers of the World Series
Designer: Peggy Davies. Ltd Ed: 750

HN 2836	1	1980	£350-£425	$750-$910

POLKA, The
Designer: Peggy Davies

HN 2156	1	1955-69	£180-£200	$385-$430

POLLY
Designer: Douglas V Tootle

HN 3178	1	1988-91	£130-£150	$280-$320

POLLY PEACHUM
Beggar's Opera Series
Designer: Leslie Harradine

HN 463	1	1921-49	£220-£260	$470-$555
HN 465	1	1921-49	£200-£220	$430-$470
HN 489	2	1921-38	£170-£200	$365-$430
HN 549	2	1922-49	£170-£200	$365-$430
HN 620	2	1924-38	£220-£260	$470-$555
HN 694	2	1925-49	£170-£200	$365-$430
HN 734	2	1925-49	£170-£200	$365-$430
HN 550	1	1922-49	£170-£200	$365-$430
HN 589	1	1924-49	£170-£200	$365-$430
HN 614	1	1924-49	£170-£200	$365-$430
HN 680	1	1924-49	£220-£260	$470-$555
HN 693	1	1925-49	£220-£260	$470-$555
Miniature Series				
M 21†	1	1932-45	£250-£350	$535-$750
M 22†	1	1932-38	£250-£350	$535-$750
M 23†	1	1932-38	£250-£350	$535-$750
†Also known as Polly Curtsey				
HN 698	3	1925-49	£180-£200	$385-$430
HN 699	3	1925-49	£180-£200	$385-$430
HN 757	3	1925-49	£250-£350	$535-$750
HN 758	3	1925-49	£250-£350	$535-$750
HN 759	3	1925-49	£250-£350	$535-$750
HN 760	3	1925-49	£250-£350	$535-$750
HN 761	3	1925-49	£250-£350	$535-$750
HN 762	3	1925-49	£250-£350	$535-$750

POLLY PUT THE KETTLE ON
Nursery Rhymes Series
Designer: Pauline Parsons

HN 3021	1	1984-87	£130-£150	$280-$320

POLLYANNA
Children's Literature Series
Designer: Pauline Parsons

HN 2965	1	1982-85	£100-£130	$215-$280

POPE JOHN PAUL II, His Holiness
Designer: Eric J Griffiths

HN 2888	1	1982-92	£130-£150	$280-$320

HN No | *Ver* | *Prod Dates* | *Market Values*

POTTER, The
Designer: Charles J Noke

HN No	Ver	Prod Dates	£	$
HN 1493	1	1932-92	£180-£220	$385-$470
HN 1518	1	1932-49	£300-£350	$645-$750
HN 1522	1	1932-49	£300-£350	$645-$750

PREMIERE
Designer: Peggy Davies

HN No	Ver	Prod Dates	£	$
HN 2343	1	1969-79	£120-£140	$255-$300

PRETTY LADY
Designer: Harry Tittensor

HN No	Ver	Prod Dates	£	$
HN 69	1	1916-38	£370-£500	$795-$1075
HN 70	1	1916-38	£370-£500	$795-$1075
HN 302	1	1918-38	£370-£500	$795-$1075
HN 330	1	1918-38	£370-£500	$795-$1075
HN 361	1	1919-38	£370-£500	$795-$1075
HN 384	1	1920-38	£370-£500	$795-$1075
HN 565	1	1923-38	£370-£500	$795-$1075
HN 700	1	1925-38	£370-£500	$795-$1075
HN 763	1	1925-38	£370-£500	$795-$1075
HN 783	1	1926-38	£370-£500	$795-$1075

PRETTY POLLY
Designer: William K Harper

HN No	Ver	Prod Dates	£	$
HN 2768	1	1984-86	£120-£140	$255-$300

PRIDE AND JOY
Designer: Robert Tabbenor

HN No	Ver	Prod Dates	£	$
HN 2945	1	1984	£200-£250	$430-$535

RDICC Exclusive

PRIMROSE
Flowers of Love Series
Designer: Valerie Annand

HN No	Ver	Prod Dates	£	$
HN 3710	2	1996	RRP	RRP

PRIMROSES
Designer: Leslie Harradine

HN No	Ver	Prod Dates	£	$
HN 1617	1	1934-49	£350-£450	$750-$965

PRINCE OF WALES, The
Designer: Leslie Harradine

HN No	Ver	Prod Dates	£	$
HN 1217	1	1926-38	£500-£650	$1075-$1395

Designer: Eric J Griffiths. Ltd Ed: 1500

HN No	Ver	Prod Dates	£	$
HN 2883	2	1981	£250-£350	$535-$750

Ltd Ed: 1500

HN No	Ver	Prod Dates	£	$
HN 2884	3	1981	£500-£600	$1075-$1285

PRINCESS BADOURA
Prestige Figure Series
Designers: Harry Tittensor, H E Stanton and F van Allen Phillips

HN No	Ver	Prod Dates	£	$
HN 2081	1	1952	RRP	RRP

Prestige Series

HN No	Ver	Prod Dates	£	$
HN 3921	1	1996	RRP	RRP

PRINCESS ELIZABETH
Tudor Roses Series
Designer: Pauline Parsons

HN No	Ver	Prod Dates	£	$
HN 3682	1	1996	RRP	RRP

Lawleys by Post

PRINCESS OF WALES, The
Designer: Eric J Griffiths. Ltd Ed: 1500

HN No	Ver	Prod Dates	£	$
HN 2887	1	1982	£500-£600	$1075-$1285

PRINCESS, A
Designer: Leslie Harradine

HN No	Ver	Prod Dates	£	$
HN 391*	1	1920-38	£750-£1000	$1610-$2145
HN 392*	1	1920-38	£750-£1000	$1610-$2145
HN 420*	1	1920-38	£750-£1000	$1610-$2145
HN 430*	1	1921-38	£750-£1000	$1610-$2145
HN 431*	1	1921-38	£750-£1000	$1610-$2145
HN 633*	1	1924-38	£750-£1000	$1610-$2145

PRINTEMPS
Les Saisons Series
Designer: Robert Jefferson. Ltd Ed: 300

HN No	Ver	Prod Dates	£	$
HN 3066	1	1987	£600-£650	$1285-$1395

PRISCILLA
Designer: Leslie Harradine

HN No	Ver	Prod Dates	£	$
HN 1337	1	1929-38	£350-£400	$750-$860
HN 1340	1	1929-49	£250-£300	$535-$645
HN 1495	1	1932-49	£300-£350	$645-$750
HN 1501	1	1932-38	£350-£400	$750-$860
HN 1559	1	1933-49	£300-£400	$645-$860
M 13	1	1932-38	£200-£250	$430-$535
M 14	1	1932-45	£200-£230	$430-$495
M 24	1	1932-45	£200-£230	$430-$495

PRIVATE 1st GEORGIA REGIMENT 1777
Designer: Eric J Griffiths. Ltd Ed: 350

HN No	Ver	Prod Dates	£	$
HN 2779	1	1977	£450-£550	$965-$1180

PRIVATE 2nd SOUTH CAROLINA REGIMENT 1781
Designer: Eric J Griffiths. Ltd Ed: 350

HN No	Ver	Prod Dates	£	$
HN 2717	1	1975	£450-£550	$965-$1180

PRIVATE 3rd NORTH CAROLINA REGIMENT 1778
Designer: Eric J Griffiths. Ltd Ed: 350

HN No	Ver	Prod Dates	£	$
HN 2754	1	1976	£450-£550	$965-$1180

PRIVATE CONNECTICUT REGIMENT 1777
Designer: Eric J Griffiths. Ltd Ed: 350

HN No	Ver	Prod Dates	£	$
HN 2845	1	1978	£450-£550	$965-$1180

PRIVATE DELAWARE REGIMENT 1776
Designer: Eric J Griffiths. Ltd Ed: 350

HN No	Ver	Prod Dates	£	$
HN 2761	1	1977	£450-£550	$965-$1180

PRIVATE MASSACHUSETTS REGIMENT 1778
Designer: Eric J Griffiths. Ltd Ed: 350

HN No	Ver	Prod Dates	£	$
HN 2760	1	1977	£450-£550	$965-$1180

PRIVATE PENNSYLVANIA RIFLE BATTALION 1776
Designer: Eric J Griffiths. Ltd Ed: 350

HN No	Ver	Prod Dates	£	$
HN 2846	1	1978	£450-£550	$965-$1180

PRIVATE RHODE ISLAND REGIMENT 1781
Designer: Eric J Griffiths. Ltd Ed: 350

HN No	Ver	Prod Dates	£	$
HN 2759	1	1977	£450-£550	$965-$1180

HN No *Ver* *Prod Dates* *Market Values*

PRIZED POSSESSIONS
Designer: Robert Tabbenor
HN 2942 1 1982 £350-£400 $750-$860
RDICC exclusive

PROFESSOR, The
Designer: Mary Nicoll
HN 2281 1 1965-81 £130-£165 $280-$355

PROMENADE
Designer: Peggy Davies
HN 2076* 1 1951-53 £800-£1000 $1715-$2145
Reflections Series
Designer: Adrian Hughes
HN 3072 2 1985-95 £100-£130 $215-$280

PROPOSAL (Female)
Designer: Unknown
HN 715 1 1925-38 £450-£550 $965-$1180
HN 716 1 1925-38 £450-£550 $965-$1180
HN 788 1 1926-38 £450-£500 $965-$1075

PROPOSAL (Male)
Designer: Unknown
HN 725 1 1925-38 £450-£550 $965-$1180
HN 1209 1 1926-38 £450-£550 $965-$1180

PRUDENCE*
Designer: Leslie Harradine
HN 1883* 1 1938-49 £300-£350 $645-$750
HN 1884* 1 1938-49 £300-£350 $645-$750

PRUE
Designer: Leslie Harradine
HN 1996 1 1947-55 £180-£250 $385-$535

PUFF AND POWDER
Designer: Leslie Harradine
HN 397* 1 1920-38 £1000-£1250 $2145-$2680
HN 398* 1 1920-38 £1000-£1250 $2145-$2680
HN 400* 1 1920-38 £1000-£1250 $2145-$2680
HN 432* 1 1921-38 £1000-£1250 $2145-$2680
HN 433* 1 1921-38 £1000-£1250 $2145-$2680

PUNCH AND JUDY MAN
Designer: William K Harper
HN 2765 1 1981-90 £150-£185 $320-$395

PUPPETMAKER, The
Designer: Mary Nicoll
HN 2253 1 1962-73 £250-£280 $535-$600

PUPPY LOVE
Age of Innocence Series
Designer: Nada Pedley. Ltd Ed: 9500
HN 3371 1 1991-94 £130-£150 $280-$320

PUSSY
Designer: F C Stone
HN 18* 1 1913-38 £2000-£2500 $4290-$5365
HN 325* 1 1918-38 £2000-£2500 $4290-$5365
HN 507* 1 1921-38 £2000-£2500 $4290-$5365

PYJAMS
Designer: Leslie Harradine
HN 1942 1 1940-49 £250-£350 $535-$750

QUALITY STREET
Designer: Unknown
HN 1211 1 1926-38 £650-£730 $1395-$1565

QUEEN ANNE
Queens of the Realm Series
Designer: Pauline Parsons. Ltd Ed: 5000
HN 3141 1 1989-93 £180-£200 $385-$430

QUEEN ELIZABETH I
Queens of the Realm Series
Designer: Pauline Parsons. Ltd Ed: 5000
HN 3099 1 1986-93 £250-£300 $535-$645

QUEEN ELIZABETH II
Designer: Peggy Davies. Ltd Ed: 750
HN 2502 1 1973-76 £1000-£1250 $2145-$2680
Designer: Eric J Griffiths. Ltd Ed: 2500
HN 2878 2 1983-90 £200-£275 $430-$590
Designer: Peter Gee
HN 3440 3 1992 RRP RRP
Designer: Alan Maslankowsi
HN 3436 4 1992- RRP RRP

QUEEN ELIZABETH THE QUEEN MOTHER AS THE DUCHESS OF YORK
Designer: Pauline Parsons. Ltd Ed: 9500
HN 3230 2 1989 £300-£350 $645-$750

QUEEN MOTHER, The
Designer: Eric J Griffiths. Ltd Ed: 1500
HN 2882 1 1980 £680-£810 $1460-$1740
. Ltd Ed: 2500
HN 3189 3 1990 £175-£250 $375-$535

QUEEN OF SHEBA
Les Femmes Fatales Series
Designer: Peggy Davies. Ltd Ed: 750
HN 2328 1 1982 £550-£600 $1180-$1285

QUEEN OF THE DAWN
Enchantment Series
Designer: Peggy Davies
HN 2437 1 1983-86 £130-£150 $280-$320

QUEEN OF THE ICE
Enchantment Series
Designer: Peggy Davies
HN 2435 1 1983-86 £130-£150 $280-$320

QUEEN VICTORIA
Queens of the Realm Series
Designer: Pauline Parsons. Ltd Ed: 5000
HN 3125 1 1988-93 £550-£650 $1180-$1395

QUEEN VICTORIA AND PRINCE ALBERT
Designer: Douglas V Tootle
HN 3256 1 1990 RRP RRP

HN No | *Ver* | *Prod Dates* | *Market Values*

QUIET THEY'RE SLEEPING
Designer: Nada Pedley
HN 3657 1 1994-95 £130-£150 $280-$320

RACHEL
Designer: Peter Gee
HN 2919 1 1981-84 £130-£150 $280-$320
HN 2936 1 1985- RRP RRP

RAG DOLL
Designer: Peggy Davies
HN 2142 1 1954-86 £60-£90 $130-$195

RAG DOLL SELLER, The
Designer: Robert Tabbenor
HN 2944 1 1983-95 £100-£130 $215-$280

REBECCA
Designer: Peggy Davies
HN 2805 1 1980- RRP RRP
Miniature Series
HN 3414 1 1992 RRP RRP

REFLECTION
Reflections Series
Designer: Adrian Hughes
HN 3039 1 1987-91 £120-£140 $255-$300

REFLECTIONS
Designer: Leslie Harradine
HN 1820 1 1937-38 £1000-£1500 $2145-$3220
HN 1821 1 1937-38 £1000-£1500 $2145-$3220
HN 1847 1 1938-49 £750-£850 $1610-$1825
HN 1848 1 1938-49 £750-£850 $1610-$1825

REGAL LADY
Designer: Peggy Davies
HN 2709 1 1975-83 £120-£160 $255-$345

REGENCY
Designer: Leslie Harradine
HN 1752 1 1936-49 £450-£550 $965-$1180

REGENCY BEAU
Designer: Harry Fenton
HN 1972 1 1941-49 £600-£800 $1285-$1715

RENDEZVOUS
Designer: Peggy Davies
HN 2212 1 1962-71 £190-£230 $405-$495

REPOSE
Designer: Peggy Davies
HN 2272 1 1972-79 £160-£180 $345-$385

REST AWHILE
Designer: William K Harper
HN 2728 1 1981-84 £130-£150 $280-$320

RETURN OF PERSEPHONE, The
Designer: Charles Vyse
HN 31* 1 1913-38 £1000-£1500 $2145-$3220

REVERIE
Designer: Peggy Davies
HN 2306 1 1964-81 £160-£180 $345-$385

REWARD
Vanity Fair Series
Designer: Alan Maslankowski
HN 3391 1 1992 RRP RRP

RHAPSODY
Designer: Peggy Davies
HN 2267 1 1961-73 £130-£150 $280-$320

RHODA
Designer: Leslie Harradine
HN 1573 1 1933-49 £180-£250 $385-$535
HN 1574 1 1933-38 £180-£250 $385-$535
HN 1688 1 1935-49 £180-£250 $385-$535

RHYTHM
Designer: Leslie Harradine
HN 1903* 1 1939-49 £850-£1200 $1825-$2575
HN 1904* 1 1939-49 £850-£1200 $1825-$2575

RICHARD THE LIONHEART
Designer: Pauline Parsons
HN 3675 1 1995 RRP RRP

RITA
Designer: Leslie Harradine
HN 1448 1 1931-38 £350-£450 $750-$965
HN 1450 1 1931-38 £350-£450 $750-$965

RITZ BELL BOY
Designer: William K Harper
HN 2772 1 1989-93 £100-£130 $215-$280

RIVER BOY
Designer: Peggy Davies
HN 2128 1 1962-75 £100-£120 $215-$255

ROBERT BURNS
Designer: Ernest W Light
HN 42* 1 1914-38 £1560-£2000 $3345-$4290
Designer: Robbert Tabbenor
HN 3641 2 1996 RRP RRP

ROBIN
Designer: Unknown
M 38 1 1933-45 £300-£350 $645-$750
M 39 1 1933-45 £300-£350 $645-$750

ROBIN HOOD
Designer: William K Harper
HN 2773 1 1985-90 £130-£150 $280-$320
Designer: Alan Maslankowski
HN 3720 2 1993 RRP RRP
Resin

ROBIN HOOD AND MAID MARIAN
Great Lovers Series
Designer: Robert Jefferson. Ltd Ed: 150
HN 3111 1 1994 RRP RRP

ROCKING HORSE, The
Designer: Leslie Harradine
HN 2072 1 1951-53 £850-£1050 $1825-$2255

HN No *Ver* *Prod Dates* *Market Values*

ROMANCE
Designer: Peggy Davies
HN 2430 1 1972-81 £130-£150 $280-$320

ROMANY SUE
Designer: Leslie Harradine
HN 1757 1 1936-49 £650-£750 $1395-$1610
HN 1758 1 1936-49 £650-£750 $1395-$1610

ROMEO AND JULIET
Great Lovers Series
Designer: Robert Jefferson. Ltd Ed: 150
HN 3113 1 1993 RRP RRP

ROSABELL
Designer: Leslie Harradine
HN 1620* 1 1934-38 £650-£750 $1395-$1610

ROSALIND
Designer: Peggy Davies
HN 2393 1 1970-75 £150-£180 $320-$385

ROSAMUND
Designer: Leslie Harradine
HN 1320 1 1929-38 £850-£1000 $1825-$2145
HN 1497 2 1932-38 £450-£550 $965-$1180
HN 1551 2 1933-38 £450-£550 $965-$1180
M 32 2 1932-45 £280-£300 $600-$645
M 33 2 1932-45 £280-£300 $600-$645

ROSE
Designer: Leslie Harradine
HN 1368 1 1930-95 £60-£80 $130-$170
HN 1387 1 1930-38 £180-£230 $385-$495
HN 1416 1 1930-49 £150-£180 $320-$385
HN 1506 1 1932-38 £200-£240 $430-$515
HN 1654 1 1934-38 £200-£240 $430-$515
HN 2123 1 1983-95 £60-£80 $130-$170
Flowers of Love Series
Designer: Valerie Annand
HN 3709 2 1996 RRP RRP

ROSE ARBOUR
Reflections Series
Designer: Don Brindley
HN 3145 1 1987-90 £80-£100 $170-$215

ROSEANNA
Designer: Leslie Harradine
HN 1921 1 1940-49 £550-£650 $1180-$1395
HN 1926 1 1940-59 £200-£250 $430-$535

ROSEBUD
Designer: Leslie Harradine
HN 1580 1 1933-38 £370-£440 $795-$945
HN 1581 1 1933-38 £250-£325 $535-$695
HN 1983 2 1945-52 £250-£310 $535-$665

ROSEMARY
Designer: Leslie Harradine
HN 2091 1 1952-59 £350-£400 $750-$860
Designer: Pauline Parsons
HN 3143 2 1988-91 £130-£150 $280-$320

Designer: Nada Pedley
HN 3691 3 1996 RRP RRP
Colourway of Claire for Birks of Canada
HN 3691 3 1995 RRP RRP
Colourway of Claire for Great Universal Stores
HN 3698 3 1995 RRP RRP
Colourway of Claire for Seaway China, USA

ROSINA
Designer: Leslie Harradine
HN 1358 1 1929-38 £450-£550 $965-$1180
HN 1364 1 1929-38 £450-£550 $965-$1180
HN 1556 1 1933-38 £450-£550 $965-$1180

ROWENA
Designer: Leslie Harradine
HN 2077 1 1951-55 £320-£380 $685-$815

ROYAL GOVERNOR'S COOK
Designer: Peggy Davies
HN 2233 1 1960-83 £180-£230 $385-$495

RUBY
Designer: Leslie Harradine
HN 1724 1 1935-49 £180-£250 $385-$535
HN 1725 1 1935-49 £180-£250 $385-$535

RUMPLESTILTSKIN
Enchantment Series
Designer: Robert Jefferson
HN 3025 1 1983-86 £150 £200 $320-$430

RUSTIC SWAIN, The
Designer: Leslie Harradine
HN 1745* 1 1935-49 £870-£1130 $1865-$2425
HN 1746* 1 1935-49 £870-£1130 $1865-$2425

RUTH
Kate Greenaway Series
Designer: Peggy Davies
HN 2799 1 1976-81 £130-£180 $280-$385

RUTH THE PIRATE MAID
Gilbert and Sullivan Series
Designer: William K Harper
HN 2900 1 1981-85 £290-£330 $620-$710

SABBATH MORN
Designer: Leslie Harradine
HN 1982 1 1945-59 £180-£200 $385-$430

SAILOR'S HOLIDAY
Designer: Mary Nicoll
HN 2442 1 1972-79 £150-£180 $320-$385

SAIREY GAMP
Dickens Series
Designer: Leslie Harradine
HN 533 1 1922-32 £55-£65 $120-$140
M 46 1 1932-83 £40-£60 $85-$130
HN 558 2 1923-39 £180-£250 $385-$535
HN 1896 2 1938-52 £180-£250 $385-$535
HN 2100 3 1952-67 £250-£280 $535-$600

HN No *Ver* *Prod Dates* *Market Values*

SALLY
Designer: Douglas V Tootle
HN 2741 1 1988-91 £100-£130 $215-$280
Designer: Unknown
HN 3383 2 1995 RRP RRP
For Freemans catalogue
Designer: Tim Potts
HN 3851 3 1996 RRP RRP

SALOME
Designer: Richard Garbe. Ltd Ed: 100
HN 1775* 1 1933-39 £1500-£2000 $3220-$4290
HN 1828* 1 1937-49 £1250-£1500 $2680-$3220
Designer: Peggy Davies. Ltd Ed: 1000
HN 3267 2 1990 RRP RRP

SAM WELLER
Dickens Series
Designer: Leslie Harradine
HN 531 1 1922-32 £55-£60 $120-$130
M 48 1 1932-81 £40-£60 $85-$130

SAMANTHA
Vanity Fair Series
Designer: Pauline Parsons.
HN 2954 1 1982-84 £130-£150 $280-$320
Designer: Peggy Davies
HN 3304 2 1990-96 £100-£130 $215-$280
Colourway of First Dance

SAMURAI
Flambé Series
Designer: Robert Tabbenor. Ltd Ed: 9500
HN 3402 1 1992-95 £200-£250 $430-$535

SAMWISE
Tolkien Series
Designer: David Lyttleton
HN 2925 1 1982-84 £200-£250 $430-$535

SANDRA
Designer: Peggy Davies
HN 2275 1 1969 RRP RRP
See also Annette (2nd version)
HN 2401 1 1983-92 £100-£130 $215-$280

SANTA CLAUS
Designer: William K Harper
HN 2725 1 1982-92 £150-£180 $320-$385

SANTA'S HELPER
Designer: Adrian Hughes
HN 3301 1 1991 RRP RRP

SARA
Designer: Peggy Davies
HN 2265 1 1981 RRP RRP
HN 3308 1 1990-96 £150-£180 $320-$385
Miniature Series
HN 3219 1 1988 RRP RRP
Michael Doulton Miniature Series
HN 3249 1 1989- RRP RRP

SARAH (in Winter)
Four Seasons Series
Designer: Peter Gee
HN 3005 1 1986 £150-£180 $320-$385
Commissioned by Danbury Mint

SARAH
Michael Doulton Series
Designer: Tim Potts
HN 3380 2 1993only £150-£180 $320-$385
HN 3384 3 1995 RRP RRP
. Ltd Ed: 1996
HN 3857 3 1996 RRP RRP
Colourway for Royal Doulton Visitors Centre

SAUCY NYMPH, A
Designer: Unknown
HN 1539 1 1933-49 £170-£230 $365-$495

SAVE SOME FOR ME
Childhood Days Series
Designer: Pauline Parsons
HN 2959 1 1982-85 £130-£150 $280-$320

SCHEHERAZDE
Fabled Beauties Series
Designer: Pauline Parsons. Ltd Ed: 1500
HN 3835 1 1996 RRP RRP
Lawleys by Post

SCHOOLMARM
Designer: Peggy Davies
HN 2223 1 1958-81 £150-£180 $320-$385

SCOTCH GIRL
Designer: Leslie Harradine
HN 1269* 1 1928-38 £870-£1130 $1865-$2425

SCOTLAND
Ladies of the British Isles Series
Designer: Valerie Annand
HN 3629 1 1995 RRP RRP

SCOTTIES
Designer: Leslie Harradine
HN 1281* 1 1928-38 £650-£850 $1395-$1825
HN 1349* 1 1929-49 £850-£1000 $1825-$2145

SCOTTISH HIGHLAND DANCER
Dancers of the World Series
Designer: Peggy Davies. Ltd Ed: 750
HN 2436 1 1978 £350-£400 $750-$860

SCRIBE, A
Designer: Charles J Noke
HN 305 1 1918-36 £500-£700 $1075-$1500
HN 324 1 1918-38 £500-£700 $1075-$1500
HN 1235 1 1927-38 £500-£700 $1075-$1500

SCROOGE
Dickens Series
Designer: Leslie Harradine
M 87 1 1949-82 £40-£60 $85-$130

HN No *Ver* *Prod Dates* *Market Values*

SEA HARVEST
Designer: Mary Nicoll
HN 2257 1 1969-76 £150-£180 $320-$385

SEA SPRITE
Designer: Leslie Harradine
HN 1261* 1 1927-38 £300-£380 $645-$815
Designer: Peggy Davies
HN 2191 2 1958-62 £180-£250 $385-$535

SEAFARER, The
Designer: Mary Nicoll
HN 2455 1 1972-76 £150-£180 $320-$385

SEASHORE
Designer: Peggy Davies
HN 2263 1 1961-65 £150-£190 $320-$405

SECOND VIOLIN
Edwardian String Quartet Series
Designer: Valerie Annand. Ltd Ed: 1500
HN 3705 1 1995 RRP RRP
Lawleys by Post

SECRET MOMENT
Reflections Series
Designer: Robert Jefferson
HN 3106 1 1986-89 £80-£100 $170-$215

SECRET THOUGHTS
Designer: Peggy Davies
HN 2382 1 1971-88 £120-£140 $255-$300

SENTIMENTAL PIERROT, The
Designer: Charles J Noke
HN 36* 1 1914-38 £1000-£1250 $2145-$2680
HN 307* 1 1918-38 £1000-£1250 $2145-$2680

SENTINEL
Designer: Unknown
HN 523* 1 1921-38 £1870-£2000 $4015-$4290

SEPTEMBER
Figure of the Month Series
Designer: Peggy Davies
HN 3166 1 1987 £130-£150 $280-$320
For Home Shopping Network, USA
Designer: Robert Tabbenor
HN 3326 2 1990 £100-£130 $215-$280
Colourway of Amanda. USA only
WIld Flower of Month Series
Designer: Peggy Davies
HN 3409 3 1991 £130-£150 $280-$320
Colourway of Beatrice for Sears of Canada

SERENA
Designer: Leslie Harradine
HN 1868 1 1938-49 £500-£640 $1075-$1375

SERENADE
Enchantment Series
Designer: Eric J Griffiths
HN 2753 1 1983-85 £130-£150 $280-$320

SERGEANT 6th MARYLAND REGIMENT 1777
Designer: Eric J Griffiths. Ltd Ed: 350
HN 2815 1 1976 £450-£550 $965-$1180

SERGEANT VIRGINIA 1st REGIMENT CONTINENTAL LIGHT DRAGOO
Designer: Eric J Griffiths. Ltd Ed: 350
HN 2844 1 1978 £450-£550 $965-$1180

SHAKESPEARE
Designer: Robert Tabbenor. Ltd Ed: 1564
HN 3633 1 1994 RRP RRP
Lawleys by Post

SHARON
Designer: Pauline Parsons
HN 3047 1 1984-95 £60-£80 $130-$170
HN 3455 1 1994 RRP RRP
Michael Doulton Exclusive Series
Designer: Nada Pedley
HN 3603 2 1994only £100-£130 $215-$280

SHE LOVES ME NOT
Designer: Leslie Harradine
HN 2045 1 1949-62 £130-£150 $280-$320

SHEIKH
Reflections Series
Designer: Eric J Griffiths
HN 3083 1 1987-89 £100-£130 $215-$280
USA only

SHEILA
Designer: Douglas V Tottle
HN 2742 1 1984-91 £100-£130 $215-$280

SHEPHERD, A
Designer: Charles J Noke
HN 81* 1 1918-38 £870-£1060 $1865-$2275
HN 617* 1 1924-38 £870-£1060 $1865-$2275
HN 632* 1 1924-38 £870-£1060 $1865-$2275
Miniature Series
Designer: Unknown
HN 709* 2 1925-38 £550-£650 $1180-$1395
M 17* 2 1932-38 £550-£650 $1180-$1395
M 19* 2 1932-38 £550-£650 $1180-$1395
HN 751* 3 1925-38 £870-£1000 $1865-$2145
Designer: Harry Fenton
HN 1975 4 1945-75 £150-£180 $320-$385
Reflections Series
Designer: Adrian Hughes
HN 3160 5 1988-89 £130-£150 $280-$320

HN No Ver Prod Dates Market Values

SHEPHERDESS
Miniature Series
Designer: Unknown
HN 708* 1 1925-48 £550-£650 $1180-$1395
M 18* 1 1932-38 £550-£650 $1180-$1395
M 20* 1 1932-38 £225-£300 $480-$645
Designer: Unknown
HN 735 2 1925-38 £810-£880 $1740-$1890
HN 750 2 1925-38 £810-£880 $1740-$1890
Reflections Series
Designer: Robert Tabbenor
HN 2990 3 1987-89 £130-£150 $280-$320
Designer: John Bromley. Ltd Ed: 12500
HN 2420 4 1991 RRP RRP

SHERLOCK HOLMES
Designer: Robert Tabbenor
HN 3639 1 1995 RRP RRP
Resin

SHIRLEY
Designer: Peggy Davies
HN 2702 1 1985 RRP RRP

SHORE LEAVE
Designer: Mary Nicoll
HN 2254 1 1965-79 £150-£180 $320-$385

SHY ANNE
Designer: Lawrence Perugini
HN 60* 1 1916-38 £750-£880 $1610-$1890
HN 64* 1 1916-38 £750-£880 $1610-$1890
HN 65* 1 1916-38 £750-£880 $1610-$1890
HN 568* 1 1923-38 £750-£880 $1610-$1890

SHYLOCK
Designer: Charles J Noke
HN 79* 1 1917-38 £1000-£1250 $2145-$2680
HN 317* 1 1918-38 £1000-£1250 $2145-$2680

SIBELL
Designer: Leslie Harradine
HN 1668 1 1934-49 £350-£450 $750-$965
HN 1695 1 1935-49 £400-£500 $860-$1075
HN 1735 1 1935-49 £400-£500 $860-$1075

SIESTA
Designer: Leslie Harradine
HN 1305* 1 1928-38 £800-£1000 $1715-$2145

SILKS AND RIBBONS
Designer: Leslie Harradine
HN 2017 1 1949 RRP RRP

SILVERSMITH OF WILLIAMSBURG
Designer: Peggy Davies
HN 2208 1 1960-83 £130-£150 $280-$320

SIMONE
Designer: Peggy Davies
HN 2378 1 1971-81 £130-£150 $280-$320

SINGLE RED ROSE
Designer: Nada Pedley
HN 3376 1 1992-95 £130-£150 $280-$320

SIR EDWARD
Age of Chivalry Series
Designer: John Bromley. Ltd Ed: 500
HN 2370 1 1979 £220-£280 $470-$600

SIR FRANCIS DRAKE
Designer: David Biggs
HN 3770 1 1996 RRP RRP
Resin

SIR JOHN A MACDONALD
Designer: William K Harper
HN 2860 1 1987-90 £120-£150 $255-$320
Made for Canada. Issued worldwide as The Statesman HN 2859

SIR RALPH
Age of Chivalry Series
Designer: John Bromley. Ltd Ed: 500
HN 2371 1 1979 £220-£280 $470-$600

SIR THOMAS
Age of Chivalry Series
Designer: John Bromley. Ltd Ed: 500
HN 2372 1 1979 £220-£280 $470-$600

SIR THOMAS LOVELL
Designer: Charles J Noke
HN 356* 1 1919-38 £1000-£1130 $2145-$2425

SIR WALTER RALEIGH
Designer: Leslie Harradine
HN 1742 1 1935-49 £550-£650 $1180-$1395
HN 1751 1 1936-49 £550-£650 $1180-$1395
HN 2015 1 1948-55 £350-£450 $750-$965

SIR WINSTON CHURCHILL
Designer: Adrian Hughes
HN 3057 1 1985 RRP RRP

SISTERLY LOVE
Reflections Series
Designer: Pauline Parsons
HN 3130 1 1987-95 £80-£100 $170-$215

SISTERS
Images Series
Designer: Pauline Parsons
HN 3018 1 1983 RRP RRP
HN 3019 1 1983 RRP RRP

SIT
Designer: Alan Maslankowski
HN 3430 1 1992 RRP RRP
USA only
Vanity Fair Series
HN 3123 1 1991 RRP RRP

SKATER, The
Designer: Peggy Davies
HN 2117 1 1953-71 £200-£250 $430-$535
Designer: Peter Gee
HN 3439 2 1992 RRP RRP

SLAPDASH
Designer: Mary Nicoll
HN 2277 1 1990-94 £130-£150 $280-$320

HN No	Ver	Prod Dates	Market Values	

SLEEP
Designer: Phoebe Stabler

HN 24*	1	1913-38	£400-£500	$860-$1075
HN 24A*	1	1913-38	£400-£500	$860-$1075
HN 25*	1	1913-38	£400-£500	$860-$1075
HN 25A*	1	1913-38	£400-£500	$860-$1075
HN 424*	1	1921-38	£400-£500	$860-$1075
HN 692*	1	1925-38	£400-£500	$860-$1075
HN 710*	1	1925-38	£400-£500	$860-$1075

SLEEPING BEAUTY
Designer: Adrian Hughes
HN 3079 1 1987-89 £130-£160 $280-$345

SLEEPY DARLING
Designer: Pauline Parsons
HN 2953 1 1981 £180-£220 $385-$470
RDICC exclusive

SLEEPY HEAD
Designer: Nada Pedley
HN 3761 2 1996 RRP RRP

SLEEPY SCHOLAR, The
Designer: William White

HN 15*	1	1913-38	£750-£810	$1610-$1740
HN 16*	1	1913-38	£750-£810	$1610-$1740
HN 29*	1	1913-38	£750-£810	$1610-$1740

SLEEPYHEAD
Designer: Peggy Davies
HN 2114 1 1953-55 £800-£1000 $1715-$2145

SMILING BUDDHA, The
Designer: Charles J Noke
HN 454* 1 1921-38 £560-£630 $1200-$1350

SNAKE CHARMER, The
Designer: Unknown
HN 1317 1 1929-38 £370-£440 $795-$945

SNOW WHITE
Disney Princesses Series
Designer: Pauline Parsons. Ltd Ed: 2000
HN 3678 1 1995 RRP RRP
For Disney stores, selected markets only

SOIREE
Designer: Peggy Davies
HN 2312 1 1967-84 £130-£150 $280-$320

SOLITUDE
Designer: Peggy Davies
HN 2810 1 1977-83 £180-£200 $385-$430

SONATA
Enchantment Series
Designer: Peggy Davies
HN 2438 1 1983-85 £130-£150 $280-$320

SONG OF THE SEA
Designer: William K Harper
HN 2729 1 1983-91 £150-£180 $320-$385

SONIA
Designer: Leslie Harradine

HN 1692	1	1935-49	£600-£650	$1285-$1395
HN 1738	1	1935-49	£650-£750	$1395-$1610

SONNY
Designer: Leslie Harradine

HN 1313*	1	1929-38	£400-£460	$860-$985
HN 1314*	1	1929-38	£400-£460	$860-$985

SOPHIA CHARLOTTE, LADY SHEFFIELD
Gainsborough Ladies Series
Designer: Peter Gee. Ltd Ed: 5000
HN 3008 1 1990-94 £200-£300 $430-$645

SOPHIE
Kate Greenaway Series
Designer: Peggy Davies.
HN 2833 1 1977-87 £100-£120 $215-$255
Designer: Douglas V Tootle
HN 3257 2 1990-92 £100-£150 $215-$320
Charleston Series
Designer: Alan Maslankowski
HN 3790 3 1996 RRP RRP
Green version
HN 3791 3 1996 RRP RRP
Blue version
HN 3792 3 1996 RRP RRP
Pink version
HN 3793 3 1996 RRP RRP
Ivory version

SOPHISTICATION
Reflections Series
Designer: Adrian Hughes
HN 3059 1 1988-90 £100-£130 $215-$280

SOUTHERN BELLE
Designer: Peggy Davies
HN 2229 1 1958 RRP RRP
HN 2425 1 1983-94 £130-£150 $280-$320
Miniature Series
HN 3174 1 1988 RRP RRP
HN 3244 1 1991 RRP RRP

SPANISH FLAMENCO DANCER
Dancers of the World Series
Designer: Peggy Davies. Ltd Ed: 750
HN 2831 1 1977 £350-£400 $750-$860

SPANISH LADY
Designer: Leslie Harradine

HN 1262	1	1927-38	£500-£700	$1075-$1500
HN 1290	1	1928-38	£500-£700	$1075-$1500
HN 1293	1	1928-38	£500-£700	$1075-$1500
HN 1294	1	1928-38	£500-£700	$1075-$1500
HN 1309	1	1929-38	£500-£700	$1075-$1500

SPECIAL FRIEND
Designer: Nada Pedley
HN 3607 1 1994 RRP RRP

SPECIAL TREAT
Designer: Nada Pedley
HN 3663 1 1995 RRP RRP

HN No *Ver* *Prod Dates* *Market Values*

SPINNING
Gentle Arts Series
Designer: Peggy Davies. Ltd Ed: 750
HN 2390 1 1984 £500-£550 $1075-$1180

SPIRIT OF THE WIND
Designer: Richard Garbe. Ltd Ed: 50
HN 1777 1 1933-39 £2500-£3130 $5365-$6715
HN 1825* 1 1937-49 £2500-£3130 $5365-$6715

SPOOK, A
Designer: Harry Tittensor
HN 50* 1 1916-38 £900-£1200 $1930-$2575
HN 51* 1 1916-38 £900-£1200 $1930-$2575
HN 51A* 1 1916-38 £900-£1200 $1930-$2575
HN 51B* 1 1916-38 £900-£1200 $1930-$2575
HN 58* 1 1916-38 £900-£1200 $1930-$2575
HN 512* 1 1921-38 £900-£1200 $1930-$2575
HN 625* 1 1924-38 £900-£1200 $1930-$2575
HN 1218* 1 1926-38 £900-£1200 $1930-$2575

SPOOKS
Designer: Harry Tittensor
HN 88 1 1918-36 £750-£1000 $1610-$2145
HN 89 1 1918-36 £750-£1000 $1610-$2145
HN 372 1 1920-36 £750-£1000 $1610-$2145

SPRING
Designer: Unknown
HN 312 1 1918-38 £720-£810 $1545-$1740
HN 472 1 1921-38 £720-£810 $1545-$1740

HN 588 2 1923-38 £650-£850 $1395-$1825
Previously known as Girl in Yellow Frock
Designer: Richard Garbe. Ltd Ed: 100
HN 1774 2 1933-39 £2500-£3130 $5365-$6715
HN 1827* 3 1937-49 £2500-£3300 $5365-$7080
Designer: Peggy Davies
HN 2085 4 1952-59 £200-£250 $430-$535

SPRING FLOWERS
Designer: Leslie Harradine
HN 1807 1 1937-59 £180-£250 $385-$535
HN 1945 1 1940-49 £350-£450 $750-$965

SPRING MORNING
Designer: Leslie Harradine
HN 1922 1 1940-73 £160-£200 $345-$430
HN 1923 1 1940-49 £250-£280 $535-$600
Elegance Series
Designer: Alan Maslankowski
HN 3725 2 1995 RRP RRP

SPRING SONG
Designer: Peter Gee
HN 3446 1 1993 £0 $0
Colourway of Danielle (2nd version) for Guild of Specialist Retailers

SPRING WALK
Reflections Series
Designer: Alan Maslankowski
HN 3120 1 1990-92 £110-£140 $235-$300

SPRINGTIME
Designer: Leslie Harradine
HN 1971 1 1941-49 £680-£750 $1460-$1610
Designer: Adrian Hughes
HN 3033 1 1983 £180-£250 $385-$535
RDICC exclusive
Four Seasons Series
Designer: Valerie Annand
HN 3477 3 1993 RRP RRP

SQUIRE, The
Designer: Unknown
HN 1814* 1 1937-49 £1100-£1400 $2360-$3005

ST GEORGE
Designer: S Thorogood
HN 385* 1 1920-38 £1000-£1250 $2145-$2680
HN 386* 1 1920-38 £1000-£1250 $2145-$2680
HN 1800* 1 1934-50 £750-£1130 $1610-$2425
HN 2067 1 1950-79 £680-£810 $1460-$1740
Designer: Peggy Davies
HN 2051 2 1950-85 £250-£350 $535-$750
Prestige Series
Designer: William K Harper
HN 2856 3 1978-94 £500-£800 $1075-$1715

STAN LAUREL
Famous Movie Comedians Series
Designer: William K Harper. Ltd Ed: 9500
HN 2774 1 1990 RRP RRP

STARGAZER
Reflections Series
Designer: Douglas V Tootle
HN 3182 1 1988-90 £100-£130 $215-$280
USA only

STATESMAN
Designer: William K Harper
HN 2859 1 1988-90 £120-£150 $255-$320
See also Sir John MacDonald

STAYED AT HOME
Designer: Peggy Davies
HN 2207 1 1958-69 £120-£140 $255-$300

STEPHANIE
Designer: Peggy Davies
HN 2807 1 1977-82 £120-£140 $255-$300
HN 2811 1 1983-94 £130-£150 $280-$320
Royal Doulton Roadshow Series
Designer: Tim Potts
HN 3759 2 1996 only RRP RRP

STICK 'EM UP
Childhood Days Series
Designer: Adrian Hughes
HN 2981 1 1983-85 £100-£130 $215-$280

STIGGINS
Dickens Series
Designer: Leslie Harradine
HN 536 1 1922-32 £55-£60 $120-$130
M 50 1 1932-81 £40-£60 $85-$130

HN No Ver Prod Dates Market Values

STITCH IN TIME, A
Designer: Mary Nicoll
HN 2352 1 1966-81 £120-£150 $255-$320

STOP PRESS
Designer: Mary Nicoll
HN 2683 1 1977-81 £150-£180 $320-$385

STORYTIME
Reflections Series
Designer: Pauline Parsons
HN 3126 1 1988-92 £80-£100 $170-$215
Designer: Nada Pedley
HN 3695 2 1995 RRP RRP

STROLLING
Reflections Series
Designer: Adrian Hughes
HN 3073 1 1985-95 £100-£130 $215-$280
Designer: Tim Potts
HN 3755 2 1996 RRP RRP

SUITOR, The
Designer: Peggy Davies
HN 2132 1 1962-71 £180-£250 $385-$535

SUMMER
Designer: Unknown
HN 313 1 1918-38 £720-£810 $1545-$1740
HN 473 1 1921-38 £720-£810 $1545-$1740
Designer: Peggy Davies
HN 2086 2 1952-59 £250-£300 $535-$645

SUMMER BREEZE
Elegance Series
Designer: Alan Maslankowski
HN 3724 1 1995 RRP RRP

SUMMER ROSE
Reflections Series
Designer: Eric J Griffiths
HN 3085 1 1988-92 £100-£130 $215-$280
Designer: Peggy Davies
HN 3309 2 1991 RRP RRP
Colourway of Denise (2nd version)

SUMMER SERENADE
Designer: Peggy Davies
HN 3610 1 1993 RRP RRP
Colourway of Beatrice for Guild of Specialist Retailers

SUMMERTIME
Designer: Pauline Parsons
HN 3137 1 1987 £150-£180 $320-$385
RDICC exclusive
Four Seasons Series
Designer: Valerie Annand
HN 3478 2 1994 RRP RRP

SUMMER'S DARLING
Reflections Series
Designer: Pauline Parsons
HN 3091 1 1986-95 £100-£130 $215-$280

SUMMER'S DAY
Designer: Peggy Davies
HN 2181 1 1957-62 £180-£230 $385-$495
Designer: Tim Potts
HN 3378 2 1991 RRP RRP

SUNDAY BEST
Designer: Peggy Davies
HN 2206 1 1979-84 £130-£150 $280-$320
HN 2698 1 1985-95 £110-£130 $235-$280
Miniature Series
HN 3218 1 1988-93 £60-£80 $130-$170
HN 3312 1 1991-95 RRP RRP

SUNDAY MORNING
Designer: Peggy Davies
HN 2184 1 1963-69 £160-£190 $345-$405

SUNSHINE GIRL
Designer: Leslie Harradine
HN 1344* 1 1929-38 £950-£1200 $2040-$2575
HN 1348* 1 1929-38 £950-£1200 $2040-$2575

SUSAN
Designer: Leslie Harradine
HN 2056 1 1950-59 £180-£220 $385-$470
Designer: Pauline Parsons
HN 2952 2 1982-93 £150-£180 $320-$385
HN 3050 2 1986-95 £130-£150 $280-$320

SUSANNA
Designer: Leslie Harradine
HN 1233 1 1927-38 £550-£750 $1180-$1610
HN 1288 1 1928-38 £550-£750 $1180-$1610
HN 1299 1 1928-38 £550-£750 $1180-$1610

SUZETTE
Designer: Leslie Harradine
HN 1487 1 1931-50 £200-£250 $430-$535
HN 1577 1 1933-49 £250-£350 $535-$750
HN 1585 1 1933-38 £250-£350 $535-$750
HN 1696 1 1935-49 £250-£350 $535-$750
HN 2026 1 1949-59 £200-£250 $430-$535

SWEET AND FAIR
Designer: Leslie Harradine
HN 1864* 1 1938-49 £550-£650 $1180-$1395
HN 1865 1 1938-49 £550-£650 $1180-$1395

SWEET AND TWENTY
Designer: Leslie Harradine
HN 1298 1 1928-69 £200-£250 $430-$535
HN 1360 1 1929-38 £250-£350 $535-$750
HN 1437 1 1930-38 £300-£400 $645-$860
HN 1438 1 1930-38 £300-£400 $645-$860
HN 1549 1 1933-49 £250-£350 $535-$750
HN 1563 1 1933-38 £350-£450 $750-$965
HN 1649 1 1934-49 £250-£350 $535-$750
HN 1589 2 1933-49 £240-£290 $515-$620
HN 1610 2 1933-38 £240-£290 $515-$620

HN No	Ver	Prod Dates	Market Values	

SWEET ANNE
Designer: Leslie Harradine

HN 1318	1	1929-49	£130-£180	$280-$385
HN 1330	1	1929-49	£130-£180	$280-$385
HN 1331	1	1929-49	£130-£180	$280-$385
HN 1453	1	1931-49	£180-£200	$385-$430
HN 1496	1	1932-67	£130-£160	$280-$345
HN 1631	1	1934-38	£200-£250	$430-$535
HN 1701	1	1935-38	£250-£300	$535-$645
M 5	1	1932-45	£200-£250	$430-$535
M 6	1	1932-45	£200-£250	$430-$535
M 27	1	1932-45	£200-£250	$430-$535

SWEET APRIL
Designer: Peggy Davies
HN 2215 1 1965-67 £220-£250 $470-$535

SWEET BOUQUET
Reflections Series
Designer: Peter Gee
HN 3000 1 1988 £120-£140 $255-$300
Commissioned by Home Shopping Network, Florida

SWEET DREAMS
Designer: Peggy Davies
HN 2380 1 1971-90 £100-£120 $215-$255
Sentiments Series
Designer: Alan Maslankowski
HN 3394 2 1992 RRP RRP

SWEET LAVENDER
Designer: Leslie Harradine
HN 1373 1 1930-49 £380-£420 $815-$900
Also known as Any Old Lavender

SWEET MAID
Designer: Leslie Harradine
HN 1504* 1 1932-38 £430-£500 $920-$1075
HN 1505* 1 1932-38 £430-£500 $920-$1075
HN 2092* 2 1952-55 £300-£350 $645-$750

SWEET PERFUME
Reflections Series
Designer: Pauline Parsons
HN 3094 1 1986-95 £100-£130 $215-$280

SWEET SEVENTEEN
Designer: Douglas V Tootle
HN 2734 1 1975-93 £110-£130 $235-$280

SWEET SIXTEEN
Designer: Peggy Davies
HN 2231 1 1958-65 £160-£200 $345-$430
Designer: Nada Pedley
HN 3648 2 1994 RRP RRP
See also Angela (4th version)

SWEET SUZY
Designer: Leslie Harradine
HN 1918* 1 1939-49 £550-£650 $1180-$1395

SWEET VIOLETS
Reflections Series
Designer: Douglas V Tootle
HN 3175 1 1988-89 £120-£140 $255-$300

SWEETING
Designer: Leslie Harradine
HN 1935 1 1940-73 £100-£130 $215-$280
HN 1938 1 1940-49 £120-£160 $255-$345

SWIMMER, The
Designer: Leslie Harradine
HN 1270* 1 1928-38 £650-£850 $1395-$1825
HN 1326* 1 1929-38 £650-£850 $1395-$1825
HN 1329* 1 1929-38 £700-£900 $1500-$1930

SYLVIA
Designer: Leslie Harradine
HN 1478 1 1931-38 £280-£310 $600-$665

SYMPATHY
Images Series
Designer: Peggy Davies
HN 2838 1 1980-86 £200-£250 $430-$535
HN 2876 1 1980-86 £200-£250 $430-$535

SYMPHONY
Designer: David B Lovegrove
HN 2287 1 1961-65 £150-£180 $320-$385

TAILOR
Designer: Mary Nicoll
HN 2174 1 1956-59 £450-£550 $965-$1180

TAKE ME HOME
Designer: Nada Pedley
HN 3662 1 1995 RRP RRP

TAKING THINGS EASY
Designer: Mary Nicoll
HN 2677 1 1975-87 £150-£180 $320-$385
HN 2680 1 1987 RRP RRP

TALL STORY
Designer: Mary Nicoll
HN 2248 1 1968-75 £150-£180 $320-$385

TANGO
Reflections Series
Designer: Adrian Hughes
HN 3075 1 1985-92 £120-£140 $255-$300

TAPESTRY WEAVING
Gentle Arts Series
Designer: Pauline Parsons. Ltd Ed: 750
HN 3048 1 1985 £400-£450 $860-$965

TEATIME
Designer: Mary Nicoll
HN 2255 1 1972-95 £130-£150 $280-$320

TEEING OFF
Designer: Robert Tabbenor
HN 3276 1 1990 RRP RRP

TEENAGER
Designer: Peggy Davies
HN 2203 1 1957-62 £160-£230 $345-$495

HN No Ver Prod Dates Market Values

TENDER MOMENT
Vanity Fair Series
Designer: Peggy Davies
HN 3303 1 1990 RRP RRP

TENDERNESS
Images Series
Designer: Eric J Griffiths
HN 2713 1 1982 RRP RRP
HN 2714 1 1982-92 £100-£130 $215-$280

TERESA
Designer: Leslie Harradine
HN 1682 1 1935-49 £550-£750 $1180-$1610
HN 1683 1 1935-38 £1000-£1250 $2145-$2680
Designer: Adrian Hughes
HN 3206 2 1989-92 £100-£130 $215-$280

TESS
Kate Greenaway Series
Designer: Peggy Davies
HN 2865 1 1978-83 £140-£180 $300-$385

TETE-A-TETE
Designer: Leslie Harradine
HN 798 1 1926-38 £650-£850 $1395-$1825
HN 799 1 1926-38 £650-£850 $1395-$1825
Miniature Series
HN 1236 2 1927-38 £500-£700 $1075-$1500
HN 1237 2 1927-38 £500-£700 $1075-$1500

THANK YOU
Designer: William K Harper
HN 2732 1 1983-86 £130-£150 $280-$320
Sentiments Series
Designer: Alan Maslankowski
HN 3390 2 1991 RRP RRP

THANKFUL
Images Series
Designer: Pauline Parsons
HN 3129 1 1987 RRP RRP
HN 3135 1 1987-94 £100-£130 $215-$280

THANKS DOC
Designer: William K Harper
HN 2731 1 1975-90 £150-£180 $320-$385

THANKSGIVING
Designer: Mary Nicoll
HN 2446 1 1972-76 £120-£150 $255-$320

THE CHARGE OF THE LIGHT BRIGADE
Prestige Series
Designer: Alan Maslankowski
HN 3718 1 1995 RRP RRP

THINKING OF YOU
Sentiments Series
Designer: Alan Maslankowski
HN 3124 1 1991 RRP RRP

THIS LITTLE PIG
Designer: Leslie Harradine
HN 1793 1 1936-95 £50-£70 $105-$150
HN 1794 1 1936-49 £180-£250 $385-$535
HN 2125 1 1984-95 £40-£60 $85-$130

TILDY
Designer: Leslie Harradine
HN 1576* 1 1933-38 £550-£650 $1180-$1395
HN 1859* 1 1934-49 £550-£650 $1180-$1395

TIME FOR BED
Designer: Nada Pedley
HN 3762 1 1996 RRP RRP

TINA
Designer: Peggy Davies
HN 3494 1 1993 RRP RRP
Colourway of Maureen (2nd version) for Great Universal Stores

TINKLE BELL
Designer: Leslie Harradine
HN 1677 1 1935-88 £60-£90 $130-$195

TINSMITH
Designer: Mary Nicoll
HN 2146 1 1962-67 £180-£230 $385-$495

TINY TIM
Dickens Series
Designer: Leslie Harradine
HN 539 1 1922-32 £55-£60 $120-$130
M 56 1 1932-83 £40-£60 $85-$130

TIP-TOE
Designer: Adrian Hughes
HN 3293 1 1990-94 £100-£130 $215-$280

TITANIA
Shakespeare's Ladies Series
Designer: Pauline Parsons
HN 3679 1 1995 RRP RRP
Lawleys by Post

TO BED
Designer: Leslie Harradine
HN 1805 1 1937-59 £110-£140 $235-$300
HN 1806 1 1937-49 £140-£160 $300-$345

TOINETTE
Designer: Leslie Harradine
HN 1940 1 1940-49 £680-£940 $1460-$2015
See also Meryll HN 1917

TOM
Kate Greenaway Series
Designer: Peggy Davies
HN 2864 1 1978-81 £200-£250 $430-$535

TOM BOMBADIL
Tolkien Series
Designer: David Lyttleton
HN 2924 1 1982-84 £200-£250 $430-$535

HN No	Ver	Prod Dates	Market Values	

TOM BROWN
Children's Literature Series
Designer: Robert Tabbenor
HN 2941 1 1983-85 £100-£130 $215-$280

TOM SAWYER
Children's Literature Series
Designer: David Lyttleton
HN 2926 1 1982-85 £100-£130 $215-$280

TOM, TOM, THE PIPER'S SON
Nursery Rhymes Series
Designer: Adrian Hughes
HN 3032 1 1984-87 £100-£130 $215-$280

TOMORROW'S DREAMS
Reflections Series
Designer: Pauline Parsons
HN 3128 1 1988-92 £100-£130 $215-$280
Images Series
Designer: Peter Gee
HN 3665 2 1995 RRP RRP

TONY WELLER
Dickens Series
Designer: Charles J Noke.
HN 346 1 1919-38 £560-£630 $1200-$1350
HN 368 1 1920-38 £560-£630 $1200-$1350
Designer: Leslie Harradine
HN 684 1 1924-38 £500-£630 $1075-$1350
HN 544 2 1922-32 £55-£60 $120-$130
M 47 2 1932-81 £40-£60 $85-$130

TOOTLES
Designer: Leslie Harradine
HN 1680 1 1935-75 £90-£110 $195-$235

TOP 'O THE HILL
Designer: Leslie Harradine
HN 1833 1 1937-71 £150-£180 $320-$385
HN 1834 1 1937 RRP RRP
HN 1849 1 1938-75 £150-£180 $320-$385
HN 2127 1 1988 £180-£200 $385-$430
Colourway for Australian Bi-Centenary
RDICC Exclusive Miniature Series
HN 2126 2 1988 £80-£100 $170-$215

TOWN CRIER
Designer: Peggy Davies
HN 2119 1 1953-76 £160-£200 $345-$430
Miniature Series
HN 3261 1 1989-91 £60-£80 $130-$170

TOYMAKER, The
Designer: Mary Nicoll
HN 2250 1 1959-73 £200-£250 $430-$535

TOYS
Designer: Leslie Harradine
HN 1316* 1 1929-38 £800-£1000 $1715-$2145

TRACY
Designer: Douglas V Tootle
HN 3291 1 1993 RRP RRP
USA only
Vanity Fair Series
HN 2736 1 1983-94 £100-£130 $215-$280

TRANQUILITY
Images Series
Designer: Peggy Davies
HN 2426 1 1981-86 £60-£80 $130-$170
HN 2469 1 1981-86 £60-£80 $130-$170

TRAVELLER'S TALES
Reflections Series
Designer: Eric J Griffiths
HN 3185 1 1988-89 £100-£130 $215-$280

TREASURE ISLAND
Designer: Peggy Davies
HN 2243 1 1962-75 £110-£140 $235-$300

TROTTY VECK
Dickens Series
Designer: Leslie Harradine
M 91 1 1949-82 £40-£60 $85-$130

TULIPS
Designer: Unknown
HN 466* 1 1921-38 £600-£800 $1285-$1715
HN 488* 1 1921-38 £600-£800 $1285-$1715
HN 672 1 1924-38 £600-£800 $1285-$1715
HN 747 1 1925-38 £600-£800 $1285-$1715
HN 1334 1 1929-38 £600-£800 $1285-$1715

TUMBLER
Reflections Series
Designer: Douglas V Tootle
HN 3183 1 1989-91 £90-£110 $195-$235

TUMBLING
Designer: Douglas V Tootle
HN 3283 1 1990 RRP RRP
. Ltd Ed: 2500
HN 3289 1 1991-94 £100-£130 $215-$280

TUPPENCE A BAG
Designer: Mary Nicoll
HN 2320 1 1968-95 £100-£130 $215-$280

TWILIGHT
Designer: Mary Nicoll
HN 2256 1 1971-76 £150-£180 $320-$385

TWO-A-PENNY
Designer: Leslie Harradine
HN 1359 1 1929-38 £950-£1100 $2040-$2360

T'ZU-HSI EMPRESS DOWAGER
Les Femmes Fatales Series
Designer: Peggy Davies. Ltd Ed: 750
HN 2391 1 1983 £600-£650 $1285-$1395

HN No	Ver	Prod Dates	Market Values	

UNCLE NED
Designer: Harry Fenton

HN 2094	1	1952-65	£180-£220	$385-$470

UNDER THE GOOSEBERRY BUSH
Designer: Charles J Noke

HN 49*	1	1916-38	£680-£750	$1460-$1610

"UPON HER CHEEKS SHE WEPT"
Designer: Lawrence Perugini

HN 59*	1	1916-38	£720-£780	$1545-$1675
HN 511*	1	1921-38	£720-£780	$1545-$1675
HN 522*	1	1921-38	£720-£780	$1545-$1675

URIAH HEEP
Dickens Series
Designer: Leslie Harradine

HN 545	1	1922-32	£55-£60	$120-$130
M 45	1	1932-83	£40-£60	$85-$130
HN 554	2	1923-39	£170-£230	$365-$495
HN 1892	2	1938-52	£170-£230	$365-$495
HN 2101	3	1952-67	£170-£230	$365-$495

VALERIE
Designer: Peggy Davies

HN 2107	1	1953-95	£60-£70	$130-$150
HN 3620	1	1994	RRP	RRP

VANESSA
Designer: Leslie Harradine

HN 1836	1	1938-49	£450-£500	$965-$1075
HN 1838	1	1938-49	£440-£500	$945-$1075

Designer: Adrian Hughes

HN 3198	2	1989-90	£100-£130	$215-$280

VANITY
Designer: Peggy Davies

HN 2475	1	1973-92	£70-£90	$150-$195

VENETA
Designer: William K Harper

HN 2722	1	1974-81	£120-£140	$255-$300

VERA
Designer: Leslie Harradine

HN 1729	1	1935-38	£400-£450	$860-$965
HN 1730	1	1935-38	£400-£450	$860-$965

VERENA
Designer: Leslie Harradine

HN 1835*	1	1938-49	£550-£650	$1180-$1395
HN 1854*	1	1938-49	£550-£650	$1180-$1395

VERONICA
Designer: Leslie Harradine

HN 1517	1	1932-51	£200-£250	$430-$535
HN 1519	1	1932-38	£310-£380	$665-$815
HN 1650	1	1934-49	£220-£280	$470-$600
HN 1943	1	1940-49	£310-£380	$665-$815
M 64	1	1934-49	£250-£300	$535-$645
M 70	1	1936-49	£300-£350	$645-$750
HN 1915	2	1939-49	£200-£250	$430-$535

Vanity Fair Series
Designer: Adrian Hughes

HN 3205	3	1989-92	£100-£130	$215-$280

VICE ADMIRAL LORD NELSON
Designer: Alan Maslankowski. Ltd Ed: 950

HN 3489	1	1993	RRP	RRP

VICTORIA
Designer: Peggy Davies

HN 2471	1	1973	RRP	RRP
HN 3416	1	1992-94	£130-£150	$280-$320

Road Show Special Gold edition
Designer: Peggy Davis

HN 3744	1	1995	RRP	RRP

Miniature
M Doulton Signature Miniature Series

HN 3737	2	1995	RRP	RRP

VICTORIAN LADY, A
Designer: Leslie Harradine

HN 726	1	1925-38	£250-£350	$535-$750
HN 727	1	1925-38	£170-£200	$365-$430
HN 728	1	1925-52	£180-£220	$385-$470
HN 736	1	1925-38	£250-£350	$535-$750
HN 739	1	1925-38	£250-£350	$535-$750
HN 740	1	1925-38	£250-£340	$535-$730
HN 742	1	1925-38	£250-£340	$535-$730
HN 745	1	1925-38	£250-£350	$535-$750
HN 1208	1	1926-38	£250-£350	$535-$750
HN 1258	1	1927-38	£250-£350	$535-$750
HN 1276	1	1928-38	£250-£350	$535-$750
HN 1277	1	1928-38	£250-£350	$535-$750
HN 1345	1	1929-49	£250-£350	$535-$750
HN 1452	1	1931-49	£250-£350	$535-$750
HN 1529	1	1932-38	£250-£350	$535-$750
M 1	1	1932-45	£180-£220	$385-$470
M 2	1	1932-45	£180-£220	$385-$470
M 25	1	1932-45	£180-£220	$385-$470

VIKING, The
Designer: John Bromley

HN 2375	1	1973-76	£180-£200	$385-$430

VIOLA
Edwardian String Quartet Series
Designer: Valerie Annand. Ltd Ed: 1500

HN 3706	1	1995	RRP	RRP

Lawleys by Post

VIOLA D'AMORE
Lady Musicians Series
Designer: Peggy Davies. Ltd Ed: 750

HN 2797	1	1976	£450-£550	$965-$1180

VIOLIN
Lady Musicians Series
Designer: Peggy Davies. Ltd Ed: 750

HN 2432	1	1972	£450-£500	$965-$1075

VIRGINALS
Lady Musicians Series
Designer: Peggy Davies. Ltd Ed: 750

HN 2427	1	1971	£450-£500	$965-$1075

HN No *Ver* *Prod Dates* *Market Values*

VIRGINIA
Designer: Leslie Harradine
HN 1693 1 1935-49 £550-£650 $1180-$1395
HN 1694 1 1935-49 £550-£650 $1180-$1395

VIVIENNE
Designer: Leslie Harradine
HN 2073 1 1951-67 £180-£220 $385-$470

VOTES FOR WOMEN
Designer: William K Harper
HN 2816 1 1978-81 £150-£180 $320-$385

W. G. GRACE
Designer: Robert Tabbenor. Ltd Ed: 9500
HN 3640 1 1995 RRP RRP
Lawleys by Post

WAITING FOR A TRAIN
Designer: Peter Gee. Ltd Ed: 9500
HN 3315 1 1990 RRP RRP
Lawleys by Post

WALES
Ladies of the British Isles Series
Designer: Valerie Annand
HN 3630 1 1996 RRP RRP

WANDERING MINSTREL, The
Designer: Leslie Harradine
HN 1224 1 1927-38 £1000-£1250 $2145-$2680

WARDROBE MISTRESS
Designer: Peggy Davies
HN 2145 1 1954-67 £200-£250 $430-$535

WATER MAIDEN
Reflections Series
Designer: Adrian Hughes
HN 3155 1 1987-91 £100-£130 $215-$280

WAYFARER, The
Designer: Mary Nicoll
HN 2362 1 1970-76 £150-£180 $320-$385

WEDDING DAY
Images Series
Designer: Douglas V Tootle
HN 2748 1 1987 RRP RRP

WEDDING MORN
Designer: Leslie Harradine
HN 1866* 1 1938-49 £600-£800 $1285-$1715
HN 1867* 1 1938-49 £600-£800 $1285-$1715
Designer: Tim Potts
HN 3853 2 1996 RRP RRP

WEDDING VOWS
Designer: Douglas V Tootle
HN 2750 1 1988-92 £120-£140 $255-$300

WEE WILLIE WINKIE
Nursery Rhymes Series
Designer: Peggy Davies
HN 2050 1 1949-53 £200-£250 $430-$535
Designer: Adrian Hughes
HN 3031 2 1984-87 £130-£150 $280-$320

WELCOME
Designer: Nada Pedley
HN 3764 1 1996 RRP RRP
RDICC

WELCOME HOME
Children of the Blitz Series
Designer: Adrian Hughes. Ltd Ed: 9500
HN 3299 1 1991-95 £150-£170 $320-$365

WELL DONE
Little Cherubs Series
Designer: Valerie Annand
HN 3362 1 1992- RRP RRP

WELSH GIRL, The
Designer: Ernest W Light
HN 39* 1 1914-38 £1250-£1500 $2680-$3220
Sometimes named Myfanwy Jones from Llnwllanwllyn
HN 92* 1 1918-38 £1250-£1500 $2680-$3220
HN 456* 1 1921-38 £1250-£1500 $2680-$3220
HN 514* 1 1921-38 £1250-£1500 $2680-$3220
HN 516* 1 1921-38 £1250-£1500 $2680-$3220
HN 519* 1 1921-38 £1250-£1500 $2680-$3220
HN 520* 1 1921-38 £1250-£1500 $2680-$3220
HN 660* 1 1924-38 £1250-£1500 $2680-$3220
HN 668* 1 1924-38 £1250-£1500 $2680-$3220
HN 669* 1 1924-38 £1250-£1500 $2680-$3220
HN 701* 1 1925-38 £1250-£1500 $2680-$3220
HN 792* 1 1926-38 £1250-£1500 $2680-$3220

WENDY
Designer: Leslie Harradine
HN 2109 1 1953-95 £50-£75 $105-$160

WEST INDIAN DANCER
Dancers of the World Series
Designer: Peggy Davies. Ltd Ed: 750
HN 2384 1 1981 £320-£380 $685-$815

WEST WIND
Designer: Richard Garbe. Ltd Ed: 25
HN 1776* 1 1933-39 £1000-£1500 $2145-$3220
HN 1826* 1 1937-49 £1000-£1500 $2145-$3220

WHAT FUN
Little Cherubs Series
Designer: Valerie Annand
HN 3364 1 1992 RRP RRP

WHAT'S THE MATTER
Designer: Nada Pedley
HN 3684 1 1995 RRP RRP

WHEN I WAS YOUNG
Designer: Pauline Parsons
HN 3457 1 1994 RRP RRP

HN No — Ver — Prod Dates — Market Values

WIGMAKER OF WILLIAMSBURG
Designer: Peggy Davies
HN 2239 1 1960-83 £130-£150 $280-$320

WILL HE WON'T HE?
Designer: Robert Tabbenor
HN 3275 1 1990-94 £100-£130 $215-$280

WILLY-WON'T HE
Designer: Leslie Harradine
HN 1561 1 1933-49 £200-£250 $430-$535
HN 1584 1 1933-49 £200-£250 $430-$535
HN 2150 1 1955-59 £150-£180 $320-$385

WIMBLEDON
British Sports Heritage Series
Designer: Valerie Annand. Ltd Ed: 5000
HN 3366 1 1995 RRP RRP

WINDFLOWER
Designer: Leslie Harradine
HN 1763 1 1936-49 £250-£300 $535-$645
HN 1764 1 1936-49 £250-£300 $535-$645
HN 2029 1 1949-52 £200-£250 $430-$535
M 78 1 1939-49 £500-£700 $1075-$1500
M 79 1 1939-49 £500-£700 $1075-$1500
HN 1920 2 1939-49 £700-£900 $1500-$1930
HN 1939 2 1940-49 £700-£900 $1500-$1930
Reflections Series
Designer: Adrian Hughes
HN 3077 3 1986-92 £100-£130 $215-$280

WINDMILL LADY, The
Designer: Leslie Harradine
HN 1400* 1 1930-38 £600-£800 $1285-$1715

WINDSWEPT
Reflections Series
Designer: Robert Jefferson
HN 3027 1 1985-94 £100-£130 $215-$280

WINNER, The
Designer: Unknown
HN 1407* 1 1930-38 £1120-£1380 $2405-$2960

WINNING PUTT
Designer: Robert Tabbenor
HN 3279 1 1991-95 £100-£130 $215-$280

WINSOME
Designer: Peggy Davies
HN 2220 1 1960-85 £130-£150 $280-$320

WINSTON S CHURCHILL
Designer: Alan Maslankowski. Ltd Ed: 5000
HN 3433 2 1993 RRP RRP

WINTER
Designer: Unknown
HN 315 1 1918-38 £720-£810 $1545-$1740
HN 475 1 1921-38 £720-£810 $1545-$1740
Designer: Peggy Davies
HN 2088 2 1952-59 £250-£280 $535-$600

WINTER WELCOME
Designer: Peggy Davies
HN 3611 1 1993 RRP RRP
Colourway of Caroline for Guild of Specialist Retailers

WINTER'S DAY
RDICC Series
Designer: Nada Pedley
HN 3769 1 1996-97 RRP RRP

WINTERTIME
RDICC Exclusive Series
Designer: Adrian Hughes
HN 3060 1 1985 £140-£180 $300-$385
Four Seasons Series
Designer: Valerie Annand
HN 3622 2 1996 RRP RRP

WINTER'S WALK, A
Reflections Series
Designer: Adrian Hughes
HN 3052 1 1988-95 £120-£140 $255-$300

WISTFUL
Designer: Peggy Davies
HN 2396 1 1979-90 £150-£180 $320-$385
Michael Doulton Series
HN 2472 1 1985 £150-£180 $320-$385
Images Series
Designer: Peter Gee
HN 3664 2 1994 RRP RRP

WITH LOVE
Sentiments Series
Designer: Alan Maslankowski
HN 3393 1 1992 RRP RRP
HN 3492 1 1994 RRP RRP
Canada only

WIZARD
Designer: Alan Maslankowski
HN 3722 1 1994 RRP RRP
Resin
HN 3732 2 1996 RRP RRP
Resin. Lawleys by Post

WIZARD, The
Designer: Alan Maslankowski
HN 3121 1 1990-95 £130-£150 $280-$320
Flambé Series
HN 2877 1 1979 RRP RRP

WOMAN OF THE TIME OF HENRY VI
Designer: Ernest W Light
HN 43* 1 1914-38 £1000-£1250 $2145-$2680

WOOD NYMPH
Designer: Peggy Davies
HN 2192 1 1958-62 £180-£200 $385-$430

WRITING
Gentle Arts Series
Designer: Pauline Parsons. Ltd Ed: 750
HN 3049 1 1986 £600-£650 $1285-$1395

HN No	*Ver*	*Prod Dates*		*Market Values*

YEARNING
Images Series
Designer: Peter Gee

HN 2920	1	1982-86	£60-£80	$130-$170
HN 2921	1	1982-86	£60-£80	$130-$170

YEOMAN OF THE GUARD, A
Designer: Leslie Harradine

HN 688	1	1924-38	£500-£560	$1075-$1200
HN 2122	1	1954-59	£400-£500	$860-$1075

YOUNG DREAMS
Designer: Douglas V Tootle

HN 3176	1	1988-92	£100-£130	$215-$280

YOUNG KNIGHT, The
Designer: Charles J Noke

HN 94*	1	1918-36	£1250-£1750	$2680-$3755

YOUNG LOVE
Designer: Douglas V Tootle

HN 2735	1	1975-90	£250-£300	$535-$645

YOUNG MASTER, The
Designer: Peggy Davies

HN 2872	1	1980-89	£150-£190	$320-$405

YOUNG MELODY
Designer: Nada Pedley

HN 3654	1	1994	RRP	RRP

YOUNG MISS NIGHTINGALE, The
Designer: Peggy Davies

HN 2010	1	1948-53	£400-£480	$860-$1030

YOUNG MOTHER WITH CHILD
Designer: Unknown

HN 1301*	1	1928-38	£750-£1000	$1610-$2145

Formerly known as Gypsy Woman with Child

YOUNG WIDOW, The
Designer: Leslie Harradine

HN 1399*	1	1930-30	£680-£750	$1460-$1610

See also Little Mother (2nd version)

YOURS FOREVER
Vanity Fair Series
Designer: Pauline Parsons

HN 3354	1	1992	RRP	RRP

YUM-YUM
Gilbert and Sullivan Series
Designer: William K Harper

HN 2899	1	2-85	£310-£340	$665-$730

Designer: Leslie Harradine

HN 1268	1	1928-38	£320-£380	$685-$815
HN 1287	1	1928-39	£320-£380	$685-$815

YVONNE
Designer: Adrian Hughes

HN 3038	1	1987-92	£100-£130	$215-$280